D1243468

Isle of Dogs

Isle of Dogs

by **LAUREN WILFORD**
and **RYAN STEVENSON**

foreword by
MATT ZOLLER SEITZ

with an
introduction by
TAYLOR RAMOS
and
TONY ZHOU

ABRAMS
NEW YORK

A FOREWORD
BY MATT ZOLLER SEITZ

I WAS THE FIRST CRITIC to profile Wes Anderson. It happened because Wes made Dallas, Texas, look like Paris, France.

It was twenty-five years ago. I was a couple years out of college and writing for the *Dallas Observer*, a free alternative newsweekly that was distributed in restaurants and bars. The city had a local film festival called the USA Film Festival. All the work being screened at that year's festival was made available to me on VHS cassette. I stacked the blocky plastic tapes in little piles in the living room of the apartment I shared with my then-girlfriend (later, wife) and fed them into the player, one by one, over the course of a few weeks, sitting cross-legged on the floor and taking notes on a little notepad.

The first thing I saw that made a strong impression on me was "Bottle Rocket," a thirteen-minute, black-and-white version of what would later become Wes's debut feature. It was the first entry that year that I immediately wanted to watch again. Filmed in 16mm, it was innocent but very assured—so much so that I was shocked to learn that, like me, Wes was twenty-four and had only recently graduated college. I'd just assumed he was some kind of professor, or maybe a local cinematographer or playwright, probably in his forties and a veteran of local film production. I also didn't know going in that "Bottle Rocket" was shot in Dallas or that its two lead actors, Luke and Owen Wilson, grew up there and went to the same school where I'd attended day camp a couple of summers as a kid. And I didn't know that Wes had met Owen at the University of Texas in Austin and shared a small apartment with him and some other guys down on Throckmorton Street, not far from where I grew up. In fact, it took me a few moments to register that what I was seeing on my TV set was the same nondescript sub-

urbanized metropolis where I'd spent most of my life: a place marked mainly by its shopping malls, chain stores, and knotted-up bundles of highway. "Bottle Rocket" made a familiar world seem new.

The whole time I was growing up, the city's politicians and businesspeople had been obsessed with making Dallas an "international city." This usually meant pushing large-scale building projects: a new airport, a new opera house, an arts district. But here was Wes photographing Dallas as if it already was an international city—a place with a rich history and powerful atmosphere; a place that kids from Rome or Tokyo or Nice might dream of visiting. Specifically, he made it look like the Paris that he fell in love with from watching one of his favorite films, François Truffaut's 1959 coming-of-age drama *The 400 Blows*.

At that point in time, Wes hadn't traveled outside the United States yet, so his only reference point for France was the movies he'd seen that were set there. His use of black-and-white was an explicit nod to Truffaut's film, but Wes went further, scoring the short with snippets of modern jazz (including a bit of Vince Guaraldi's score from *A Charlie Brown Christmas*), mimicking specific shots (such as the sequence of close-ups of a pinball machine), and editing the whole thing in a faintly French New Wave style that was fleet-footed and playful, and that made the main characters, a couple of petty thieves, seem charming, even oddly touching, rather than pathetic.

There was no readily identifiable logical connection between this material and the aesthetic that Wes had chosen. He did it that way because it felt right. He shot "Bottle Rocket" that way because he loved *The 400 Blows* and François Truffaut and black-and-white and jazz. He treated all the culture he'd consumed up to then as part of an artist's supply kit: an assortment of paints and brushes, charcoals and pencils and erasers that he could use as he saw fit.

When "Bottle Rocket" became a feature, Wes wanted to keep it in black-and-white but shoot it in CinemaScope, a wide format. He was told he couldn't do that because it was too technically complicated and uncommercial. His fallback position was to model the visuals on Bernardo Bertolucci's 1970 drama *The Conformist*. If there were ever two movies that could be said to have nothing in common, it's *Bottle Rocket* and *The Conformist*, an emotionally and visually intense classic of Italian cinema, set against the backdrop of rising Fascism. But Wes and his soon-to-be-regular cinematographer Robert Yeoman printed out a series of color stills from *The Conformist* and taped them to the side of the camera as reference points. Certain signature qualities of Bertolucci's film—costumes, decor, the rich color palette—were lifted out of their original context and put to uses that the creators could never have foreseen.

In film after film, Wes makes choices like this. *Rushmore* is shot in Wes's hometown of Houston, Texas, one of the largest and most sprawling cities in the United States. It was more architecturally notable and historically conscious a place than Dallas, a city where one of my favorite burger joints as a teen in the eighties had a sign out front, bragging, "A Dallas tradition since 1972." Undaunted, Wes presents Houston as a dream space, never saying the word "Houston" onscreen, just as he never said "Dallas" in either version of *Bottle Rocket*; in the end, you do feel as if you dreamed that place, and that story. *Rushmore* has CinemaScope compositions, radiant colors that are often reminiscent of David Hockney's paintings, camera movements that evoke films by Martin Scorsese, Jacques Demy, and Jean-Luc Godard, and a British invasion–heavy soundtrack. If somebody who knew nothing about Wes Anderson's own history told an uninitiated viewer that they were about to see a fantasy vision of Houston by a French

or Italian filmmaker who'd never lived there, the viewing experience would sell the illusion. Wes's third movie, *The Royal Tenenbaums*, stirs influences as varied as Orson Welles, Woody Allen, E. L. Konigsburg, J. D. Salinger, *The New Yorker* magazine, *Peanuts*, and *The French Connection* into a magisterial family drama set in an alternate New York, with invented landmarks like Archer Avenue, the 375th Street Y, and the Lindbergh Palace Hotel, and perhaps no Statue of Liberty (Kumar Pallana blocks the monument in the one scene where you might be able to see it). The words "New York" are never spoken. A close-up of a publication modeled on the layout of the Sunday *New York Times Magazine* is titled simply *The Sunday Magazine Section*. This world is New York but not New York, just as the Houston of *Rushmore* was Houston but not Houston.

When we get to *The Life Aquatic with Steve Zissou*, things get much weirder. Wes had originally imagined that film (one of several scenarios that he dreamed up while in college with Owen Wilson) as an American tale that would likely be shot off one of the US coasts. But then he toured the festival circuit in Europe and fell in love with Rome. He decided to shoot the film at Cinecittà, where Federico Fellini made one of the great ship movies, *Amarcord*, and film most of the sailing scenes in the Mediterranean Sea. Wes's wanderlust prompted an even more sudden and drastic change of scenery for *The Darjeeling Limited*. He devised the story while traveling across France on a commuter train with Roman Coppola and Jason Schwartzman, and originally envisioned the story being set there. Then he attended a screening of a newly restored version of Jean Renoir's *The River*, about a family of farmers in India, and was so moved and impressed that he decided right then and there that the film should be shot in India instead. The resultant film—a comedy about squabbling, grieving brothers who remain largely oblivious to the culture that they pass through—is set in a dazzling variety of locations throughout the subcontinent and borrows a lot from the work of international auteurs like Renoir and Satyajit Ray. But you can also detect elements of the John Cassavetes male bonding dramas that he and Owen Wilson used to watch on VHS in college. Cinema history, real history, and personal history again combine to form a vast archive that Wes mines for imagery and ideas.

The everywhere-and-nowhereness of Wes Anderson's films starts to seem increasingly integral by this stage. The ordinary otherworldliness of his most recent features—*Moonrise Kingdom*, *The Grand Budapest Hotel*—is rooted in their sense of history/ not history and geography/not geography. *Moonrise Kingdom* is set in September 1965, on the cusp of cultural and generational upheaval, and the entire story is laid out for us by a historian who ties important events, past and present, to a map of the nonexistent New Penzance Island; but there's ultimately no sense of the film's events fitting into a specific real-world narrative, and the film's insistence on letting us know precisely where everything is happening ultimately becomes a humorous acknowledgment that for these characters (as for us), it's the heart, not the compass, that fixes one's position in the world. As with *The Darjeeling Limited*, it's the way the camera celebrates places, the way cinema remembers history, that inspires Wes's wanderlust.

The Grand Budapest Hotel is arguably Wes's most aggressively "meta" film, a story about storytelling. The region has a rich history that we learn about in due course, and many key plot twists are driven by travel from point A to B, the breaching of borders by armies, and matters of citizenship and identification papers. The entirety of Europe has been given the 375th Street Y treatment. World Wars I and II have somehow been combined, with the Prussians, the Fascists, and the Communists blurring into one persistent threat to happiness. There's even a rapprochement of Europe and the Middle East, represented in the character of Zero, who's somehow simultaneously a Jew (like Stefan Zweig, the Austrian author, who inspired the movie but whose plots have little to do with the screenplay) and a Muslim. Billy Wilder, Max Ophüls, Jacques Becker, and Ernst Lubitsch all influence the storytelling: four European masters, two of whom resettled in the United States and were ultimately accepted as Americans. Both Wes's seventh and eighth films are

obsessed with history and maps, even as their stories lament how such artificial demarcations constrain affairs of the heart.

Isle of Dogs expands Wes's reach even further. The thoroughness of the film's references outdoes any previous Wes Anderson film. Students of Yasujiro Ozu, Akira Kurosawa, and Mikio Naruse might not necessarily expect to see all three directors, and others, acknowledged in a single feature—one that also happens to be animated; to owe a lot to Richard Adams's animal novels *Watership Down* and *The Plague Dogs*, John Carpenter's *Escape from New York*, and *kaiju* films like *Gorath* and *Monster Zero*; and to pay simultaneous homage to touchstones of anime, including *Akira*, *Perfect Blue*, and *Neon Genesis Evangelion*.

The entire idea of the film comes out of Wes's love of Japanese cinema, animated and live-action, as well as films from other countries (including the United States) that influenced them. When Wes "does" Kurosawa or Honda here, stop-motion animated and with scruffy yet adorable dogs, cinema's time-spanning, ocean-hopping chain of aesthetic influence gains yet another link. Here is an American translating and reconfiguring work by directors who were themselves strongly influenced by American directors, many of whom were, in turn, borrowing from the Germans, the French, and others who produced images that sparked their own imaginations. The Japan of *Isle of Dogs*, the Europe of *The Grand Budapest Hotel*, the Mediterranean of *The Life Aquatic*, the India of *The Darjeeling Limited*, and the New York of *The Royal Tenenbaums* are all ultimately Dallas as Paris, as dream-spaces and mindscapes. Wes is a citizen of the world now. His mind accepts no border.

AN INTRODUCTION

BY TAYLOR RAMOS
AND TONY ZHOU

THEY SAY THERE'S NOTHING quite like the relationship between a boy and his dog, which is perhaps why we've had so many animated films about it.

In the last twenty years alone, American filmmakers have explored a dozen variations: a boy and his giant robot (*The Iron Giant*), a boy and his medium-size robot (*Big Hero 6*), a boy and his dragon (*How to Train Your Dragon*), a boy and his monster dog (*Frankenweenie*), and in a slight inversion, a dinosaur and his feral boy (*The Good Dinosaur*). In all of these films, the gulf between the human world and the dog/robot/dinosaur world is the source of much comedy and drama.

At first glance, *Isle of Dogs* is Wes Anderson's foray into similar territory. This time, the variation is that Atari and Spots (the Boy and His Dog) are separated at the beginning, and the rest of the film is the journey to reunite them.

But this turns out to be a bit of a feint. The real dog in the story is Chief, a stray who helps the boy on his quest across Trash Island. And the relationship between Atari and Chief takes longer to develop, because it's so obvious that they come from different worlds.

For *Isle of Dogs* is not just about This Boy and This Dog, but also about the environments and backgrounds that formed them. The film takes place in a Japan "20 years in the future," though the exact date is nebulous. The retro-futuristic setting offers a way to explore two societies: the world of dogs on Trash Island and the world of humans in Megasaki City. Each has its own hierarchy and power structure, outcasts and agitators.

As for those environments and backgrounds and humans and dogs, they're all handmade, at tiny scale. Anderson made this film by employing stop-motion animation, his second feature (after *Fantastic Mr. Fox*) to be done entirely using the process.

Isle of Dogs, then, is not just the meeting of a boy and a dog, but also of an artist and a medium.

About that medium: stop-motion is the most physical form of animation, with its own quirks and limitations. Traditional hand-drawn animation (think Studio Ghibli) is limited only by what the artist can draw on paper. Computer 3-D animation (think Pixar) is limited by the capabilities of the software.

Stop-motion, on the other hand, is built entirely in the physical world. The puppets are real and have weight, everything is tactile, and the images have an imperfect quality that comes from real light passing through glass.

The limits of stop-motion, then, are the limits of the physical world: The fur moves with every touch, the puppets get dirty and worn, and the lenses can only focus so close. Every choice of composition and production design is a negotiation between the desire of the filmmakers and the elements of their craft.

Some of Anderson's choices are a natural fit for this process; others are not. Part of the fun in watching the film and reading this book is to tease out which visual effects were simple to pull off and which were very complicated. And yet this, too, says something about the filmmakers—the willingness to embrace the restrictions of the medium and turn them into something else.

Just one example: in *Fantastic Mr. Fox*, the fur on the puppets moved whenever it was touched by the animators. This is called "boiling" and is, technically speaking, a mistake. On *Isle of Dogs*, the boiling fur offers multiple functions: It's an aesthetic stamp, a form of worldbuilding, and ultimately, a beautiful thing just to look at.

But why stop-motion? Anderson says he was inspired to try the medium because of his childhood memories of Christmas specials on TV, specifically the ones made by Rankin/Bass Productions. Those Christmas specials—including *Rudolph the Red-Nosed Reindeer* (1964), *The Little Drummer Boy* (1968), and, our personal favorite, *The Life and Adventures of Santa Claus* (1985)—have been an annual tradition on American TV since the 1960s.

On the surface, *Isle of Dogs* would seem to have nothing in common with those films. But a closer examination reveals a subtle connection: Even though the Rankin/Bass stop-motion specials are considered quintessentially American, they were actually animated by a service studio in Japan—MOM Film Studio. Indeed, the puppet makers and animators of MOM were all trained in Bunraku, a traditional Japanese form of puppeteering, according to Rick Goldschmidt's book on the making of *Rudolph the Red-Nosed Reindeer*. And this tradition of Japanese craftsmanship worked its way into the look of the characters and the way they moved. By setting *Isle of Dogs* in Japan and including many traditional types of Japanese art, Anderson has closed the loop on one of his own key influences.

Furthermore, in the 1960s, Rankin/Bass began using a production pipeline spread across three countries. The story was written and the characters were designed in New York; the voices were recorded in Toronto; and the puppets were built and animated in Tokyo. Today, this type of pipeline—with the story written in one country but animated elsewhere—has become commonplace.

Isle of Dogs, then, is a snapshot of how international the animation industry (and animated storytelling) has become. The film was animated in London, directed from points all across the globe, and cowritten by three Americans and a Japanese man. The dogs in the film all speak English and the humans all speak Japanese, but neither can understand the other. Anderson's trademark labels appear in Japanese (and a moment later, in parenthetical English). And the filmmakers' key influence ended up being Akira Kurosawa—a Japanese filmmaker who adapted stories by Shakespeare, Dostoyevsky, Maxim Gorky, Dashiell Hammett, and Ed McBain.

When Anderson first embarked on *Fantastic Mr. Fox*, the running joke among his critics was that he had at last found his perfect medium. Surely, they said, a filmmaker who focused on precise composition and detailed production design was going to love a process that gave him total control.

But what becomes apparent to any filmmaker who works in animation is that it is impossible to have total control. No two animators work exactly alike, and thus, no two scenes will have the exact same sensibility. The director can supervise, correct, make choices, but the process of turning something inanimate into something believable ultimately lies in the hands of others.

Indeed, "total control" may not even be the point. As Anderson himself once remarked in an interview with ARTE Cinéma, "directing is organizing chaos, but it's also creating new forms of chaos." Perhaps we can surmise that Anderson chose stop-motion because it creates his preferred forms of chaos. If filmmaking is about problem-solving, then these are the types of problems that attract Wes Anderson's attention: Can we achieve deep focus in this shot with this lens? Can we make the buttonhole on Mayor Kobayashi's suit that fine? How many freckles can we put on exchange student Tracy Walker's face?

What seems to have happened, all those years ago, was that Wes Anderson and stop-motion (like Atari and Chief) met, got to know each other, and discovered that the things they didn't expect were part of the fun. And this is a truth well worth acknowledging.

For film critics, it is often tempting to look at a finished film and say, "This was the result of a single creative vision." At its most extreme, the auteur theory—the argunent that the director is the author of the film—can treat the many people who worked on a production as mere executors of one person's will.

At the same time, the aphorism that "Filmmaking is collaborative!" leaves out the fact that most productions have a chain of command. The director doesn't collaborate with every single person, but with a smaller group of people who then fan out and work with others. Decisions generally come from the top down, but any good command system also leaves room for bottom-up moments of inspiration.

Indeed, the artists can often be at their most open and inspired when there is a strong general with a clear vision. Instead of trying to please five or six people who may disagree, the artists basically answer to one person. And once they learn what she likes, they know how they can best offer their talents.

Call it the *filteur* theory, after Terry Gilliam's remark (in an interview with Intelligence Squared): "People think I'm an auteur . . . The ideas come from everybody, and I get the credit or the blame." In this schema, it's not the director's job to know every answer, but to establish a framework that allows everyone else to do their jobs. Periodically, they go back to him: "Is this what you wanted?" He makes comments or adjustments, then lets them go back to their work. This allows for serendipity and discovery;

the film is not just an execution of a preexisting idea, but a living, constantly evolving thing.

So consider *Isle of Dogs* not as a fait accompli, but as the end result of a very long process of figuring out "How do we make this film?" Yes, there are the daily choices of "Where do we put the camera?" and "How do we light this?" but there are also managerial decisions like "How do we set up a chain of command so that each person can do her job?"

And it shows that we can understand the filmmakers not just by their finished film, but through the systems and processes they employed to make it: What problems were they trying to solve? What restrictions did they place upon themselves? And what mistakes did they find and decide to keep?

For Wes Anderson does not shy away from the most visceral element of watching stop-motion: that we can literally see the human touch onscreen. In choosing to make *Isle of Dogs* this way, he is inviting the viewer to witness both the story and its making simultaneously—one snapshot of boiling fur at a time.

A PREFACE:
WES ANDERSON, AKIRA KUROSAWA, AND THE MAKING OF A STOP-MOTION FEATURE

ONCE I ASKED *about what a certain scene in a prior picture had meant, and he said: 'Well, if I could have answered that, it wouldn't have been necessary for me to film the scene, would it?' I may have had my theories about my subject, but he was not interested in theory.*

He was interested only in practice—how to make films more convincing, more real, more right. He would have agreed with Picasso's remark that when critics get together they talk about theory, but when artists get together they talk about turpentine. He was interested in focal lengths, in multiple camera positions, in color values, just as he was interested in convincing narrative, inconsistent characters, and in the moral concern that was his subject."
—Donald Richie, "Remembering Kurosawa," an essay for Criterion

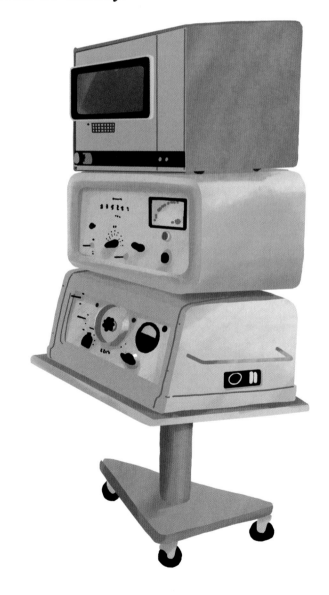

If you want to understand a director's movies, it helps to know about the movies the director loves.

This is especially true when a film director loves movies as much as Wes Anderson does. If you want to understand why he made *Rushmore*, and what it means to him, it'll help to watch *The Graduate* and *Harold and Maude*. If you want to understand *The Royal Tenenbaums*, you'll want to know what Wes thinks of *The Magnificent Ambersons* and *You Can't Take It with You*. If you want to write a book about *The Darjeeling Limited*, it's also going to be a book about the films of Satyajit Ray, whose family dramas have been touchstones for Wes and whose catchiest compositions make up the *Darjeeling* soundtrack. And if you want to talk to Wes about the movie he's making right now, it helps to have seen the movies that are on his mind, because he's going to want to talk about them.

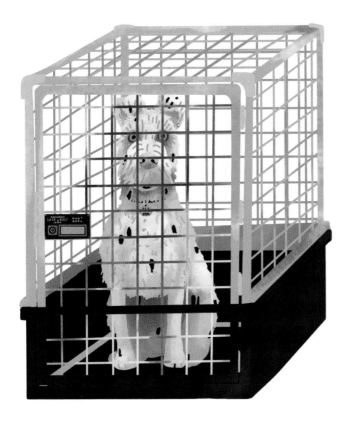

in Kurosawa's *Drunken Angel* and Hitchcock's *Rear Window*, what lessons a production designer like Paul Harrod takes from Tarkovsky and James Bond movies, what an animator like Gwenn Germain loves in Miyazaki, are often things that critics might not notice or cherish in the same way. For a film-maker, these elements are not just beautiful and meaningful, but useful, educational, relevant to their daily work.

This is a book about that daily work. If you're reading this book, you've likely already seen its results. The project of the critic is usually to discuss those results, but at the time of these interviews, neither I nor the filmmakers I talked to have seen their finished film. The job of the interviewer is usually to ask filmmakers about what they've done, and perhaps how it came to be. This book, instead, is a chance to see how filmmakers analyze and discuss their process while they're in the midst of it—what they're doing, how they're doing it, and why they love it. It's a book about the turpentine.

Wes's desire for *Isle of Dogs* was not so much to make a film set in Japan as to make a tribute to the golden age of Japanese cinema—above all, to Kurosawa, with nods here and there to Ishiro Honda, Yasujiro Ozu, Masaki Kobayashi, and more. *The Grand Budapest Hotel* was the same kind of project: both a portrait of old Europe and a tribute to the filmmakers who captured its glamour—Ernst Lubitsch, Max Ophüls, Jean Renoir. Like the Europeans, the great Japanese auteurs offer Anderson a litany of historical details to respect, a wealth of techniques to learn, and a high bar to aim for as an artist. And so, being a book about *Isle of Dogs*, this is also a book about Akira Kurosawa—interpreting key themes of his work, investigating his world and his times, and identifying elements of his filmmaking technique.

Like other books in *The Wes Anderson Collection*, this book is a chance to see what stands out to filmmakers when they watch movies—the focal lengths and color values as well as moral concerns and convincing narratives. What Wes latches onto

A NOTE ON AUTHORSHIP AND VOICE: The text of the book was cowritten by Lauren Wilford and Ryan Stevenson, and is the product of our collaboration and shared experiences. We visited 3 Mills Studios in May/June 2017 and conducted most interviews there jointly. A few interviews were conducted later in the summer and fall, including the interviews with Wes Anderson that Lauren conducted alone in Paris and Rome. For ease of reading, we've formatted interview questions to come from a single "voice" and have opted for "I" for any first-person statements in the text.

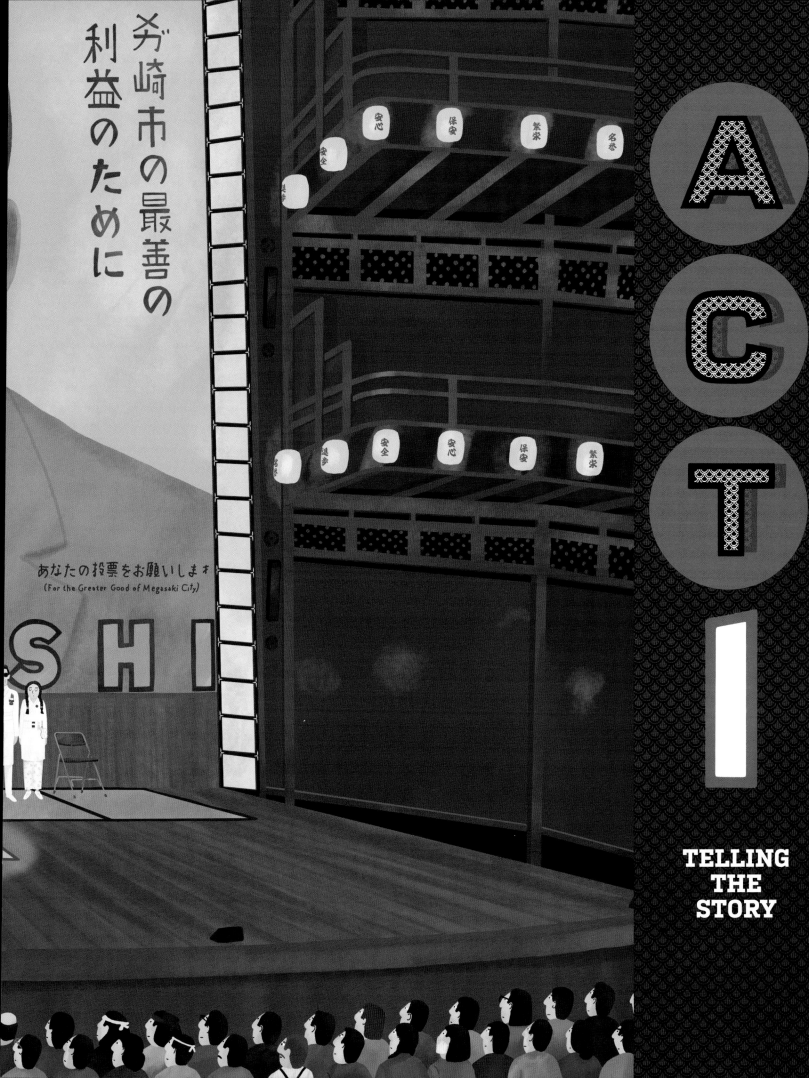

WHAT HAPPENS NEXT?

AN INTERVIEW WITH
Wes Anderson, Roman Coppola, AND Jason Schwartzman

WES ANDERSON is staying at an apartment at the dead end of a long Roman *traversa*. I cross the Tiber on my way there. The street slopes upward toward a green hilltop, and on my way up I pass stucco buildings colored pink and rust and mustard, with wooden shutters and art deco street lamps, window gardens, and overgrown ivy. At the end of the street, where the greenery is thickest, I find the door to Wes's place.

As I linger outside, a little too early, I notice two figures in the distance advancing up the hill. As they approach, I notice a dynamic, even from afar. The shorter of the two is more animated; he is telling jokes or spinning yarns or otherwise spitballing. The taller one is occasionally nodding, asking questions, arms crossed or hands in pockets, considering. They are, it is becoming

Roman Coppola with Chief,
Wes Anderson with Atari, and
Jason Schwartzman with Spots

increasingly apparent, Jason Schwartzman and Roman Coppola.

As they draw near, Jason immediately goes in for the chummy jugular: a hearty handshake, a "Hi, I'm Jason!" delivered right from the bottom of his heart. Roman is cordial and grounded, and makes a note that the first order of business is to figure out how to get into this joint.

Wes has passed along instructions to all of us for entry to the apartment; there are buttons and keys and doors and a rope. The email describing the process begs for a quick-patter delivery by Edward Norton, each instruction shot as its own insert. We are deliberating over the first step when a voice calls out above us. We whip-pan to our left, tilt up, and see Wes, hoisted half out of a second-story window, long hair dangling. He wears round glasses and a look of deep amusement.

We tell him that we are trying to figure out which button to press. "Well, you don't have to press the button now," he says. "I'll go pull the rope." He disappears back into the window.

The big wooden door eases open, and Jason, Roman, and I file in, only to find ourselves in a small vestibule shrouded in near-total darkness. Jason, not missing a beat, starts banging on the walls, adopting a thick British accent for the bit: "All right, Wonka, very funny!" Once we find the key, we open a door onto a white staircase flooded with soft light that bounces off pink walls, and we ascend up to Wes, who is waiting at the top, offering to make us coffee. He's dressed casually: a dusty-red button-up not buttoned to the top, soft yellow linen pants, yellow socks, cobalt blue slippers.

The obvious thing would be to say that this all felt like a beat out of one of Wes's films. (It did.) But in the moment, it feels more like the reverse—that these sorts of moments in the films must be inspired by moments from Wes's real life. All at once it seems clear that the wry humor in the films isn't mannered or contrived or really even invented—that it must just be the outgrowth of a genuinely funny way of being, which people like Jason and Roman are part of and party to.

Roman and Wes go to attend to the coffee, and Jason and I go to sit in the apartment's living room. Floor-to-ceiling windows open onto a rooftop garden. Jason, who is clearly an expert befriender, peppers me with questions until Wes and Roman come back with coffee. (I didn't realize until this moment that "coffee" implied freshly pulled espresso macchiato. But when in Rome.)

So this is your first writing collaboration as a threesome since *The Darjeeling Limited*?

WES ANDERSON: Yes. Roman worked with me on *Moonrise Kingdom*. And here we also have another collaborator, Kun Nomura.

For *Darjeeling*, **I know you guys did a lot of traveling and working in close quarters to get in the headspace of what you were doing. What was the approach to** *Isle of Dogs*, **as opposed to** *Darjeeling*? **Were you physically together this time?**

ROMAN COPPOLA: For *Darjeeling* we had certain trips where we were all together for a really focused time, and this one seemed like it was over a more extended timeframe. It feels like we worked on this longer.

WA: Well, we started working on it together, to invent the story, and then we've had different sessions in different places, just when we find ourselves together. And we had the time with Kun in England, not so long ago. I mean, the thing with an animated movie is, you're kind of rewriting it—you're reworking it as you go along. So the writing process goes into the shooting process.

But don't you record the voiceover before you do the shooting?

WA: Yes, but then you add more and change it around and so on. We actually haven't recorded all the voices yet, *still*. A lot of the dialogue is in Japanese, and we've been retranslating the translations and refining them and tinkering with them for months. Because it needs to work in Japanese, but it also needs to work *not* in Japanese. It's extremely complicated, but we've had fun trying to get it to operate right. We've learned an awful lot, too.

JASON SCHWARTZMAN: Also, with *Darjeeling*, because there was a start date where a whole crew and all these actors and all these people were gonna be assembled—with this, there's obviously a start date and people working on it, but the way it works is different. If there's a scene that needs specific attention, or a part—

OPPOSITE: **Shots from a montage that establishes the symptoms of Dog-Flu. The crew refers to this sequence as "Miserable Dogs."**

WA: It's a longer shooting process, and it's prepared so differently, so you can review it and study it before it's really finished. Before it's really shot, even.

I think the actual workflow for a collaborative writing process is something that's kind of mysterious to people, and it's different for each group of collaborators. How does it work for you guys?

RC: Usually it's a lot of banter and discussion, and then sometimes we'll improvise in the spirit of a character. On *Darjeeling* we did that because we kind of each had our character that we represented or we thought on behalf of. But usually we talk, there's banter, discussion, and then when something feels right, Wes will make a note of it in his notebooks. And then there's a gestation period of gathering material, and then there's another phase where it's more written. Was that accurate to say?

JS: I think so.

WA: We started with two things, I think. We had a Dog Movie, and a Japan Movie. Right?

RC: And there was always a science-fiction feeling to it.

WA: Yes. We wanted to do something sort of futuristic. Originally it began with a narrator saying, "The year 2007." That was meant to be some years in the future, but from the '60s. But then we sort of thought, "Are we going to confuse everybody too much?" I mean, would you have been confused by that? "The year 2007."

So we had the idea of a Dog Movie, the story about dogs and the garbage dump and everything. And you could set that anywhere, anywhere that has—

RC: Dogs.

WA: —government of this kind. And dogs and buildings.

RC: And garbage.

That leaves you with a lot of options.

WA: Yes. The Japanese setting came about simply because we wanted to do something related to Japanese cinema. We all do especially love Japan, but we wanted to do something that was really inspired by Japanese *movies,* and so we ended up mixing the Dog Movie and the Japan Movie together.

So who makes the first move? How is that first move made?

RC: We're looking for what sort of feels right, and it's a hard thing to define because we don't really know, but we'll talk and then something will stand out—

So it comes from conversation.

RC: Pretty much.

WA: We wanted to do a story where we had dogs and garbage. Does that sound very appealing to people? [LAUGHS] I don't know.

People love dogs *a lot*, so—

WA: Yes. I mean, I don't know why this *was* interesting to me or why I thought it was a good setting, to have these dogs that are living among garbage. But I always liked Oscar the Grouch when I was a kid. Or, like, *Sanford and Son*.

RC: Junkyards.

WA: Or *Fat Albert*.

JS: Who were those two puppets who lived in a junkyard? Were they at *Fraggle Rock?* They wore trash.

So the concept of trash as a playground—

WA: Yes. Trash is complicated; it has its own life. Isn't there a Beckett play where he's in a garbage can? *Endgame*. Those were all aspects of it, I think. Trying to make a world of abandoned, mistreated dogs, and I think some sort of sad setting for the story. And we did all have some separate particular affinity for Japan, before this movie.

Roman, you visited Japan when you were quite young, didn't you?

RC: I went there for the first time in 1979, so I was twelve or so, or fifteen—something like that. But yeah, we went there for Christmas one year as a family and visited Kyoto and Tokyo. My mom has always had a particular interest in Japanese culture and food, and textiles and art, so I think I've inherited her interest in that as well.

OPPOSITE TOP: **In Sofia Coppola's** *Lost in Translation*, **Bill Murray plays an American actor doing a Japanese commercial for Suntory Whisky, just as Sofia's father, Francis, had once done.**

OPPOSITE ABOVE: **Akira Kurosawa appeared in several print and television ads for Suntory in the '70s and '80s.**

ABOVE LEFT: **Concept drawing of Tracy, by Félicie Haymoz.**

ABOVE RIGHT: **Alexia Keogh plays author Janet Frame as a child in Jane Campion's** *An Angel at My Table*, **based on Frame's autobiographies. Wes used her as an inspiration for foreign exchange student Tracy Walker, another young writer who goes abroad.**

Your father is partially responsible for Akira Kurosawa's renaissance in the '80s. Did you get to meet him?

RC: I did get to meet him. He was very tall, as I recall, a very elegant guy. My dad did a commercial with him in our living room for Suntory whisky, which suggested the idea for Sofia's movie [*Lost in Translation*], where Bill Murray did the Suntory commercials.

"Passion knows no limits" was the tagline in the Kurosawa commercial, I think. They're on YouTube now.

RC: Yeah, I saw them a few years ago. "Suntory Reserve." That was shot in our living room. You know, my dad—and George Lucas, obviously—idolized Kurosawa as a great world cinema figure, so in the '80s, when he had a hard time with financing, when they could lend their names to sort of help, obviously they were delighted to do so.

JS: [PERTURBED] It's crazy that Kurosawa could have trouble making—I feel like there are certain people that should just be allowed to make movies, and it should be funded by, like, the government or something. There should be grants—

Like certain people could earn a lifetime pass—

JS: There are people out there who are struggling to make movies that should just . . . be able to make movies. Just so the rest of us can see what they're thinking about.

RC: It's hard. But yeah, I remember Kurosawa was kind of an interesting, imposing figure. You're aware that he's an important man, so that rubs off on you.

JS: Had you seen his movies?

RC: I hadn't seen them at that time particularly, but when I went to NYU, I took a Kurosawa class, so I saw all his movies in that class and enjoyed them very much.

Which ones are your favorites?

RC: My favorite is *Throne of Blood*. That's the one with all the arrows shooting at Toshiro Mifune? It has kind of a ghost element. . . .

So much mist. So much fog.

RC: Yes, and they're kind of riding around in the forest, getting lost, and that one I particularly like.

And then of course all the great ones. We had a dog named Yojimbo.

Did you guys watch movies together at all when you were doing the writing process for this?

RC: Once in a while we would see something—

JS: I feel like our time was so precious that we were really just trying to focus.

RC: What about the Kurosawa kidnapping movie?

JS: *High and Low*. We watched that one. But sometimes it's less for inspiration and more to create a vibe, to kinda—

RC: But also just to rest your brain.

JS: For me, it's fun because I feel like, lately, I don't get to see as many movies, so I love when we say, "Should we put on a movie?" It's the ultimate luxury.

I wanted to ask about the decision to do the languages the way that you did, as far as having the Japanese characters speak Japanese and using the translators. At what point in the process was that decision made? Was there ever any consideration to do something else?

WA: We always wanted the humans to speak Japanese. The question was, "How are people who don't speak Japanese going to know what's going on?" For some scenes, like in the Municipal Dome, it made sense that we could have an interpreter, United Nations–style. On TV, we could have it make medium-sense that these things could be translated for English-speaking viewers. But then at some places—

RC: The Simul-Translate.

WA: Yes, a translating machine. Who is it translating to? I don't know. And there's a foreign exchange student. That's why Greta Gerwig's character came from Cincinnati. But then, I think, we were also drawn to the idea of their international romance. Across the borders of Ohio and Megasaki.

RC: We didn't want subtitles, and we wanted people to understand it, so that was the challenge.

Was that partly for kid reasons? Because kids might not be used to subtitles?

WA: Partly, but mostly it was more about: what's there for us to use? To keep it dynamic. Other ways of subtitling. We sort of use every method! Usually, subtitles are there when a movie is being shown to audiences who don't speak the language the thing was made in. For us, this was the *version originale*. Eventually, translation became part of our subject matter, I think. Every now and then, of course, we just use subtitles, anyway.

AN INTRODUCTION TO AKIRA KUROSAWA

> "He is an artist, and he is demanding; a man more full, more whole, both more self-willed and more compassionate than most men are."
> —TOSHIRO MIFUNE, IN HIS PREFACE TO DONALD RICHIE'S *The Films of Akira Kurosawa*

JAPAN'S most legendary director is traditionally depicted wearing a bucket hat and a bemused smirk, or, in his later years, a fishing cap and sunglasses. The photographs sometimes fail to give a sense of his height: a gangly, stoop-shouldered boy who grew into a lanky, stoop-shouldered man, who filled out into a solid, stooped, but still tall old-timer. He always looks wry and proud in repose, exhilarated on set—it's easy to see why Toho Masterworks' documentary series on Kurosawa is named for his saying, *"It is wonderful to create!"*

What we don't see in the photographs are his rages, his shouting, his implacable fits of perfectionism. The photographic evidence does not explain the disparaging nickname *Kurosawa-tenno*, Emperor Kurosawa. His critics meant that he was irascible, demanding, sometimes even a bully. He was also charismatic, compassionate, a great soul. If he was imperious on set, his loyal crew protested, it was in service of the awesome responsibility of the work itself.

The quality of that work is partly a testament to his eye for talent. He rode to success at the head of a powerful scrum of regular collaborators, the *Kurosawa-gumi*, or Team Kurosawa. He kept a stable of great cowriters, writing in groups of two, three, or five at a time; a rotating coterie of great cinematographers, frequently working in tandem, manning the two or three cameras Kurosawa liked to have shooting at once. In front of the cameras, his repertory company: the magnetic Toshiro Mifune and trusty Takashi Shimura, joined later by the great Tatsuya Nakadai, and backed by a dozen handpicked character actors returning for film after film. The same art director, special effects man, and script supervisor for decades. A production team and crew so fluent in Kurosawa's methods that they could make a Kurosawa movie together (*After the Rain*) even after Kurosawa's death.

A film is the work of dozens of artists laboring over a single artwork, and also, at the same time, the work of a single artist practicing dozens of art forms at once. At the center of this central paradox of filmmaking stands the director. A director needs administrative skills, trust, and humility to address this first reality—many artists, one art. At the same time, a director will fall short of the task if he or she is merely an administrator and not a hands-on practitioner of each of cinema's constituent art forms, separately and in concert—many arts, one artist.

In this, *Kurosawa-tenno* was really something of an emperor among directors, seemingly born for the role. A single defining trait as a great film craftsman would be impossible to pinpoint—Kurosawa was one of the all-time greats at directing the camerawork, one of the all-time greats at blocking, one of the all-time greats at pulling powerful performances from actors. At shooting in color, at shooting in black and white; at vertical compositions in Academy ratio and at perfectly balanced framings in anamorphic widescreen. At quick cutting, at holding a long take, at movement, at stillness. At using score, at sourcing music, at choosing and mixing sound. At deeply researched period pieces, at portraits of modern life; at using complex sets, at finding stunning locations. At wrangling even the weather itself, his constant bane and frequent boon—his scenes are set by wind-whipped grass, muddy cloudbursts, volcanic steam and eldritch ice-mists, heatstruck streets and frostbitten hinterlands, lung-spasmingly brisk autumn air. What he couldn't find, he made. What he couldn't make, he waited for.

He wrote or cowrote every screenplay. He rehearsed his actors for weeks—to this day, still rare in cinema. Not only did he edit his own films, he did it while he was shooting them—today, all but unheard of. He'd stay up at night with an old Moviola editing machine and have a rough cut just about ready by the time production had wrapped. He was constantly playing with technology—new uses of slow motion, wipe transitions, reflected light, telephoto lenses, Dolby sound, digital video—and he continually reinvented his visual style. Great careers could be, and have been, made by excelling at a single trick he mastered and moved on from.

As a storyteller, too, he constantly switched his genre and approach. His worldwide reputation was made on samurai films like *Rashomon* and *Seven Samurai*, but he also aced the sports story (*Sanshiro Sugata*) and the film noir (*The Bad Sleep Well*), the realist problem play (*I Live in Fear*) and the neorealist social drama (*One Wonderful Sunday*). He filmed Shakespeare (*Throne of Blood*, *Ran*) and Maxim Gorky (*The Lower Depths*), adapted Ed McBain (*High and Low*) and arguably Dashiell Hammett (*Yojimbo*). He tackled Dostoyevsky's *The Idiot* (his preferred cut, now lost, was nearly five hours long). He helped invent the conventions of the buddy-cop movie (*Stray Dog*), the yakuza film (*Drunken Angel*), the blood-spurting black-comedy action flick (*Yojimbo* and its sequel, *Sanjuro*), and the big damn adventure blockbuster (*The Hidden Fortress*, which inspired *Star Wars*). Some of his most moving films—tender, meandering hagiographies like *Red Beard*, *Dersu Uzala*, and *Madadayo*, or vivid motion-paintings like *Dreams*—remain without genre or easy comparison.

His works and methods were not always well received. Years of failed negotiations with Hollywood producers and risk-averse Japanese studios in the late sixties left him with a reputation for unreliability and without access to funds. He was fired from an American co-production, *Tora! Tora! Tora!*—the producers said, and the press wrote, that he must be mentally ill. His gorgeous first color film, *Dodes'kaden*, failed at the box office. He attempted suicide. He recovered quickly (the company of his beloved dogs helped) but the resurrection of his career took time.

Unexpectedly, he was invited to direct a story of his choosing with Soviet funding—a year and a half of shooting in Moscow and Siberia produced *Dersu Uzala* in 1975. He began writing scripts again, illustrated by sweeping, hypersaturated paintings of the shots he still feared he might never see on screen. When Japanese producers doubted the practicability of his planned samurai epics, his longtime admirers George Lucas and Francis Ford Coppola stepped in, securing financing and distribution for 1980's *Kagemusha* and reintroducing his art to the world.

Kurosawa's private interests were no less varied than his professional skills—a painter, a mountaineer, a knowledgeable amateur of classical music, a passionate drinker of whiskey, a devourer of cultural experience. He was an ardent student of Japan's traditional art forms—Noh, kendo, haiku, ceramics—and a thorough scholar of Japan's history. He bristled at the indignity, the irony, the absurdity of the charge leveled by snooty French critics of the fifties—and repeated by American hipsters ever since—that his films were not truly Japanese; that they were gross fare for Western tastes, popcorn for the hoi polloi, and nothing to the rarefied pleasures offered by authentically Japanese filmmakers. Over whiskeys with the critic Donald Richie, Kurosawa complained that what Westerners perceived as "authentically Japanese" subtlety and restraint in the work of his colleagues was often just emotionally uninvested filmmaking—a sign that his fellow directors simply had too little interest in *people*.

Kurosawa's unqualified passion for people manifested on every scale, and reviewers around the world often knocked him for it—his directing was too excessive, too indulgent, too sentimental; his moral statements too clear and assured for critical tastes. Kurosawa continually proved he was capable of crafting tight, intricate, jewel-movement domestic dramas but always disdained to be subtle or small for small or subtle's sake—like Shakespeare, he knew when it was high time for a tavern song, a round dance, a sword fight, a thunderclap. Filmmakers around the world, though, worship him,

THE FILMS OF AKIRA KUROSAWA

for the same reason they do homage to other easy pleasures like Hitchcock and Spielberg: his absolute command of film craft and his knack for spinning a yarn.

Kurosawa's stories rush into the midst of a crisis—sometimes grand, sometimes quiet. He shamelessly hits you, floors you, with the exposition of the problem right up front, so he can get on to the business of watching how his characters deal with it. Whether he was adapting another's work or inventing his own plot from scratch, he started his screenplays at the first scene, with the problem, with the thing that arrested his attention; he didn't let himself decide the end in advance. The result is that even the logline of a Kurosawa movie can make you sit up in your seat: A rookie cop loses his gun—he finds out someone's committed murder with it. A straightlaced medic accidentally cuts himself while operating on a soldier, and discovers he's contracted syphilis from his blood—he decides what to tell his fiancée. A ruffian is groomed to be a noble lord's decoy—the warlord is killed and the ruffian must continue to impersonate him. A kidnapper demands a king's ransom from a wealthy businessman—the boy he kidnapped is not the businessman's son, but the kidnapper wants the ransom anyway, or the boy dies.

"I suppose all of my films have a common theme," he told Donald Richie. "If I think about it, though, the only theme I can think of is really a question: Why can't people be happier together?"

It was not an idle question. His films offer dozens of answers—some sweet, some bitter, all of them poignant, incisive, and true, and all of them quietly troubling, too. Only in his last films, made when Kurosawa was in his eighties, does he seem to make peace with the question. *Dreams*, based partly on his real dreams, partly on his fears, partly on his childhood memories, ends with the protagonist passing through a poor village that seems to exist outside of time. He meets an old man there, not unlike one Kurosawa himself had met in a similar poor village as a teenager. The old man is 103, and is getting ready for a funeral parade for an old girlfriend who only made it to ninety-nine. As he suits up in festive clothes, he shrugs off the Kurosawa character's worries. "Some say life is hard. That's just talk," the old man says. He picks a bunch of roadside flowers as the marching band makes its way down the road. "In fact, it's good to be alive," he remarks as he departs. He turns over his shoulder to add, "It's exciting."

1943

SANSHIRO SUGATA

1944

THE MOST BEAUTIFUL

1945

SANSHIRO SUGATA, PART 2

1945

THE MEN WHO TREAD ON THE TIGER'S TAIL

1946

NO REGRETS FOR OUR YOUTH

1947

ONE WONDERFUL SUNDAY

1948

DRUNKEN ANGEL

1949

THE QUIET DUEL

1949

STRAY DOG

1950

SCANDAL

1950

RASHOMON

1951

THE IDIOT

CONTINUED

THE FILMS OF
AKIRA KUROSAWA

CONTINUED

1952

IKIRU

1954

SEVEN SAMURAI

1955

I LIVE IN FEAR

1957

THRONE OF BLOOD

1957

THE LOWER DEPTHS

1958

THE HIDDEN FORTRESS

1960

THE BAD SLEEP WELL

1961

YOJIMBO

1962

SANJURO

1963

HIGH AND LOW

1965

RED BEARD

1970

DODES'KA-DEN

1975

DERSU UZALA

1980

KAGEMUSHA

1985

RAN

1990

DREAMS

1991

RHAPSODY IN AUGUST

1993

MADADAYO

At this point, Wes's eighteen-month-old daughter, Freya, comes toddling into the room, all sunshine in a delicate floral onesie. She's followed by Wes's partner, Juman Malouf. Freya is about to go down for a nap but wanted to say good night first. She's toting a pink Pegasus and repeating the phrase "horsie, horsie, horsie" in a near-inaudible whisper. "She's been obsessed with horsies," Juman explains. Wes and Jason join in the quiet chorus of "horsie" until Freya shifts the subject: "doggies!"

"Oh, yes, she's wanting to watch the movie doggies," Wes explains. She likes to watch the Isle of Dogs *dailies with Wes. "We'll watch the doggies after your nap."*

That's nice that she likes the doggies.

WA: She likes to sit and watch them, yes.

[TO JASON AND ROMAN] I don't know how much we talked about Miyazaki during the process. Lately I've been feeling more and more . . . We always talked about Kurosawa in relation to this, but Miyazaki is at least as much of an inspiration.

JS: Yeah, there's a great Miyazaki documentary called—

The Kingdom of Dreams and Madness.

JS: Yeah, did you see it?

I did.

JS: It's great, right?

Yeah, it's good.

JS: [INCREDULOUS] It's "good" [LAUGHS]. No, it's *great*. I love it because it gives you such access to him—just watching him work and just feeling like you're really in the hands of a master. Like, a person who's literally talking and looking up like this [JASON IMITATES MIYAZAKI DRAWING AND TALKING AT THE SAME TIME]. He's *so* good at what he does.

But the script is not written. That's the only thing that's confusing—

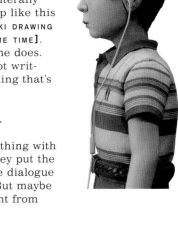

That's a crazy thing to me.

JS: They do the whole thing with no script, and then they put the script in. They put the dialogue in as they go, right? But maybe that's not that different from anything else.

WA: Well, that's the way most animated movies are done. They have a story, they have their characters and things, they start developing the look of the characters, and they work in sequences and they do the boards; that's their script, really. And then they record—

JS: I'm playing dumb for the benefit of having it explained to the reader. [LAUGHS]

WA: But we don't do it that way. We do it with a script.

The way they work nowadays, like Pixar for instance, there's a lot of interaction between drawing and recording and rewriting and reboarding, and it's always being worked out that way. And it makes sense, because they usually have a large staff. They staff up the thing, and they develop the images and the characters and all those things at the same time because it's such a long process that they need those things to get started. So before they even have the story fully developed, they have visuals that are already developed. And we do this much, much less than they do. They actually work much more freely in a way, the Pixar guys—

JS: Well, the infrastructure is crazy. They have a whole setup to be like that.

WA: It's set up to be like that, yes. And also, it's set up to not just do *a* movie.

The Interpreter (BELOW) is voiced by Frances McDormand. Jake Ryan voices the Junior Interpreter (FAR RIGHT). The Simul-Translate machine (ABOVE), which appears in the scene between the films' villains, is voiced by Frank Wood.

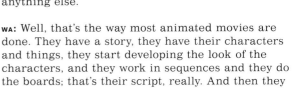
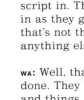

JS: Exactly.

WA: All movie studios used to be like that. But they aren't now. Only the animation studios are like that.

JS: Even in something as recent as *Inside Out*, in the original version, I don't think Joy was the star of it—there was a different emotion that was the star of it, and they switched. So *huge* changes happen while you're doing it. Pretty interesting.

Where do the changes happen in your writing process? How do you decide something isn't working, or where does a better idea come from? Is there an example you can think of in the *Isle of Dogs* script where that happened?

WA: I think for us it's more about what's going to happen next. And that's enough, that's a big enough challenge to say, "Who are they, and what's going to happen, and then what, and then what, and then what, and then what?"

And then, when you have the whole story together, it's like, "OK . . . the thing that we wrote in the first scene, we actually never *did* that. The thing we said is going to happen, we did a slightly *different* thing. And now we need to go back and figure out . . . it sounds so *good* the way we set it up, and it's actually not what we did."

I feel like, for a certain kind of storyteller, they set out to do something and they *do* the thing they set out to do. And then sometimes, other kinds of storytellers, you're searching for it as you do it—as you tell it, I guess. And when you're doing that, you sometimes have to re-find it. Does that make any sense?

JS: It does make sense. And, in a weird, mysterious way, to go along with that, it also feels like you're trying to find this thing that already exists, somehow? Like, there's a movie *there*, you're just trying to

ABOVE: **Hayao Miyazaki in Mami Sunada's 2013 documentary *The Kingdom of Dreams and Madness*, which chronicles the production of *The Wind Rises* at Studio Ghibli.**

CASTELLO CAVALCANTI

WES test-drove the bilingual concept in a 2013 short film, "Castello Cavalcanti" (TOP), which pays the same tribute to Federico Fellini that *Isle of Dogs* does to Kurosawa. (BOTTOM, a still from the Mille Miglia race scene in Fellini's *Amarcord*.) It stars Jason Schwartzman and Giada Colagrande, an Italian director who's married to Anderson regular Willem Dafoe.

Most people in many countries around the world prefer to watch foreign films dubbed into their own language. Americans are an exception. If we're purists, we Americans tend to feel that a dubbed performance is an inauthentic approximation of the actor's work. Even those of us who aren't purists tend to be put off by the mismatch between the soundtrack and the mouth movements.

Italian audiences, historically, haven't cared. (In Fellini's time, recording the dialogue in postproduction was the norm, even for Italian films with Italian actors.) Italian audiences have always tended to be much more put off by the thought of looking away from the actor's face. A subtitle is a distraction from the actor's authentic *nonverbal* performance.

For "Castello Cavalcanti," Wes went for a third option: no dubbing, no subtitles. Instead, clever, deliberate screenwriting, precise direction, and a cast of smart actors ensure that the dramatic beat is always clear. The tempo is never rudely subdivided by the interruption of a new line of text. The performances come through much more vividly: There's no need to take your eyes off the gestures and glances, no need to take your ear off the pauses and understated inflections.

uncover it? So when you *hit* it, it's almost like hitting a nerve or something. It's like digging and going, *"Ding ding ding!* I think we found something here!"

Have any of you read *In the Blink of an Eye* **by Walter Murch?**

JS: Yes. [NODS FROM WES AND ROMAN]

There's a section where he talks about "dreaming in pairs," a kind of dream therapy technique where in order to figure out what someone's dream was, you make guesses. If they say, "I was in an airplane," then you, the dream therapist, say, "So the airplane, was it going to crash?" And then the dreamer will correct you: "No, no, it was doing this or that." So you can guide someone to remember a dream by asking questions about it. The dream rises to defend itself.

WA: What's the context of him telling that?

Well, he's speaking as an editor—

WA: He's asking the director what he would want.

Yes. But I think it applies to storytelling as well, especially in a collaborative way.

JS: Yes.

WA: [INTERRUPTING] Is that moleskin? These trousers. [TOUCHING JASON'S PANTS]

JS: No, it's cotton, I think.

WA: Because I was going to say, they could be very, very warm.

I am gonna bring it back to the screenwriting thing—

JS: [ADOPTING A MOCK-SAGE SERENE VOICE] But you must look at it like this: this *is* the screenwriting thing.

You're right, actually. This is a good point. With this movie, were you thinking of it as a Hero's Journey kind of a story?

RC: I don't really think in those terms. We don't talk in themes or big concepts.

It's just, "What's gonna happen?"

RC: Well, that's just the way it is: We just talk in very practical terms. Even with *Darjeeling* and other projects like *Moonrise Kingdom*, it's not like we're thinking, "What are they going through?" There's never any real discussion about anything other than, "Where are they? What's happening? What could happen next? What would be interesting? What feels right?" You know, very practical things.

There aren't any screenwriting principles that you apply, like, "We need a turning point" or "We need—"

RC: Never. It never comes up. I mean, sometimes there'll *be* some turning point, or maybe we intuitively recognize, "Oh, that's the right thing to have in this place."

JS: So much of the time I feel like we're talking about something that is *real*, even though it has a magical quality. I always feel like we're thinking, "What happened next to these people?"

It's like you're trying to remember it?

JS: It's like we're ten feet behind them, on their tail or something, trying to investigate it. Do you know what I mean? It feels like we're putting together a crime. Trying to figure it out. So that's, at least to me, why we don't talk in themes. You can't think about themes until you even have a . . .

I think that it's a tendency of viewers and critics to want to talk about themes and ask about themes—but it sounds like what you're saying is, "We were just figuring out what happened to the dogs."

RC: Exactly. That would probably be accurate.

I've been reading about Kurosawa's screenwriting process—

WA: Tell us about it.

Well, I'm wondering if it resembles yours at all, because he always worked with cowriters.

WA: It's not necessarily common in Japanese cinema, but with Kurosawa, they're often filmmaking *groups*. And the Italian cinema, you look at the credits, and then you see young Bertolucci, Pasolini. I mean Fellini—who did Fellini write for?

Rossellini.

WA: Rossellini. Yes! You know, those are the guys in the restaurants across the river somewhere in those days, sitting around. But anyway, go ahead.

I think that one of the things that sets Kurosawa's work apart is that the screenwriting is really good. The screenplays are tight, and they kind of hit you in the gut.
   I read this memoir by Shinobu Hashimoto, who wrote *Rashomon* **and** *Ikiru* **and** *Seven Samurai* **and a couple others with Kurosawa. Kurosawa, apparently, would kind of pick collaborators by asking himself, "Who do I think is going to be the right fit, personality-wise? How do I want the room to feel when we're holed up in there writing?" So he'd pick the team, and they'd get a room at an inn. Kurosawa and Hashimoto would write things, passing them back and forth and giving each other thoughts and corrections.**
   And they had a third guy, Hideo Oguni, who didn't write anything. But he was credited as a screenwriter. They called him "the command tower."

RC: The command tower would give comments and . . . ?

WA: Yes, what did Oguni do?

He was the comment person. Apparently, they sat across a table, and Hashimoto and Kurosawa would write, and—

JS: In front of each other? They'd just write in front of each other?

Yeah! Like, at the same table. And then Oguni would sit across the room from them with his back turned, and he'd be reading something else.

RC: Like on the Internet or something.

So Hashimoto and Kurosawa would kind of go back and forth between each other, but then they would pass their finished stuff to Oguni. And then he would kind of redirect the course.

JS: "Command tower." Like if he felt something was not right, he had a lot of say—

Yeah, he had kind of veto power, or yes-or-no; he could say, "This is all wrong."

WA: Like editing.

JS: Was there always a command tower?

No, actually. So this is the premise of this memoir by Hashimoto, that they switched to a different system after *Seven Samurai*. *Seven Samurai* was the hardest thing they'd ever done—

WA: And it was just the three of them?

It was the three of them. But they were all so proud of it, they felt like they had achieved the greatest thing they were going to achieve. After that point, Kurosawa said, "What if we try a different system?" Because they were all so *tired* from making *Seven Samurai*, which is this super-long script. Hashimoto said, "What if we have Oguni write with us too? Instead of having him as the editor, we'll just all kind of make stuff up, and we'll all kind of write the screenplay together." So it didn't go through these

rounds of edits. And their next movie was *I Live in Fear*, which turned out to be a huge flop.

WA: Yes, but it's interesting—I mean, also, that movie's such a dark . . . [TO ROMAN AND JASON] You know what that one is? The old man is *obsessed* with nuclear disaster. And "I Live in Fear" is a description of his state of mind. He's afraid for his family.

He wants to move his family to Brazil, and so his family wants to have him declared insane so that they don't have to deal with him.

RC: Wow.

WA: Yes. And that's already . . . I don't see *money*.

RC: [WEIGHING] Yeah, *Seven Samurai* . . . to *I Live in Fear*.

JS: Sounds great, though.

WA: Yes, it's a very interesting movie.

JS: So what happened then?

WA: They switched back again?

No, they kept doing it that way.

WA: What comes after *I Live in Fear*?

Throne of Blood, and then in the same year *The Lower Depths*, which is also a pretty dark, hard-to-get-into kind of—

WA: But, you know, that's a good one too.

Well, I guess I bring it up because—

ABOVE: Artist's impression of Hideo Oguni, Akira Kurosawa, and Shinobu Hashimoto writing the screenplay for *Ikiru* in 1952 or *Seven Samurai* in 1953. The setup was the same. A story idea was chosen. Kurosawa had Shinobu Hashimoto write a first draft based on that idea. Hashimoto and Kurosawa got a room at a *ryokan*, a traditional Japanese inn. Kurosawa and Hashimoto would then be joined by Hideo Oguni, senior member of the writing team. Together they'd rewrite the script from scratch. They worked for seven hours a day, seven days a week, and didn't check out until they had a final draft, no matter how long that took. They'd pass their work counterclockwise as they wrote, to be reviewed by each writer in order of seniority, until every page passed muster. Hashimoto describes the trio's writing process and seating plan in his memoir *Compound Cinematics: Akira Kurosawa and I*, published in 2006 and in English in 2015.

OPPOSITE: In a shot from *I Live in Fear* (ABOVE), the stubborn septuagenarian Nakajima (played by Toshiro Mifune) faces a team of court mediators. In a shot from *Isle of Dogs* (TOP), Chief faces the rest of the pack.

JS: Can I say one thing? Did Kurosawa have the initial nugget for the idea?

Usually, yes.

JS: OK. Because his mind was probably going in a different place too—it's not just the command tower's fault [LAUGHS]. It's easy to point the finger at the new addition.

WA: But I like having the command tower in the room.

JS: Do you think the command tower, though, felt like his time was being wasted?

Well, apparently Hashimoto thought that he was lazy, at first. He was kind of like, "What's this guy doing? Why is he getting paid more than me to just sit there?"

WA: He was paid *more*?

Yeah!

WA: Why was he paid more?

He was just more established. I don't want to be, like, lecturing you guys on Kurosawa history!

WA: No, I mean, I think that that's good for the book.

I bring it up just because I've read this script a couple of times, and I find it to be very tight. And I think that this is true of pretty much all of the scripts that you guys have worked on, that Wes has made. I think that you are, maybe, even on the opposite pole from something like a Miyazaki film, which feels very free-form, where that kind of "What happened next?" energy is the whole thing. Whereas *Isle of Dogs* . . . I feel like it sets out to do a certain thing, and it loops back to certain themes, and it really does feel like a whole *piece*. So did it go through several drafts? Was there a refining process?

WA: I don't think we work in drafts, exactly. Once we reach the end, we start reworking it. I mean, even *now*, when we change something in the movie, or cut something, then I usually go back into the script and modify. It is constantly reworked. And then there usually are some big problems that we're struggling with and trying to figure out. Usually, those problems don't just get *solved*. I feel like it gets pushed a little this way, and reshaped, and then eventually, the problem is *absorbed*, and redirected, and eventually you look at it and say, "Well, now it seems OK that that happens." And often it's like, enough *little* things make a difference, you know? Does that make sense?

JS: [JUMPING IN] And can I say one thing, that probably is wrong?

Go for it.

JS: But in this moment I feel that it's right?

WA: Please.

JS: Initially, when you were talking about just kind of blasting out ideas, and then you have these problems later on . . . I find this to be true in life, too. It's like a puzzle, and you were looking at it in the wrong way. And all of a sudden you realize, "Oh wait! We've always had this notion about something, we just didn't know how it fit. And *now* . . . it just didn't have the proper things around it, and now all of a sudden it fits." So I think that's also an interesting thing, that you're always creating and always changing and rethinking.

But there's always a little pile of ideas that were there from the *very* beginning. That happened with *Darjeeling*. Like, there are these *principles* that end up being a very big part of the movie—

WA: Usually we have them sort of in a list.

JS: Exactly.

WA: A list that keeps getting remade. And we'll say, "Wait, what are we trying to do again? Was it like this? Or like this? Or like that?" Some version of this list appears maybe six different times in the notebooks that the movie comes out of.

The list of core ideas? What's in the list?

WA: It could be anything. It could be that we wanted a character like such-and-such, or that we wanted to have this thing visually happen—

RC: Or a narrator saying a certain phrase.

WA: Yes. It could be a phrase . . .

Feel free to hit me with specifics!

WA: [AS IF RECITING A LIST, RATTLING THINGS OFF] Well, I think for this, it was that we have these alpha dogs—Chief, Rex, King, Duke, Boss—this list of dogs that are all named as if they were the top dog. That there were fleas, worms, ticks, lice, a garbage dump. . . . That we had a political—

RC: Atari was always a boy pilot who was on a quest.

WA: Yes, the pilot. What were some of the other things?

RC: I cut you off, but the political situation—

WA: That there was some political crisis. That there were trams that carry garbage around.

RC: That there had been some testing, and that there was sort of an "Outer Cuticles" area that had this deeper mystery.

WA: Animal testing was always part of it.

Does that come from *The Plague Dogs*?

WA: It relates to *The Plague Dogs*, for sure, and we did talk about it. I love *The Plague Dogs*, I love *Watership Down*. But I feel like that aspect of the thing, the laboratory testing thing and all that, is more from *The Secret of NIMH*.

JS: When we're writing and we get stuck, we can just think, "What was on that list?" It's reassuring sometimes, to know what some of those ideas were, the ones that you had at the most basic version of the movie.

Because you can forget.

JS: It makes you feel like you're onto something. It's nice to be realigned with yourself, or something.

WA: Well, also, sometimes there's a solution to a problem, and it would be easy to just decide, "Let's do *this!*" Let's do the thing that someone just suggested would make it make sense to them. But we don't want to do it.

RC: There was one thing that would have solved a lot . . . that seemed so obvious—

WA: Is it that we would make it really about replacing dogs with robot dogs?

RC: Exactly.

WA: Yes, and often it was like, that would give motivation to everything in the story. They want to get rid of the real dogs and replace them with robot dogs because they want to sell robot dogs. And there's a kind of little current of that in it. But that's not actually the feeling of the movie. So it's a little more vague. *Why* are they doing this?

They just hate dogs.

WA: They hate dogs! [LAUGHS FROM THE GROUP] Yes, that's what it is. They hate dogs.

JS: Have you ever met someone who hates dogs, by the way? Because when you *do,* they can't really tell you why they hate a dog. They just hate dogs.

WA: Well, some people don't like dogs because they find them scary.

Would you guys all consider yourselves dog people?

JS: [IMMEDIATELY] Yes.

RC: [WITH CALM CONVICTION] I'm not a dog person.

WA: [CONSIDERING] Not really. I mean, I *like* dogs, but I don't desperately need to have dogs around me.

Roman, you're not a dog person?

RC: I prefer cats. I have a cat. I don't dislike dogs. Jason—

WA: Jason is a dog person because Jason has a very close relationship with his dog.

JS: I grew up with dogs, like, I've always had them.

You seem like a dog person.

JS: I can't imagine my life without a dog.

Well, I ask because the screenplay is so much about loving dogs—this almost moral urgency or beauty to the relationship between a dog and a person. I think that it's probably going to be kind of emotional for dog people to watch this movie.

WA: [PLAINTIVELY] I hope so.

RC: [ALSO PLAINTIVELY] "Whatever happened to man's best friend?"

You said that in a way that made it sound kind of jokey, but at least on the page, it reads as very sincere.

RC: No, it's very sincere.

WA: I don't think we want to go jokey with it at all.

JS: This is a powerful thing to talk about, this movie.

WA: We shouldn't even make light of it in front of Jason. It upsets him.

So Jason is your core dog-lover for this script.

WA: He's the command tower for dog lovers. Yes. I mean, Jason's always had a big note on this movie, which is, "Why would they *do* this?!"

At this, I put my hand to my heart, and let out a touched laugh. Jason's face is very sincere.

WA: [STILL IMITATING JASON, SQUEAKING] "No one would do this!" [LAUGHS FROM THE GROUP]

Well, there's a lot of cruelty—

JS: [IMMEDIATELY] There is a *lot* of cruelty!

—in the way that you guys were talking about the things on your list—there are dogs, and they're mistreated, and there's trash. . . . I mean, it's an animated movie, and kids are going to see it, and I can picture it being kind of a formative, potentially slightly disturbing experience for young people—

WA: I don't know how old they should be to see it, you know.

JS: Could we invent our own MPAA rating? Like you can't see this unless you're—

RICHARD ADAMS

Martin Rosen's 1982 film version of The Plague Dogs

RICHARD ADAMS is known for his animal novels—tales about rabbits, bears, horses, and dogs with echoes of ancient epics and religious stories. With his master's degree in history and his experience serving in the British army in World War II, many have interpreted his books—particularly his most famous, *Watership Down*—as political allegories.

But Adams, too, is a practitioner of Wes, Roman, and Jason's "what happened next?" school of storytelling.

"I want to emphasize that *Watership Down* was never intended to be some sort of allegory or parable," Adams says in the preface to the 2005 edition of the book. "It is simply the story about rabbits made up and told in the car." He told new bits of the story to his daughters every time they drove to school, over a period of months. Eventually, at their urging, he turned these stories into the Carnegie-medal winning novel—his first, published in 1972, when Adams was fifty-two years old. Like the *Iliad* and the *Odyssey*, the finished novel is

almost too structurally sophisticated to believe that it was ever an oral tale. Seemingly modeled, *Aeneid*-style, on both of the Homeric epics at once, it follows the bedraggled wanderings of a band of exiles and culminates in a war for the fate of a nation.

The Plague Dogs, published in 1977, is a simpler, bleaker tale: it follows the exploits of two dogs that have escaped from an animal testing facility, on the run from authorities who believe they're carrying bubonic plague. Both books were adapted into animated films by Martin Rosen, and both films are famous for traumatizing a generation of unsuspecting children who thought they were sitting down to watch something more cuddly and less bloody.

Adams made sure to do research into the lives and habits of animals, wanting to avoid the anthropomorphic tendencies of most animal fiction. In *Watership Down*, the rabbits have rabbit needs and rabbit problems: they want to mate, to find a warren, to avoid being hunted, to eat tasty vegetables. *The Plague Dogs*, like *Isle of Dogs*, is about domesticated dogs that have experienced trauma and are learning to fend for themselves for the first time. The book's heroes, Rowf and Snitter, have dog desires: the more naive of the two, Snitter, longs to return to his master. Near the book's end, the two

take to the sea in an effort to escape their pursuers. Rowf asks Snitter where they hope to arrive. "There's an island," Snitter says. "They're all dogs there."

"Men aren't allowed there unless the dogs like them and let them in."

"I never knew. Just out there, is it, really? What's it called?"

"Dog," said Snitter, after a moment's thought. "The Isle of Dog."

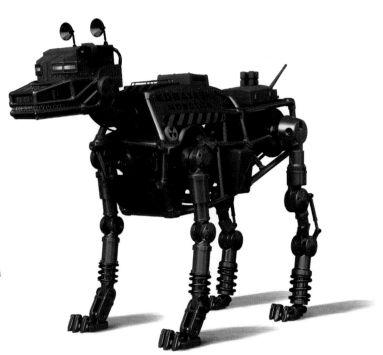

WA: PG-9.

JS: Nine years old.

That seems fair to me. It makes me think of, I don't know, like, *E.T.* or something. You know, that's a movie for—

RC: That sounds good.

WA: Yeah, that's good box office. [LAUGHTER]

RC: But I think a lot of the kids' movies, or literature—and we've talked about this with *Moonrise Kingdom*—the things we're drawn to as kids often have an edge, or they have some dark quality.

WA: But you mean children's literature that's filled with violence and stuff like that.

Like Roald Dahl.

WA: And everything before. [LAUGHS]

JS: Or like movies from my childhood, like *The Secret of NIMH.*

Oh yeah. All the Don Bluth stuff—

JS: But also, more than anything, as a kid, what I remember from those movies is like, a *loneliness.* Even the way that the sound is recorded—like water will be dropping, like [IMITATES THE SOUND OF ONE LONELY WATER DROPLET AFTER ANOTHER]. And there's a little reverb on it. The first movie I ever saw in theaters was *The Last Unicorn.* And my daughter just brought the DVD home from the library and said, "Can we watch this?"

How old is your daughter?

JS: Six and a half. So we were watching it, and there's a real sad, lonely thing about it . . . I'm telling you, it's so weird, even just talking about the sounds—those movies have just a lot of sonic space. Like, an animal just eating grass. There's not a lot of other stuff going on.

WA: Well, this is something that Miyazaki has always had.

JS: Space.

WA: Quiet, and the willingness to take a moment. I mean *My Neighbor Totoro*, one thing that's very different is that it's such a quotidian sort of . . . They arrive in a new house. They start cleaning it.

That's the plot. [LAUGHS]

WA: Yes! I mean, there are some interesting discoveries to be made in the neighborhood, but a lot of it is these kids moving into their new house and adjusting to life in the country. I think their mother is in the hospital. That's not the rhythm of American animated movies. It's not even that it's a slow-paced

story, it's that the events are quite low key, up to a point. Then you find a giant creature—

Right, it's not as if nothing happens, but the film is interested in the same things a child that age is interested in.

JS: I don't know, but can I say one thing? Which is that, like, when Wes was talking about this story idea in the very beginning, and as we've been working through it, even though I hadn't rewatched *The Secret of NIMH* and those things, there was something that appealed to me about this, which was just in some way having something that is connected to a type of movie that's animated, that has these types of . . . *feelings.*

A tradition of a cinema of—

WA: Yes, those feelings.

JS: Sort of, and I mean, just in a vague way—I *miss* that. I connected with that—

WA: Emotionally.

JS: That sense, that sensation.

Tell me about writing the scene where Atari meets Spots.

WA: [TO ROMAN AND JASON] Do we remember cooking that up?

PREVIOUS SPREAD: Dog tags for Rex, Duke, King, Boss, and others

TOP: A robot-dog puppet

LEFT: ***Mrs. Frisby and the Rats of NIMH***, a 1971 children's novel by Robert C. O'Brien, tells the story of a widowed mouse trying to save her family's home from a farmer's plow. But the most memorable part is a long flashback about the titular rats, in which they're subjected to tests by the National Institute for Mental Health (NIMH) and, as a result, become intelligent. The rats are happy to escape from NIMH, although in the book, they were treated reasonably well, all things considered. In his 1982 animated film adaptation, ***The Secret of NIMH***, Don Bluth shortens the flashback into a quick montage but ratchets up its shocks and spooks, as he does throughout the story. The book's ending, in which the intelligent rats sensibly relocate Mrs. Frisby's house for her, is livened up with magic, swordplay, and sociopathy.

The Secret of NIMH, Bluth's first feature, is a relic of a period of children's animation that more freely featured jump scares, gloom, and frank cruelty—though *NIMH* is a less famously scarring childhood memory than Martin Rosen's film versions of ***Watership Down*** and ***The Plague Dogs***.

THE FILMS OF HAYAO MIYAZAKI

1979

THE CASTLE OF CAGLIOSTRO

1984
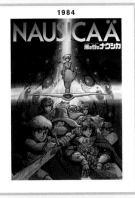
NAUSICAÄ OF THE VALLEY OF THE WIND

1986

CASTLE IN THE SKY

1988

MY NEIGHBOR TOTORO

1989

KIKI'S DELIVERY SERVICE

1992

PORCO ROSSO

1997

PRINCESS MONONOKE

2001

SPIRITED AWAY

2004

HOWL'S MOVING CASTLE

2004

PONYO

2013

THE WIND RISES

THE animated films of Hayao Miyazaki are very big, and very small. They're about princesses and warriors, witches and gods; they're also about toddlers and ten-year-olds and teenagers. They feature pirates and explosions and high-speed chases; they also show us butterflies landing, plants sprouting, characters quietly eating alone. Frequently, they feature flight—Miyazaki, fond of vintage aircraft, likes to make films about pilots. His storytelling often feels airborne as well: his stories are unbounded by traditional plot structures, and his characters are free to explore for exploration's sake.

Miyazaki is the director of eleven feature films, perhaps best known for 1988's *My Neighbor Totoro* (which established the character Totoro as an international icon and perennially popular plush toy) and 2001's *Spirited Away* (which won the Academy Award for Best Animated Feature and remains the highest-grossing film of all time in Japan).

A recurring feature of his work (seen in *Nausicaä of the Valley of the Wind, My Neighbor Totoro, Princess Mononoke, Spirited Away*, and *Ponyo*) is an encounter, and then a relationship, between a young protagonist and an animal or spirit. Sometimes the animals are spirits, or the spirits appear as animals. In Shinto, the *kami* are the gods, forces, or spirits that dwell in, and are inseparable from, nature; some of Miyazaki's films feature kami explicitly (*Princess Mononoke, Spirited Away*), others implicitly or suggestively (*My Neighbor Totoro, Ponyo*).

In all of these films, the kami or kami-like creature invites the hero, in one fashion or another, into the realm of nature or spirits, and then the hero must serve as the go-between for the needs of the animal (or animal population) and the human population. The hero of a Miyazaki film is a young person straddling the line between human and animal, between human and nature, and having to advocate for the needs of both. *Isle of Dogs*'s Atari fills this classic Miyazakian role, as the liaison between Megasaki and Trash Island, between the human world and the dog world.

The bustling "human worlds" of Miyazaki's films (*Nausicaä*'s Tolmekia, *Mononoke*'s Irontown, *Spirited Away*'s present-day Japan) are associated with technology, industry, and the military, and are represented with ambivalence at best. In this, we can sense some of Miyazaki's feelings about his country—Japan's rural green spaces are teeming with life, imbued with very old power. Its urban centers are doggedly modernizing at too great a cost. It is the young protagonist's job to make sure, against all odds, that the humans don't forget about the world of tradition, the world of nature, the world of the kami.

Miyazaki also respects children and animals enough to put them in very difficult situations and to allow them to encounter suffering. *Isle of Dogs* shares with Miyazaki's work a juxtaposition of darkness and tenderness, a commitment to rendering the full spectrum of human experience in a form sensible to young people. *Princess Mononoke* is a violent, often bloody film, but Miyazaki told the *New York Times* in a 1999 interview that he envisioned its audience as "anyone over the age of ten." He continued:

"I think that if you are very genuine in doing films for young children, you must aim for their heads, not deciding for them what will be too much for them to handle. What we found was that the children actually understood the movie and what we were trying to say more than the adults."

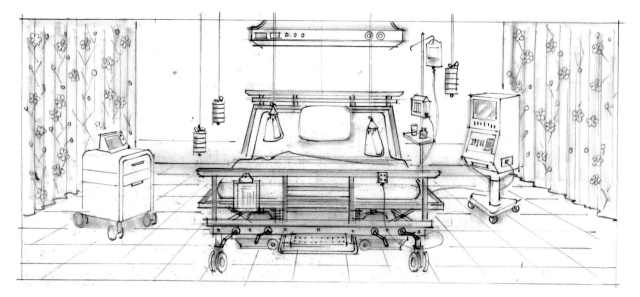

RC: I remember being moved by it. I always thought that was very sweet and genuine. I'm trying to remember . . .

JS: Well, I could be wrong about this, but wasn't part of the thing that led to that scene is, we were talking about how Atari became the ward of Kobayashi, like how he fell into his life. That's sort of what led us down that road, with his parents, that was the real—

He's an orphan, which is now the third orphan in one of your screenplays?

WA: Is that right? I know we had the orphan in *Moonrise Kingdom* . . .

And Zero.

WA: Oh, Zero's an orphan too! That character's an orphan. Yes. Orphans! [LAUGHS]

RC: I think all the Disney movies have orphan protagonists.

WA: Only orphans.

Well, loneliness is the thing that Jason identified, and they do—

WA: Yes, this poor kid, he's sitting in a hospital with a broken leg, and he's got—he spends the whole movie with a piece of metal stuck in the side of his head.

JS: Yeah, he gets beat up a little.

WA: Yes, it's quite rough on him. And his parents have died. And his distant uncle is not nice to him.

The love of this dog, which is also still being sort of denied to him by Major-Domo, is kind of—

WA: He's given a dog that he's told is not his pet. And then the dog's taken away from him and sent to a garbage dump. [LAUREN LAUGHS, JASON MAKES A SAD SIGH] So really, it's rough. But he also has a pilot's license.

RC: I think it's a junior pilot's license.

WA: Yes, some type of permit.

But the scene really kind of establishes the human-dog connection. There's just this purity to it, is what I read off it.

WA: Well, that's good. That could be good.

Well, I haven't seen it yet. [LAUGHS]

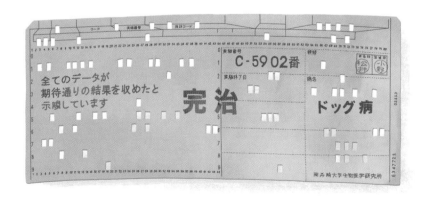

ABOVE: Concept drawing of the hospital where Atari meets Spots. Concept art by Carl Sprague

OPPOSITE: Atari offers a hand to his new bodyguard-dog.

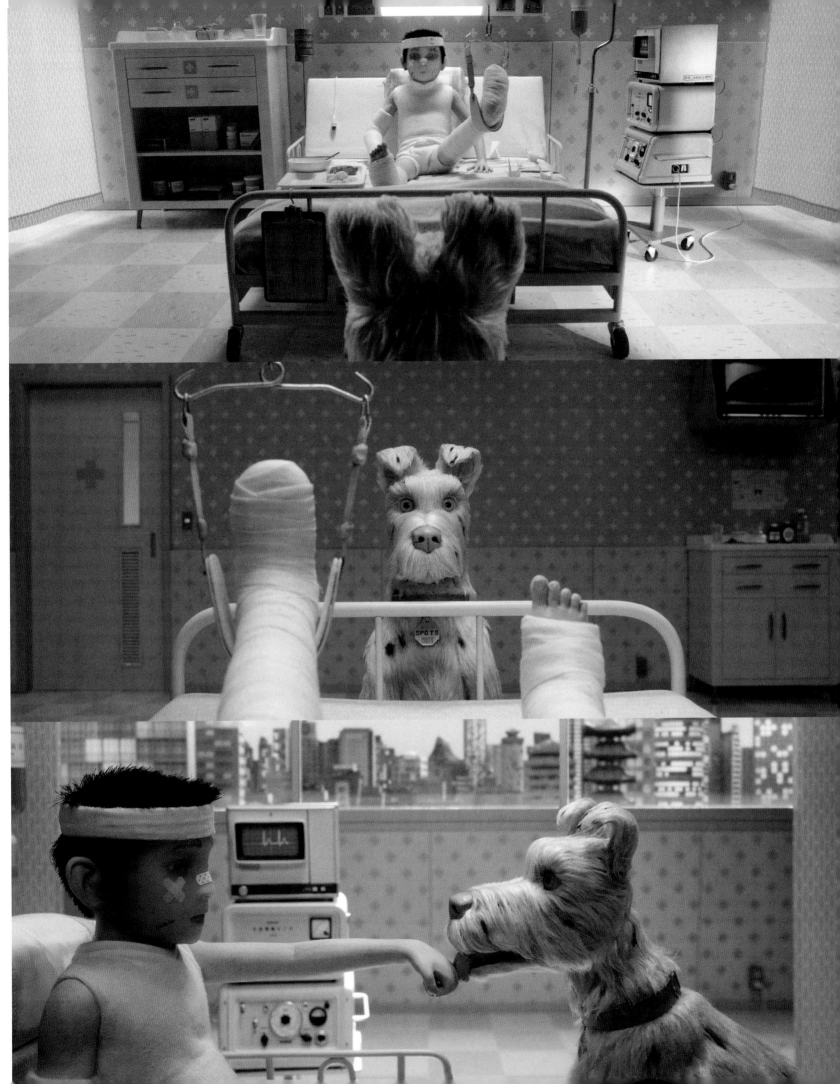

HOSPITAL ROOM

1. OVER SPOTS AT FOOT OF BED OF ATARI IN TRACTION & MAJOR DOMO TALKING.

2. ATARI'S FEET, SPOTS, (T.V. & DOOR IN B.G.)

3. ATARI SITTING IN BED, CRY SPOTS ENTERS, PETTED, ETC, BOTH LOOK, ALARMED, OVER MIDDLE OF CAMER TO:

4. LOW ANGLE OF MAJOR DOMO SCOLDING

5. TIGHTER OF ATARI AS MAN WIRES HIM.

BEGINS TO

 THEN BACK TO 3. SPOTS BACKS AWAY OUT OF CAMERA RIGHT.

THEN BACK TO 2. SPOTS BACKS UP TO HIS ORIGINAL SPOT AS MAN COMES IN W/ WIRES.

CUT BACK TO 4. DOMO INSTRUCTING.

BACK TO 2. FINISHES WIRING SPOTS.

THEN TO 5.

BACK TO 4. DOMO STILL TALKING. STOPS.

BACK TO 5. (ALONE) PAUSE. WHISPERS.

BACK TO 2. AS MAN EXITS. SPOTS REPONDS.

6.

END W/ CLOSE-UPS.

7.

18.

Atari's deceased parents at their wedding; footage of a traditional Japanese funeral; a post-card-image of the imposing, Gothic mayoral residence; and Spots' official wood-block-print press-portrait.

                    INTERPRETER (V.O.)
          -- and also the intention of his
          distant-uncle, Mayor Kobayashi, to
          personally adopt him as ward to the
          mayoral-household. Upon his release
          from Megasaki General, Atari (who
          suffered the loss of his right kidney
          and numerous broken bones in the
          crash) will live in sequestered
          quarters within the confines of Brick
          Mansion, where he will be educated in
          solitude by private tutors. Atari has
          also been assigned a security-detail
          for his own protection in the form of
          a highly-trained bodyguard-dog named
          Spots Kobayashi.

INT. HOSPITAL ROOM. DAY

Atari lies in traction propped-up on an electric bed with both legs elevated by pulleys and harnesses, one broken arm encased in a plaster-cast, and a swirl of bandages wrapped around his head. Spots waits, obedient, on the floor. He looks worried and sad. In a scratchy, sinister voice (in Japanese), Major-Domo explains the details of the current situation to both the boy and the dog. Spots adds gently:

                    SPOTS
          You're my new master. My name is
          Spots. I'm at your service. I'll be
          protecting your welfare and safety on
          an ongoing-basis. In other words: I'm
          your dog.

Atari hesitates. He extends his good hand, palm down. Spots promptly approaches, licks the back of Atari's hand, and bows, deferential. Atari strokes the top of Spots' head and scratches under his chin. Against their best efforts, they both begin to quietly cry.

Major-Domo watches, mortified. He interrupts with a sudden question in Japanese. Atari and Spots both look at him. They hesitate. Major-Domo explodes (subtitled in English):

                    MAJOR-DOMO
          Security-detail! Bodyguard-dog! Not
          pet!

Silence. Atari and Spots look at each other again, confused and troubled. They do not know what to do.

OPPOSITE: **Wes's early story-board for the first hospital scene**

THIS PAGE: **An excerpt from this scene in the *Isle of Dogs* screenplay**

19.

A technician enters the room carrying two secret-service-type earphones. He installs one in Atari's ear and one in Spots'. (The diode-light on each wire activates, blinking green.)

Major-Domo instructs Atari briefly. Atari reluctantly puts his finger to his earphone and, looking to Spots, speaks at a low whisper. A few words of distinct Japanese crackle from Spots' earphone. His eyes light-up. He blurts eagerly, moved:

                    SPOTS
          I can hear you, Master Atari-san!

Atari's eyes continue to well-up with tears. His lips quiver as he whispers to his dog; and Spots' body shakes as he listens, nodding and repeating softly:

                    SPOTS
          I can hear you. I can hear you. I can
          hear you.

CUT TO:

The dog-skeleton.

Atari unzips a pocket and produces a small, orange locker-key labeled: Master Pass-Key. He kneels and pulls a safety-catch before unlocking the bolt and flipping open the door. The living-dogs groan and grimace with frustration. Rex mutters:

                    REX
          You need a key.

Atari wipes away his tears with his sleeve. He turns and walks away. Rex, King, and Duke follow him. They stride past several on-looking-dogs -- including Chief, who, at some point, has seated himself in the path behind them. He does not acknowledge them as they pass.

Boss pokes his nose into the cage. He looks down at the dirty I.D. tag.

INT. LABORATORY. DAY

A hydraulic sliding-door opens, and Professor Watanabe and Yoko-ono enter a bright-white scientific research facility. A junior-scientist gives a progress-report about a research-dog with tubes in its nose, I.V. drips in its legs, pulse-sensors on its paws, and a thermometer in its mouth. The junior-scientist checks the dog's temperature and injects it with a shot of blue serum. He hands Professor Watanabe a computer punch-card.

INSERT:

The punch-card. There is text all over it in Japanese. The one sentence in English is a bold-faced:

          Dog-Flu: CURED.

MONTAGE

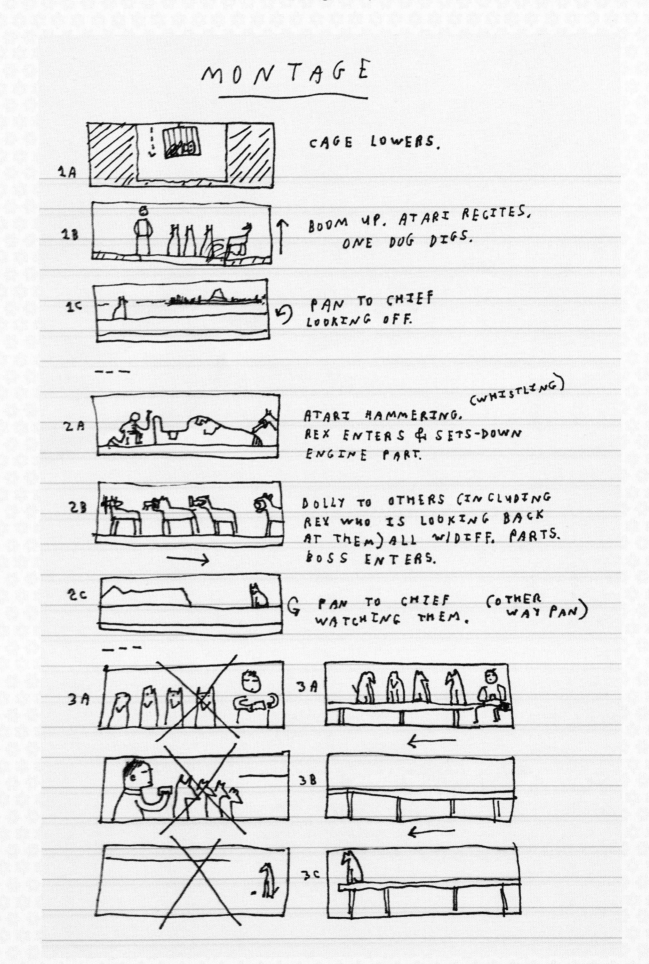

1A CAGE LOWERS.

1B BOOM UP. ATARI RECITES, ONE DOG DIGS.

1C PAN TO CHIEF LOOKING OFF.

— —

2A ATARI HAMMERING. (WHISTLING) REX ENTERS & SETS-DOWN ENGINE PART.

2B DOLLY TO OTHERS (INCLUDING REX WHO IS LOOKING BACK AT THEM) ALL W/DIFF. PARTS. BOSS ENTERS.

2C PAN TO CHIEF WATCHING THEM. (OTHER WAY PAN)

— — —

3A **3A**

3B **3B**

3C **3C**

OPPOSITE: The pack helps Atari bury a dog skeleton and rebuild his plane.

THIS PAGE: Wes's early storyboard for this sequence

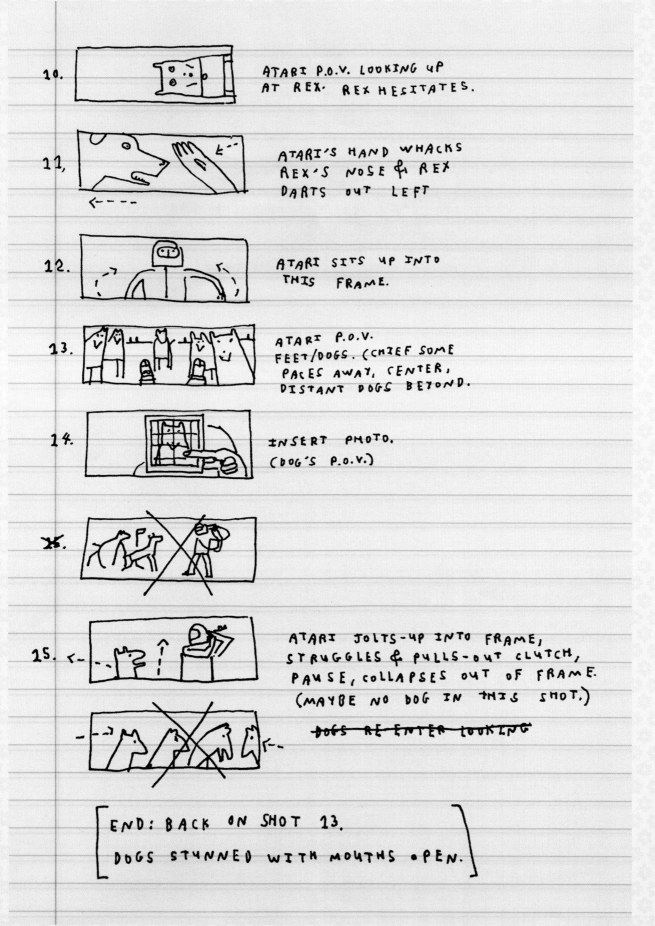

10. ATARI P.O.V. LOOKING UP
AT REX. REX HESITATES.

11. ATARI'S HAND WHACKS
REX'S NOSE & REX
DARTS OUT LEFT

12. ATARI SITS UP INTO
THIS FRAME.

13. ATARI P.O.V.
FEET/DOGS. (CHIEF SOME
PACES AWAY, CENTER,
DISTANT DOGS BEYOND.

14. INSERT PHOTO.
(DOG'S P.O.V.)

15. ATARI JOLTS-UP INTO FRAME,
STRUGGLES & PULLS-OUT CLUTCH,
PAUSE, COLLAPSES OUT OF FRAME.
(MAYBE NO DOG IN THIS SHOT.)

~~DOGS RE-ENTER LOOKING~~

[END: BACK ON SHOT 13.
DOGS STUNNED WITH MOUTHS OPEN.]

THIS PAGE: Wes's early
storyboard for Atari's
landing

OPPOSITE TOP: Concept
drawing for the wide
view of Atari's takeoff.
Concept art by Victor
Georgiev

OPPOSITE MIDDLE AND
BOTTOM: Frames from
Atari's landing scene

FINDING TRANSLATIONS
AN INTERVIEW WITH Kunichi Nomura

IT'S HARD to sum up what exactly Kunichi Nomura does, and probably better to wonder what it is he *doesn't* do. He's an interior designer. He edits a magazine. He's on Instagram rubbing elbows with actors, modeling hip threads, and promoting local artists in his native Tokyo. And there are few things Wes hasn't got him doing on *Isle of Dogs*—he worked on the story, translated dialogue, helped cast the Japanese voice actors, and, unexpectedly, wound up voicing the main villain.

So how did you first get to know Wes?

I knew Sofia Coppola first. I worked on *Lost in Translation.* I think she wrote the script based on her memories of staying in Tokyo in the '90s. But when she came back for location hunting, most of the places were gone. And she tried to explain to the location people what she really wanted, but they really didn't know. So she asked me to help, and I found locations that were similar to the ones she wrote about in the script. Then she gave me a role too. So I had a cameo in the film.

Afterward, she would write me randomly, "Hey, Kun, my friend is coming to Tokyo, can you look after him or her?" And those people are such random people. Some could be her friends from film, or they could be just her regular friends.

One time, she emailed me, like, "My friend is coming to Tokyo for the first time, look after him." And that was Wes. But he didn't mention who he was. He's just, like, "Hi, I'm Wes. Can I see you?" So I saw him. I didn't know who he really was. I just took him around and went bar-hopping. The next day, he emailed, like, "Oh, I had fun. Can we meet again?" That's how I got to know him. Then eventually he asked, "Oh, do you like movies?" I said, "Sure, yeah." "Do you want to see my film?" Then I realized, "Oh, that's . . . Are you Wes Anderson?"

So you didn't realize that you had taken Wes Anderson bar-hopping until days later?

Days later, yeah. But you know, it's kind of the best way to get to know people—when you don't know who they are, when they don't know who I am, and when you get along, you just become friends, right?

So that's how I met Wes. And he's, like, "Oh, Kun, when you come to New York, you know, give me a call. We'll get dinner." I go to New York quite often, so when I'm there, I call him and we go out. When he was in Paris, I was in Paris—I hit him up, like, "Ça va?" We have many friends in common, so that makes it easier, you know?

I looked at your Instagram, and I saw that you both had dinner with Spike Jonze?

I've known Spike a long time too. That's a longer story. Wes invited me to appear in *The Grand Budapest Hotel*, but he didn't tell me what for. His emails are always short. It's like, "Hi Kun. Are you coming to Germany any time soon?" It was maybe four years ago. So I said, "Well, I'm going to Paris in January"—you know, Fashion Week—"Maybe I can stop over in Germany, just have a connecting flight." And he said, "Oh, that's great. Let's meet up."

Then his assistant, or somebody, emailed me: "I heard you've been assigned a cameo for his new movie." It's like . . . "Oh."

"News to me!"

"Really? All right . . . And where?" "Near the border of Poland. And Kun, you have to come here on January 12," or something. I said, "No, I can't, because I've got to go to Paris." Then they emailed me: "OK. So you're going to find your own costume in Japan. You need to find a 1960s breeches suit, the color code is brown, like this Pantone orange . . . " I said, "No way."

But Band of Outsiders gave me a kind of brown velvet suit. So I brought it with me. And when Wes saw it, he said, "Oh, that's perfect! But let's cut three inches off your trousers." Because he has to be like that. [LAUGHS]

That's kind of how Wes wears his pants, right? They're a little bit short?

Yeah. Yeah. They have to be. So I cut my suit, and that's what I wore for the movie. And I did all the promotion for the Japanese market.

For *Grand Budapest*?

Yes. And you know, he didn't come to Japan—he doesn't like flying. I had to do a little talk about the film at the premiere screening in Japan. And Spike was in Tokyo promoting his movie *Her*, so I invited him, but I didn't know if he was coming or not. When we were doing a kind of Q&A, he came into the room, raised his hand, and started questioning me. And everybody was like, "Wow, that's Spike Jonze." So when I went to New York, I told Wes, "Wes, you owe me dinner, the rest of my life," and he agreed. Then I knew Spike was in New York, so I explained, "You know, because of Spike, our

premiere became big news, and we should invite Spike too." So we did. And it became this pretty fun dinner, so we did it a few times—me, Spike, and Wes.

Just out of curiosity, where is your cameo in *Grand Budapest*? Where can we see you, if we want to?

In the opening scene, I was a Japanese traveler in a hallway. And when Jude Law and F. Murray Abraham are talking in the banquet room, I was behind them eating a cold German soup for six hours.

So it seems like, from what I've gathered about you, that you and Wes share a passion for style. Wes's taste, of course, really mixes modern and vintage. And it seems like you might be interested in those elements too? Am I right in saying you're involved with a throwback American-style breakfast restaurant in Tokyo?

I don't know . . . I do many things. I write for magazines, I edit for magazines, I do branding. I do interior design. I have my own radio show.

That's so many things.

I'm maybe an old-fashioned guy, you know? I love old American cars. I drive a prewar Ford in Tokyo. You know, the breakfast joint is—I just love a regular, old kind of diner. But for my job, I design in many different styles. I design retail, like the North Face store in Japan. Just random things. So I don't know . . . Maybe Wes and I have something in common in the way we love old things. I'm just a really curious guy, with many things. You know what I mean? My taste changes every day. And that's pretty natural, no? I don't have to be somebody, to try to prove myself to be somebody. I'm, like, a fluffy person.

At what point were you called in to help with this project? How did that work?

At first, Wes sent me another short email: "I'm thinking of making this stop-motion film set in Japan. Would you help?" And a short email from Wes is a bad sign. Because he's going to start a whole thing. And I said, "Yes." Then he sent me a rough script, and somebody had to translate it, so I did. It took time. Because I know who Wes is. His dialogue and writing is . . . He has his own character.

I've done some work with subtitles for American movies. But translating Wes's script is something so different. I know him kind of well. I know what kind of sense of humor he has. So . . . It wasn't something like, "Ah, it's really easy to translate." I have to modify it, and I have to talk to him a lot.

Because you have to translate his sense of humor in a particular way, when you're translating it into Japanese?

Yeah—I can't just make it in Japanese and make it short or anything. Because then you lose the humor

OPPOSITE TOP: Kun's cameo in *The Grand Budapest Hotel*

OPPOSITE ABOVE: Back in its heyday the Hotel Okura played a brief but decisive role in *Walk Don't Run*. The whole place is booked for the 1964 Tokyo Olympics; Cary Grant can't get a room when he arrives two days early for his business trip, and that sets the whole romantic comedy in motion.

of the old dialogue. And then he started sending me more emails, and asking about all the references too. Like, "Can you send me a traditional Japanese department store uniform from, let's say, the '50s and early '60s?" It's really difficult. He always has specific ideas for what he wants. Then he's like, "Can you record these five or six characters' voices on your iPhone and send it to me?" So I did a few. I also have my own radio show, which I prerecord every week. So I went to the radio station and asked the technician, "Can I stay half an hour more, and can you record . . ."

They were so curious because, in the recording booth, I suddenly started to yell . . . The technician was like, "What's this for?" I was like, "Uh—it's a secret." But they were so confused because I did Mayor Kobayashi, Professor Watanabe, and some women, you know, because Wes wanted to see how it sounds. And also, they wanted to kind of calculate how long the lines were.

I thought, "Wow, that really short email has led to a lot of time-consuming things." Then Wes just kept me as Mayor Kobayashi. He said, "Well, Kun, you've got a really low voice. So you sound like a mayor, even though you are much younger than the actual Mayor Kobayashi." And I said, "All right."

But then he says, "OK, we have many Japanese roles. Each role has maybe one line, but we have, like, twenty Japanese roles. Can you—can you organize that?" So I did. I know many Japanese artists, musicians, actors . . . I tried to find people who were the same age as the characters.

So you had to do casting?

You know, I'd ask Wes, "So who is this Junior Scientist? What do you think? How old is he?" "Uh, he could be, like, early thirties. Maybe he speaks really fast or with a high-pitched voice . . ." Then I'd just call them, like, "Hey, I'm working on an American movie. I can't show you the whole script or tell you what it's all about, but can you record it?" I think their agents were pissed off that I didn't ask the proper way. But I could get away with it.

Who are some interesting people that ended up lending their voices to this, that you helped coordinate?

I coordinated pretty much all the Japanese casting, except Assistant-Scientist Yoko-ono and Major-Domo. The Old Woman is voiced by Mari Natsuki. She was the witch in Hayao Miyazaki's movie *Spirited Away*. And I got two brothers, the sons of Yusaku Matsuda, who was a yakuza in Ridley Scott's *Black Rain*. And we have a fashion model, who is the daughter of Yokozuna, a sumo wrestler. The anchorman in the movie is a singer from the bestselling rock band in Japan last year who did the soundtrack for *Your Name*, which is going to be adapted into an American movie. Then I also cast the designer of the brand Undercover. And we also have Glamour Nobu [Nobuhiko Kitamura], who was also in *Lost in Translation*. I thought it would be cool to have a connection since we met through Sofia.

Wes is always working with the same kind of group of people, people who know each other. So I wanted to create the same kind of vibe in Japan, as well.

What is it like to see your performance in Kobayashi's body?

I didn't know what he looked like until last December. So when Wes showed me, I just laughed. Like, this is me? [LAUGHS] I mean, you hate hearing your own voice, you know? And today, we've been in the studio all day. And I've been listening to my voice for, like, ten hours total, and I used to be really uncomfortable. But now I'm kind of used to it. As long as Wes and Roman say, "Oh, it sounds really good," that makes me happy, even though they don't understand what the hell I'm saying in Japanese. But they trust me. "Kun, you really sound like a mayor." I'm like, "All right."

Since you were involved in the story and helped consult on the setting, I wanted to ask for your thoughts on the world of *Isle of Dogs* and specifically, on any elements from history in the story. I know Wes usually draws on the past in his movies and I wondered how Japanese history plays a role here.

There are many elements—bits and pieces. But I told Wes, "Don't worry about it too much," you know? We always appreciate different perspectives. For a foreigner who's been to Japan, and seen the country, and read about it, and just created his own world using his imagination, it's really fascinating. I'm glad that this movie has that kind of 1960s, after-the-war element, which I love, but which is disappearing from Japan.

Did you hear about the Hotel Okura? Hotel Okura was a midcentury-style, really good hotel in central Tokyo. The design was beautiful. But nobody cared. And over the last ten years, a lot of big hotels came to Japan and opened up, and all the rich Japanese and the tourists tended to stay in the new hotels. So Hotel Okura lost so many customers. In the end, like a few years ago, they said, "Oh, we're gonna tear it down and build a high tower building." And then suddenly there were designers and foreign artists protesting around the world, like, "Why would you do this? This is a beauty of Tokyo. Like, really authentic design." And that made the Japanese pay attention again.

That has a lot in common with the story of the Grand Budapest, of course.

It's happening everywhere in the big cities. I've been to New York, like, ninety times. Every year I've gone there like five times, over the last twenty years. And it has changed so much. It's—it's really losing its charm. You know, like, an old neighborhood, a beautiful block; now, demolition, building some stupid condo. And people don't realize it until they lose it.

And Wes captured the beauty of mixing old and new, you know? There's all the imagination you see in the comic books from those days, and maybe in Kurosawa, when he was in his heyday in the '60s. Then Wes, of course, researched things—the design, the history. The background elements he researched from history. But everything doesn't have to play in order or be perfectly matched with history. It's based on the facts of history, but what's in *Isle of Dogs* is what he created. And I'm more than grateful to see his creation, especially based on my own country.

And I appreciate how he sees things. It's just so interesting—it reminds me of things I completely forgot about. Like, "Oh, I remember those kinds of comic books from back when I was a child, where they'd describe what direction the future is going."

I remember my father-in-law watched *Moonrise Kingdom* and said, well, in some important way, that *is* what it was like to be in the Boy Scouts in the '60s—the pup tents, the whittling knives, his crushes, his coke-bottle glasses. And if you're a New Yorker watching *The Royal Tenenbaums*, that is what New York used to be like, kind of. Not exactly—there's an element of fantasy that comes from Wes's sensibility. But there's a pleasure of recognition and maybe a pleasure of being recognized, too. It's kind of touching to watch a movie and realize that someone has paid close attention to something you have grown up in and loved.

I mean, his movies are so detailed, and those detailed elements somehow attach to people in unique ways. You can always find a way to relate to his films, I think. Like, it reminds you of your childhood, and it's very, very unique for me. And I'm so amazed that so many people love his work.

Like, I have—Lauren, I have *really* random friends. When I go to New York, I hang out with everyone from teenage skaters to old punk rockers,

ABOVE LEFT: Wes and Kun direct Akira Takayama, who voices Major-Domo.

ABOVE MIDDLE: Character sketch of Auntie, by Félicie Haymoz. "If I could walk away with one puppet from this film, it would be Auntie," production designer Paul Harrod told me, when I asked him if he had a favorite character. "You look at that face, and it's just like . . . That puppet has lived."

ABOVE RIGHT: Character sketch of the News Anchor, by Félicie Haymoz

OPPOSITE TOP LEFT: Auntie is voiced by Mari Natsuki, who voiced the twin witches Yubaba and Zeniba in Hayao Miyazaki's *Spirited Away*.

OPPOSITE TOP RIGHT: The News Anchor is voiced by Yojiro Noda, lead singer for the rock band RADWIMPS.

OPPOSITE MIDDLE AND FAR RIGHT: Jun Takahashi, designer for the brand Undercover, voices a drone pilot.

OPPOSITE BOTTOM: The first Junior Scientist is voiced by actor Takayuki Namada. The second Junior Scientist is voiced by Kozue Akimoto, a model whose father is sumo grand champion Chiyonofuji Mitsugu. The third and fourth Junior Scientists are voiced by actors Shota and Ryuhei Matsuda, sons of the actor Yusaku Matsuda. Character designs by Félicie Haymoz

KUROSAWA'S VILLAINS

THE corrupt corporate vice president Iwabuchi in Kurosawa's *The Bad Sleep Well*. Like Kobayashi, he is willing to move against a young member of his own family to protect his interests. Unlike Kobayashi, he succeeds with no regrets. Western critics saw parallels to Shakespeare's *Hamlet*, which Kurosawa did not particularly have in mind.

LIKE Mayor Kobayashi, General Washizu is a tyrant toppled by those closest to him. Kurosawa's *Throne of Blood* is a deliberate retelling of Shakespeare's *Macbeth* with an important difference: Washizu's orders are resisted by his own soldiers, who silently turn on him en masse before the battle can even start.

IN *The Hidden Fortress*, Kurosawa shows that villains are not beyond redemption. If you look at *Star Wars* as George Lucas's loose remake of this samurai adventure, that would make General Hyoe Tadokoro the film's Darth Vader. Returning, dark and disfigured, to execute the captured heroes at the film's climax, Tadokoro feels a pang of conscience, throws his political loyalties to the wind, and risks his life to protect them in a thrilling escape.

designers, bankers . . . I am a social butterfly. Anyway, they all have watched Wes's films, and every single one of them has their own opinion and love toward his movies. "Oh, my favorite is this." "Oh, my favorite is that." But it's really interesting how his films attach to people's emotions. You know, some hardcore skater dude, he discovered that I'm working with Wes, and it's like, "Hey man! I love your friend's work." And I say, "You like Wes's films?" And he says, "*Hell* yeah!"

You were talking about the '60s and the after-the-war setting. I'd been thinking about the student protesters in *Isle of Dogs*, and how they're kind of like the Zengakuren: the *Daily Manifesto* and Editor Hiroshi leading a group of young student Marxists.

We had protests here in the '60s, same as in the United States. There were a lot of antiwar protests, and about Anpo, which was the pact between Japan and America about the army. Many students were against that. But the same thing happened around the world. I think around that time, people were idealistic, and young people believed that they could change the world.

And *Isle of Dogs* is an optimistic portrayal of student protests. They actually win and end the corruption.

Yes, that's how it should be. It didn't happen like that in the past, but it's cool that the protesters win in the end.

I wanted to ask about Mayor Kobayashi as a character and as a figure of corruption, kind of like one Kurosawa has in *The Bad Sleep Well*, which Wes has mentioned as a primary influence on this film. There's a quote from Kurosawa about that movie, where he shows that he was much more personally interested in real-world political issues than a lot of viewers in America might assume—it's not just a film noir or a retelling of *Hamlet*.
He says here, "I wanted to make a film with some social significance. At last, I decided to do something about corruption because it always seemed to me that grift, bribery, etc. on a public level is the worst crime that there is." Mayor Kobayashi seems to represent the specific connection between *The Bad Sleep Well* and this film.

Yeah, yeah. I agree. I mean, it happens everywhere, no? In the United States too. There's a small number of people who always have power, and you just don't know. Mayor Kobayashi is a good example of power with corruption. But as you say about the school protesters, it's optimistic because Mayor Kobayashi wasn't one hundred percent that guy, in the end.

Right. He actually has a change of heart . . .

Yeah, change of heart. Gave the kidney. And he wasn't happy being in prison, but, you know, he's following the rules. It's not something that happens in this real world. You know, once people have that kind of power, they're just corrupt.

ABOVE: **Character design of Mayor Kobayashi, by Félicie Haymoz**

KOBAYASHI

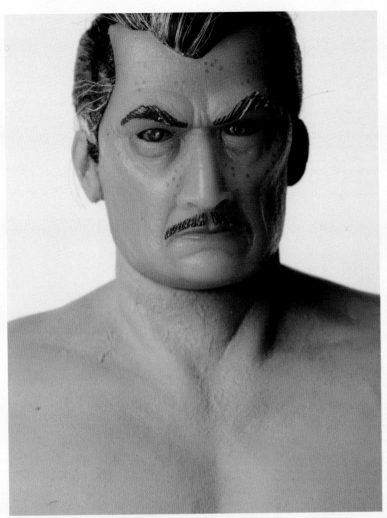

The face of a medium-scale Kobayashi puppet

High and Low plays like a Sophoclean tragedy for its first hour, a police procedural for its second. The first act obeys a tense, claustrophobic unity of time and place: we watch, cooped up with Kingo Gondo in his stylish, palatial home, as he's sadistically forced to choose between his position, his reputation, and his entire fortune on the one hand, and on the other, the life of a child. At first, we're afraid he'll pick the wrong one.

It seems certain that Kobayashi will make the wrong choice, too. But like Kingo Gondo, and King Creon in Sophocles's Antigone, *and Darth Vader, he feels the gut pull of paternal (or as the case may be, avuncular) love wrench him away from the darkness and into the light. It's an archetypal story too rarely filmed: the father rescued by the helplessness of the son.*

Toshiro Mifune as shoe magnate Kingo Gondo in Kurosawa's High and Low

Kobayashi soaks in an ofuro tub.

locals, random strangers. Once the sculptors get to work, they depart from the original, and each puppet becomes a unique individual. But some of the old personality shines through.

Toshiro Mifune was Kurosawa's leading man in sixteen films, from *Drunken Angel* in 1948 to *Red Beard* in 1965. He played a vast range of characters for Kurosawa—samurai, businessman, ruffian, a snarling young gangster dying of tuberculosis, a suave motorcycle-riding young painter caught in a sex scandal, a clean-cut young doctor, a brusque old bearded one, even an ornery seventy-year-old patriarch when the actor was only thirty-five. There was one constant that Kurosawa couldn't have trained out of him even if he'd wanted to: whether his character is swinging a katana to save a village from bandits or swinging a loan to finance a leveraged buyout, Mifune has more swagger than you can shake a stick at. He's lent some of it to Mayor Kobayashi.

In particular, Kobayashi's pencil mustache, barrel chest, pomade, and panache are a nod to Kingo Gondo, the wealthy shoe magnate Mifune played in 1963's *High and Low* (JAPANESE THEATRICAL POSTER AT LEFT).

WES'S puppet modelers often start with real faces. At the studio in London, there's a wall in the art department workshop with glossy headshots tacked up for inspiration: famous actors, dead and alive, from around the world, as well as friends, acquaintances,

Kobayashi's also got a lot in common with Charles Foster Kane, played by Orson Welles in his masterpiece Citizen Kane. *Like Kane—another tycoon with a mottled soul and a smart mustache* (TOP LEFT)—*Kobayashi has never let his political ambitions distract him from his vast, diversified, and surely ill-gotten business empire. He shares Kane's monogram, too—shown here on the gate of Kane's estate at Xanadu* (ABOVE LEFT) *and Kobayashi's pharmaceutical factory on Trash Island* (ABOVE RIGHT). ***Kobayashi Testing Plant concept art by Victor Georgiev***

STUDENT PROTESTS

OF ALL the fanciful things that happen in *Isle of Dogs*, perhaps the least fanciful is the part where a dour group of hardline teenage Marxists commandeer a classroom for their headquarters, expose a perversion of the democratic process, incite a citywide protest, lead it to the halls of power, and successfully oust the head of government.

Student activism of the sort practiced by Editor Hiroshi and the *Daily Manifesto* staff has a long history in Japan. The student Marxists will probably be as recognizable to Japanese audiences as *Moonrise Kingdom*'s Khaki

Scouts are to American viewers—they're not exactly supposed to represent the real thing, but we all know their type.

Zengakuren, a nationwide association of students, was formed in 1948, though its forebears were raising hell against bad pedagogy, lack of student self-government, and the militarist regime all the way back in the prewar days—the first formal socialist and communist organizations in Japan were founded by university students in the 1920s. The Zengakuren rank and file often joined the association just for the group sings, cheap thrills, and opportunities to fraternize with the opposite

sex, but the leaders were diehards, both extremely serious and extremely specific about their own extremely particular brands of revolutionary vanguardism.

Zengakuren students didn't just fight for their own cause: they linked arms with any protest they deemed worthy. There were plenty of protest movements to link up with in the 1950s, and Zengakuren made sure it was on the front lines against bourgeois-capitalist-imperialist oppression in any form.

The ultimate showdown between Zengakuren and the establishment was the Anpo protest in 1960—both a tactical failure and Zengakuren's finest

hour. The ruling party's desire to renew the Security Treaty with the United States (called Anpo for short) incensed activists on both the right and left who wanted to protect Japanese national sovereignty. But the hugger-mugger way the politicians did it offended any citizen with respect for the proper functioning of democracy. They turned off their televisions and took to the streets. In the end, the Security Treaty was renewed, but the clamor raised by protesters, with Zengakuren always at their forefront, forced the resignation of the prime minister shortly after.

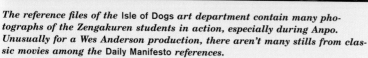

The reference files of the Isle of Dogs *art department contain many photographs of the Zengakuren students in action, especially during Anpo. Unusually for a Wes Anderson production, there aren't many stills from classic movies among the Daily Manifesto references.*

"It is interesting to note," wrote university student Masahiro Nakanishi in 1970, "that whereas there have been many books published in Japanese on the student movement, articles in newspapers and magazines, programs on television and radio, no one has yet tried to make a full-length feature film for the popular cinema. It seems there just aren't any more Kurosawas."

Nakanishi passes over an important exception: Nagisa Oshima, one of Japan's greatest filmmakers and nearly Kurosawa's equal in reputation. Oshima himself had been one of Japan's student radicals in the 1950s, and he told the story of a group of young activists in 1960's Night and Fog in Japan (TOP AND ABOVE LEFT). *The film only shows the Anpo protests elliptically and impressionistically, with light and sound in a pitch-black studio soundstage. Even still, the studio withdrew the film from theaters within a week, feeling that the political climate was too hot for it. It's likely that young Nakanishi had not seen it. (You can read his essay and others like it in* Zengakuren: Japan's Revolutionary Students, *a collection of firsthand accounts written by undergraduates in Tokyo.)*

There were other protest films of this period that made reference to the Anpo protest or channeled its spirit to critique American foreign policy—films like Kinji Fukasaku's investigative journalism thriller The Proud Challenge *and Kei Kumai's* The Japanese Archipelago—*but to this day, they remain little known and are often hard to find.*

Anpo protestors have a brief cameo in Oshima's Cruel Story of Youth (TOP AND MIDDLE RIGHT), *also released in 1960. Oshima was one of a number of young maverick filmmakers who emerged in the late 1950s and shaped Japanese cinema of the 1960s. They're known as the Japanese New Wave (*nuberu bagu *in Japanese, after the French* nouvelle vague *filmmakers). Masahiro Shinoda, another New Wave director, told the story of a particularly far-out, opportunistic student radical in his second feature, 1960's* Dry Lake, *also known as* Youth in Fury (BOTTOM RIGHT). *A real bad egg, disaffected and equally comfortable with any political extreme, the protagonist is flippant to his fellow radicals and posts pictures of Trotsky, Castro, and even Hitler on his apartment walls.*

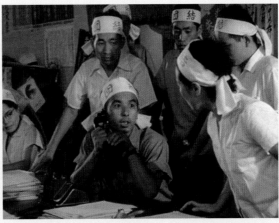

One of the flashpoints of conflict in postwar Japan took place at Miike coal mine in 1960: a ten-month strike led to internecine violence between protesters. Novelist Kobo Abe wrote a surreal television drama inspired by the events that director Hiroshi Teshigahara filmed as the movie Pitfall in 1962 (ABOVE). In the film, as they did in real life, the striking miners wear hachimaki, or head-bands. Hachimaki are meant to encourage perseverance and pride. They're worn by protesters as a demonstration of solidarity and strength in numbers, by artisans as a mark of dedication to their craft, and by students buckling down for exams. Both the pro-dog and anti-dog factions wear them in Isle of Dogs.

Kurosawa himself fell in with a group of radicals as a young man, back when he aspired to a career as a painter. He lost touch with his underground Marxist contacts after a prolonged illness and was never doctrinaire about his politics, but later in his life he admitted to retaining some sympathies for the outlook of those young Marxists. His 1946 protest film No Regrets for Our Youth (TOP LEFT AND ABOVE), his first film after World War II, offers a heartfelt salute to the student activists of the 1930s struggling under the shadow of militarism. Oshima remembers being deeply affected by the film as a teenager.

The art department's research files also contain material from May 1968, when an explosive series of protests in France threatened to the bring down the government. A year before the protests broke out, Jean-Luc Godard saw the writing on the wall and shot La Chinoise (ABOVE). In the film, a small cell of young Marxist-Leninists share an apartment, hand out copies of Mao's Little Red Book on the street, and give each other daily lectures on film history and American imperialism.

PRAY FOR ATARI AND SPOTS

NUTMEG

BANDIT

ZAP

HUGS

TOP: The classroom headquarters of the *Daily Manifesto*

MIDDLE: The *Daily Manifesto* staff poses for a press photo on the heels of their Atari Lives! campaign.

BOTTOM AND OPPOSITE BOTTOM: The students' pro-dog protest signs designed by the graphics department

OPPOSITE: Tracy Walker and Editor Hiroshi of the *Daily Manifesto*, protesting the Trash Island Decree at the start of the film (TOP) and the rigged election near the end (MIDDLE)

Spots, the Hero Pack, and the
Aboriginal Dogs about to receive a
message from a concerned owl

THE THROWAWAYS

AN INTERVIEW WITH Bryan Cranston

RYAN CRANSTON, Academy Award–nominated and Tony and Emmy Award–winning actor, is in London to play mad-as-hell newsman Howard Beale in the National Theatre's stage adaptation of *Network*. Bryan took a bit of time out of his rehearsal schedule to reminisce about playing Chief back in June 2015—in a small soundproof room, with a cast of four, for an audience of one.

Do you remember how you first heard about *Isle of Dogs*?

Well, it was Wes Anderson's name that first rang my chime. I actually thought that *Grand Budapest* was the best movie I had seen the year before. His body of work was very interesting to me. I really enjoyed *Fantastic Mr. Fox*. Wes is very unique, in his voice, and in his expression. So I was all-in.

Just from the name.

OPPOSITE: Bryan Cranston with Chief

ABOVE: Like Kikuchiyo in Kurosawa's *Seven Samurai*, Chief likes to keep his distance.

From his involvement, knowing that he takes meticulous care of his stories, which are very personal and often internal. And he doesn't succumb to any outside pressures of "Well, we need to put in more jokes here, in this story," or "It needs to be sadder." He's an auteur. He has his own sensibilities

that he is responsible to and that he lives up to. I think he has a very high bar that he sets for himself which he aims to meet or exceed each time. And I like working with people like that, that expect a lot of themselves. When you're around someone like that, it rubs off.

How would you characterize Wes's approach to directing, at least as far as directing voice acting?

What's great about Wes is that he is specific but not rigid. And that those aren't contradictory things. You can know what you want, and yet the pathway to get what you want doesn't have to be predestined.

If I'm in the booth with him, and I say something that Wes has a visceral reaction to—good or bad—and makes an adjustment to, it's not even ultimately

necessary for me to completely and fully understand where he's going. Just as long as Wes knows where he's going.

Fantastic Mr. Fox has received some recognition for its recording process—there were several actors in the same room, instead of individual actors recording their parts separately. Was that your experience on this one?

It was. I was there among actors who I'm a fan of, who I revere. I look over, and there's Wes sitting in a chair looking at us. To my far left was Bob Balaban. Next to me, on my left, was Edward Norton. And then I look to my right, and it's Bill Murray. And I thought, "This is fantastic. I'm in the room with these actors, all of whom I just admire so much," in the presence of Wes Anderson, who is so interesting, and such an outlier to his Texan roots. He doesn't seem like he's from Texas in any way, shape, or form, or whatever cliché anybody thinks about a Texan. He's very worldly, with a sweet kind of disposition. A pleasant comportment. And unassuming. He's very nattily dressed. You know, he has that very specific kind of style to his appearance, and to his hair.

He's a bit of a conundrum, I think, and he takes that kind of curiosity into his work. Because a lot of it is curious, and odd at times. But the thing that he maintains is a dedication to the development of a character or a plot that is consistent. He doesn't do odd or strange for its own sake or for shock value. It's followed through. A character may have a very different appearance, a very different way of seeing life, but it's consistent throughout his storytelling.

Usually, the quirkier the character, the harder it is to invest in them, from an audience standpoint. Because they're not so easy to relate to. They're so different from me. But Wes is able, underneath the surface of the quirkiness, to tap into a humanity with his characters that still draws you in and makes you invest in them.

I think that's true of all his work, but this one, at least on the basis of the screenplay, often seems even warmer, more humanistic, than the other things he's done. Particularly in the way that he's rendering the relationship between the dogs and the humans, and particularly between Atari and Chief. I'm thinking of the scene in the script where Chief kind of has a change of heart, where Atari gives him his first bath.

[LAUGHS] Right . . .

On the page, that struck me as one of the sweeter things that Wes has ever written. I'm also thinking of the scene where the dogs each talk about their favorite food, and Chief gets his big speech about biting the boy and the old woman who made him chili. Do you remember recording that one?

I do remember it . . . It was like—it's specific to the character of a dog. And that's what I was speaking to just now, relating to the quirkiness of it: How do human beings watching this movie relate to characters who are dogs?

And I think that's the effect that we're going for here, is that you have a story of displacement, of disenfranchised dogs. And that's a very real experience that human beings are feeling in every country. They're disenfranchised. The throwaways. The ones that are considered—well, in the case of this movie, literally less than human. And it's about the demagoguery of fear. I think it is very timely.

Your character, Chief, is kind of a classic type in samurai films and westerns—the ruffian, the outcast, the lone wolf who eventually has to learn to step up and accept some responsibility.

Yes, right.

Kurosawa's canon has a lot of these types. I don't know if Wes made you watch _Seven Samurai_ during this process . . . ?

[LAUGHS] No . . . I've seen it before. But that wasn't a requirement.

He's talked about _Seven Samurai_ in relation to this movie, and I guess that makes Chief the Kikuchiyo character—he's the stray, the castaway runt, the odd one out.

But perhaps the one with the most nobility.

Right, and it's nice to watch that come out through the doppelgänger plot. It's kind of _A Tale of Two Cities_—Chief as the Sydney Carton to Spots's Charles Darnay.

Yeah, it's sweet. It's a sweet revelation to it, to see that. And it also presents the theme of second chances. That with hope comes the possibility of a second chance.

And on top of that there's the plotline of the rescue: the Search for Spots. Almost a _Saving Private Ryan_ thing, I suppose, which you were in.

When I was doing it, I didn't think of _Saving Private Ryan_ as much as I thought of an old film like _The Dirty Dozen_. Because those men were throwaways as well. They were incarcerated with no hope of a future. And they were told, "We'll give you that sliver of hope for a future, if you do this task and make it out alive." So this kind of felt like, "Wow . . . " Despite the fact that someone—in this case, a dog—someone is down and out, and seemingly without hope, there still lies a level of ambition to accomplish something in life. And I think that's what makes us, ultimately, human, the desire to get up every morning, to attempt something. Whether or not that ever comes to fruition is almost immaterial. Almost unimportant. The important part is that you have the ambition, the will, the fortitude, the strength, the tolerance of life in order to put one foot forward in front of the other and march on.

STRAY DOG

SOME people claim Kurosawa's warrior stories are chiefly about the theme of honor. Others put a finer point on it and say that Kurosawa's moral fixation is duty. I've always preferred the word "responsibility."

The greatest Kurosawa heroes, the ones the director himself seems to envy and marvel at, do more than their duty, more than what's asked by their lord or by their job—they feel compelled to do what no one's asked, but what they know they could do, or could have done. They feel responsibility, even anxiety and shame, for the furthest and most tenuous consequences of their actions, their inactions, their friends' and families' actions, even the actions of strangers they think they could have influenced. They can't look at a problem and leave it for another to fix. They don't let themselves off the hook, even for an honest mistake. They carry their own burdens, then take an extra helping of the world's karma onto their shoulders.

Kurosawa's films, like Dostoyevsky's novels, ask us to study these strange, hypersensitive, unusually strong men and women. There's the agonized young cop Murakami in *Stray Dog*. There's the preternaturally innocent Kinji Kameda, straight from Dostoyevsky's *The Idiot*. There's Dersu Uzala, the Siberian guide whose heart breaks for even plants and animals. There's gruff Dr. Red Beard. *Dodes'ka-den* has wise old silversmith Mr. Tamba. *The Most Beautiful* has stolid young lens technician Tsuru Watanabe, who leads her team of factory girls as courageously and thoughtfully as modest Kambei leads the team of *Seven Samurai*. Obi-Wan Kenobi seems to be one of their lineage. Spots Kobayashi is perhaps another.

Kurosawa juxtaposes these warrior-saints and divine physicians with aggressive wild cards, chaotic neutrals, diamonds in the rough who need a good polish. The surly gangster Matsunaga from *Drunken Angel*, who must decide whether to give his life before he loses

it to tuberculosis. The slimy, dipsomaniacal lawyer Hiruta from *Scandal*. The reckless ersatz samurai Kikuchiyo from *Seven Samurai*. Kurosawa never judges them. They're strays. They're fearful. That's why they bite.

Each must learn a hard lesson through hard knocks: to become courageously kind, ruthlessly self-critical, never aloof, universally responsible. To wade into the messes that others may have made, and declare, "I am involved."

One of the pleasures of reading the *Isle of Dogs* screenplay, and one of its most Kurosawa-like touches, is the way the focus shifts from apparent protagonist to apparent protagonist. Each one, in turn, is forced to make a choice: whether to hang back and guiltily watch a tragedy befall someone else, or to risk danger and declare, "I am involved." We see this choice come to Spots and then to Atari, then to Rex, then to Tracy, then to giant Gondo and his tribe of former lab-test dogs, and, then, most powerfully, to the reluctant Chief and even to

the villain, Kobayashi. In the end, even when it's not their duty, they all choose to make it their responsibility.

A few of Kurosawa's most fascinating characters are both good dogs and strays at the same time. The best known is Sanjuro, an unwashed and irritable son of a gun who stars in *Yojimbo* and its sequel *Sanjuro*. He is the original Man with No Name—Sanjuro, "thirtysomething," seems to be a nonspecific nom de guerre he tosses out when pressed. No doubt partly inspired by the gunslingers from Kurosawa's beloved Westerns, Sanjuro provided the model for Clint Eastwood's most famous role: the Man with No Name in Sergio Leone's *A Fistful of Dollars*. (The film was a totally unauthorized beat-for-beat remake of *Yojimbo*.) Sanjuro's younger relations include such scruffy-looking strays as Han Solo and Mad Max, taciturn badasses who, like Chief, are almost surprised to learn that they're too soft-hearted to walk away from a crisis.

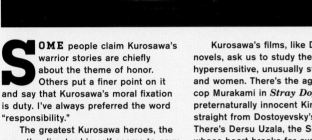

Sanjuro, a ronin with no master to serve and no particular place he has to be, is a quick-draw iaijutsu master and tactical genius who'd rather just take a nap if anyone would leave him alone. In Yojimbo, or "The Bodyguard," he singlehandedly saves a small village by renting his services to two rival gangs and playing them off each other until not a man is left standing. In the sequel Sanjuro (ABOVE), he finds himself mentoring a group of eager but incompetent young noblemen on a mission to root out corruption, more because he feels sorry for them than anything else.

Kagemusha—the title means "The Shadow Warrior" or, more idiomatically, "The Body Double" or "The Decoy." The film stars Tatsuya Nakadai in a dual role: the mighty historical warlord Takeda Shingen and a vulgar, nameless thief. The warlord's brother finds the thief at the execution grounds—at first, "I wondered if our father might have had another son somewhere," he says. The thief looks almost exactly like Lord Shingen. He's spared from crucifixion and groomed to be the lord's kage-musha, his double in situations where there's too great a risk that Shingen could be killed. But Shingen unexpectedly dies, and the thief has to decide whether to accept the responsibility of taking the lord's place until his clan is safe from its enemies. Shingen's toddler grandson unexpectedly takes to the kagemusha, and the thief's love for the boy prompts him to grow into the dead lord's role.

"Why should I?" Chief asks Nutmeg. "Because he's a twelve-year-old boy," Nutmeg replies. "Dogs love those."

THE BATTLE FLAG

AN INTERVIEW WITH LEAD STORYBOARD ARTIST Jay Clarke AND ANIMATIC EDITOR Edward Bursch

OPPOSITE: Chief prepares to confront a robot-dog in the animatic (TOP) and in the finished film (BOTTOM).

TOP: Tracy explains her hunch to the *Daily Manifesto* staff in the animatic (LEFT) and in the finished film (RIGHT).

BOTTOM: Atari and Chief face down a pack of robot-dogs at the causeway in the animatic (LEFT) and in the finished film (RIGHT).

IN THE WES ANDERSON school of filmmaking, you start with a screenplay. Then you make a movie. Then you make a movie out of that movie.

This "movie before the movie" is called an animatic, which is a set of moving storyboards timed out to a voice track. These days, nearly all animated films, stop-motion or 2-D, use an animatic. Storyboards are an important part of the preproduction process for most movies, but they're vital for animated films, where everything in every shot needs to be made or drawn. Most animatics are provisional and unpolished, and they are put together by a large team.

Wes's method is different. He works with an unusually small team to create animatics that are unusually detailed and thorough. By the end of the animatic process, the team has made a prototype of the entire film—framings, camera moves, sound design, and all—before the start of production proper. Wes first used an animatic on his first animated feature, *Fantastic Mr. Fox*, but he's used animatics to plan the shooting of his live-action films ever since. Key scenes for *Moonrise Kingdom* were laid out and choreographed with animatics, and editor Edward Bursch estimates that 90 percent of *The Grand Budapest Hotel* was rendered as a preproduction animatic, something that lead storyboard artist Jay Clarke says is quite rare.

Sometimes the plan for a scene will start to depart from the animatic, but even then, Wes prefers to go in and change the

animatic first, so that it can continue to serve as a reference for the rest of the crew.

Jay Clarke has worked as a storyboard artist on stop-motion films for ten years, with credits on Aardman Animation productions like *Wallace and Gromit's World of Invention* and *Shaun the Sheep*. Edward Bursch's career began with an internship on *The Darjeeling Limited*, which turned into an assistantship with Wes, which led to his current gig as Wes's animatic editor. Jay, Edward, and Wes made their first movie-before-the-movie together on Wes's last film, *The Grand Budapest Hotel*, and they reunited in 2015 to start work on *Isle of Dogs*.

Normally, from what I understand, an animatic involves a whole team of people, but for *Isle of Dogs*, Jay was the sole artist and Edward was the sole editor?

JAY CLARKE: Yeah, Eddie was the sole animatic editor. Sometimes, on a big animated feature film, there'll be maybe two directors; there's just more of an infrastructure there. With a project like that, you might have up to seven or eight storyboard artists, and you might just be trying out lots of different things, trying to find that story, because they just make many different versions of the film. Whereas with Wes, it's slightly different. He's very confident with the story; he knows the story that he's telling. It's just all about the detail within—what shot sells that particular moment and things like that.

On *Isle of Dogs*, since everything was going through Wes, it naturally had a small setup to begin with, which is fun. We'd worked together before, on *Grand Budapest Hotel*, so we had a sort of shorthand among Wes, Eddie, and myself. Initially, when I came on, Wes just wanted to start, to see if this was going to work as a project; I didn't think that we would continue on with our "just-the-three-of-us" dynamic. But I could just about stay ahead of schedule.

Is an animatic a normal thing for almost every animated film?

JC: Yes. You usually only find it in live-action features that are special-effects heavy and storyboarding stunt sequences. But Wes sort of figures out the rhythm of the film with these animatics. That seems to be the thing that you kind of go over and over again: how long a shot lasts, and what follows it. It's very satisfying because it feels like every shot is worthwhile; there's nothing in there that's taken for granted. The staging is so strategic, whether it's a wide shot or a close-up. We've got to earn every shot.

EDWARD BURSCH: You can save a lot of production costs—and time—if you know exactly what needs to be in every frame of every shot, and if you only

shoot what's necessary. You're not building some gigantic set that you only end up seeing a portion of in the final movie.

I've definitely gotten the impression from the crew that the animatic really feels like a film, and that it's been an important resource for them.

JC: I always try to bring quite a lot to the storyboards because, ideally, it'll start everyone off on a higher plane. I feel like everything's just going to get better from the animatic on: the set dressers are going to make even wilder, more amazing sets, and the character designers are going to take it to that next level.

But this does mean that every shot in the animatic goes through a massive process. I would do a pass on it; Wes would take it and move things around; it would come back to me; and then I would have to make that look good. Hopefully, over time, I've been able to get on his same wavelength—I kind of got the look he was going for. Obviously, sometimes you can be way off. But you're really just looking to help the director. I think Wes enjoys the process, so that's good. I've worked with other directors, and it's very easy to *not* enjoy it. We're literally going through every tiny little thing, every single shot—I mean, I can almost visualize them now, in my head, *all* of them, you know? [LAUGHS] So by the time it gets to the guys at 3 Mills [Studios], they'll be able to take it that step further.

Editing is generally considered a part of postproduction. But you're editing as part of preproduction. That's sort of unusual, isn't it?

EB: It's doubly unusual—not only to be editing as a part of preproduction, but also then to have another

ABOVE: **Nutmeg and Chief in the animatic (TOP) and in the finished film (BOTTOM)**

editor who will cut together the actual film footage. With an animated movie, however, it's good to edit the whole thing before actually doing the time-consuming stop-motion work—to know exactly how many frames you're going to shoot and plan every single shot down to a "T."

Jay, you mentioned that Wes was still feeling out whether this was going to be his next project. I'm curious about what existed before you two came on board. Was there concept art? Were there chicken-scratch storyboard drafts that Wes had done? What was presented to you?

EB: The first thing I received, on April 12, 2015, was the script from Wes along with a number of reference images and a reference video. The reference images were just a few Japanese woodblock prints, and then a picture of a dog, and then a picture of a dog statue in Japan. The video was of three taiko drummers drumming this ferocious beat, which was the kind of thing that the movie begins with. He sent that to set the mood.

JC: I got some early script pages and thumbs from Wes, and there were some visual references that production designer Adam Stockhausen had begun to gather, especially for the island; I specifically remember getting reference for the trash trams.

The first shot I worked on was the opening shot: Megasaki City, where you see the dome and everything in the city center. I knew that Wes wanted a "future from the '60s" type of look. We had to figure out what the characters would look like in the animatic because the character design process hadn't begun—we just needed to get something down. So Wes would be sending images, a lot of them actors from Kurosawa films, and then I would kind of base some of those initial character sketches on those actors.

I went out and bought the big Kurosawa DVD box set and dove into those films. I then drew with those movies playing in the background, on a TV. A lot of those movies are black and white, and the animatic is black and white, so it all helped me to get into that kind of Kurosawa mood.

Initially I asked the question, "Are these dogs in costume?" Because I wasn't sure if it was like *Fantastic Mr. Fox*—"Are they on two legs?" And Wes was like, "No, these are real dogs, on four legs"— that sort of thing.

So aside from the thumbs that Wes had done, you were the first person to draw these characters? They hadn't been at all designed yet?

JC: Yeah—often it happens that way. Sometimes you'll come on to a project and they've been doing some character design already. But we obviously went through that design process as the film evolved.

Was there a particular look Wes was aiming for at this stage?

JC: Wes mentioned that it might be quite good if the style of drawings in the animatic could resemble Japanese woodblock prints, or look a bit like that style. I took that on board and used certain digital pens to get that inky look.

Wes and Adam had collected a lot of the woodblock prints together, and I referenced them and found others as I was drawing backgrounds and characters. I also visited the Victoria and Albert Museum, which has a permanent exhibition of Japanese art, and I filled a sketchbook there studying them. It was a real inspiration to see that artwork in person.

In terms of the look of the animation, I know that Wes is fond of the Bill Melendez *Peanuts* animated specials, which I obviously love—that kind of design, that simplicity.

Personally, I like simple graphic character designs and expressionistic set design—just enough in the storyboard to convey the emotional atmosphere the shot requires. My type of animation isn't very showy. Sometimes in animatics, the animation can be really over the top, and Wes said quite early on, on *Grand Budapest*, that that's not what he wanted. He wanted it to be quite subtle. And so that just kind of carried over into this.

Are there other cinematic influences you drew from?

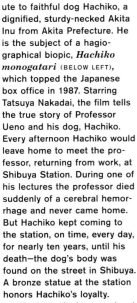

No discussion of Japan, dogs, or dedication to duty would be complete without a brief tribute to faithful dog Hachiko, a dignified, sturdy-necked Akita Inu from Akita Prefecture. He is the subject of a hagiographical biopic, *Hachiko monogatari* (BELOW LEFT), which topped the Japanese box office in 1987. Starring Tatsuya Nakadai, the film tells the true story of Professor Ueno and his dog, Hachiko. Every afternoon Hachiko would leave home to meet the professor, returning from work, at Shibuya Station. During one of his lectures the professor died suddenly of a cerebral hemorrhage and never came home. But Hachiko kept coming to the station, on time, every day, for nearly ten years, until his death—the dog's body was found on the street in Shibuya. A bronze statue at the station honors Hachiko's loyalty.

Easier to find in your local library is the 2009 remake, *Hachi: A Dog's Tale*—a film that is no less weepy than the original, nor should it be. Starring Richard Gere and directed by Lasse Hallström, the film was shot in Rhode Island. Another memorial to Hachiko, sculpted by Darren Hussey and pictured here in a photo by the author (FAR RIGHT), now stands outside the Woonsocket Depot, a pilgrimage site for Hachiko's American devotees.

JC: There were certain films in the '30s that used a particular kind of staging. *King Kong* was interesting to look at because it has stop-motion animation in it. Another film that comes to mind is *20,000 Years in Sing Sing*. The thing about both of those was the staging: A moment plays out in one shot, over a period of time, and it would have a quite dense, deep staging. Detail in the extreme foreground would be quite dark, almost like a framing device. Then you would have a middle ground where there was, perhaps, some action going on with actors. And then you would have that really interesting background detail.

At a later stage in the process, Wes wanted to go back into some shots that were already approved and just weave this technique in. He would reference things like *Citizen Kane* a lot, especially in the early—

For the Municipal Dome scene?

JC: Yeah, absolutely. *The Manchurian Candidate* is a good one for that technique too—lots of Dutch angles that you film from a low angle, in the shadows a bit. And Sidney Lumet's *The Hill*. It's a very unsettling way of filming people, with a dramatic wide-angle lens and deep-focus framing.

One film Wes didn't mention but that *Isle of Dogs* made me think about was Martin Scorsese's *Gangs of New York* because of the barren New York landscape and all the different gangs. And, of course, thinking about Wes's films in the past. I like when he uses techniques from his back catalog—but with a twist—for a new film. Like the red theater curtains opening to reveal new scenes in *Rushmore*; he's applied the same idea here, except this time with Japanese screens sliding open. But like a few things, this was cut from the final film.

How do you edit an animatic together?

EB: I get Photoshop files from Jay, and those files will have different layers. Say there's a character who's supposed to be walking through a shot; he'll send me a file that has the character on a layer separate from the background in the scene. And I use an Adobe software called After Effects to move that character, and then export that file for Avid, which is what the real editors over in London use to edit

the whole movie together. And then I cut it together with the sound design.

Do the programs that you're working with allow you to do camera movement, like pans and zooms? So that's all built into the animatic?

EB: Exactly. That's all pretty much ironed out before they shoot. And I try to differentiate between a zoom and a dolly shot by using 3-D effects in After Effects. And then I cut it together with the sound design. Wes does the voice work, the first pass of the voice work, before the actors actually go into the studio and record.

So you're just working with Wes's line readings at first?

EB: At first, exactly, yes. The actors didn't record their voice work in the studio until we'd already been working on the animatic for a few months. So, in the meantime, Wes would act out the scenes—just, like, on an iPhone or something—and we would use his voice tracks, temporarily. And then we would add the sound design, cut it together, and decide what shots to trim or extend; we'd begin the whole editing process.

How's Wes's voice acting?

EB: It's great because he nails the pacing. He has a very distinct idea for how lines should be delivered,

BELOW LEFT: *Chidori Birds*, by an artist of the school of Katsushika Hokusai (1760–1849)

BELOW: *Cock*, attributed to Hokusai

BOTTOM: A concept drawing of the hardened lava on Trash Island. Concept art by Turlo Griffin

and for the pace of the line. A lot of the time, we cut the actors' performances together to match Wes's initial reading. He knows exactly how they should sound, and it sounds great. [LAUGHS]

How did you figure out the initial sound design?

EB: Wes would often send me music tracks that we wanted to use, and many of them are still in the cut that they have right now, as they're assembling the movie. A bunch of music from the scores of Kurosawa films, and then some other Japanese taiko drumming tracks. But mostly tracks from Japanese films. Those just came from Wes; he emailed me these tracks and said, "Let's try this for this scene; let's try beginning at this point in the track, to this point; let's try looping this. . . ." He was very, very precise about the music he wanted to use and where he wanted to use it.

Were there any recurring types of sounds that you were putting in? Can you describe the provisional soundscape that you created?

EB: Wes was pretty particular about wind; it took a while to find the right wind tone and texture. We wanted something that captured the feeling of a barren wasteland, but also had a texture. It took a while to find just the right wind sound. For live stage performances, they use these wind machines that create this kind of up-and-down *whoooosh* sort

of sound, which worked nicely. Another sound that we hear a lot is this humming drone—or drones, plural—throughout the film because we see drones a number of times in the movie.

Kurosawa was very big on storyboards. Jay, did you get to look at any of his?

JC: Yeah, I have. I'm happy you brought them up. I had forgotten, but they were very much in mind for this project, as we were thinking about Kurosawa so much. They're so full of expression and energy that any storyboard artist would draw inspiration from them.

There's footage of him on the set of *Ran* doing sketches. He'll draw something so that he can show it to his director of photography, and say, "I want it to look like this." When I watched the Kurosawa documentary *For Beautiful Movies*, by his son Hisao, I took down a quote of Kurosawa's about this: "Drawing a storyboard requires you to make ideas more precise. So showing the storyboard helps the crew to understand what I want. It's the simplest way to achieve that, and the simplest way to show them an idea."

JC: That just about sums it up, doesn't it? I remember talking to Paul [Harrod], the production designer, and a few others in the art department; they were really positive about the animatic, saying how useful it was, even just as a starting point. But

TOP: A frame from the animatic featuring the dogs in deep-focus group composition

BOTTOM: A still from Sidney Lumet's *The Hill* (LEFT) and a wide-angle group shot from Martin Scorsese's *Gangs of New York* (RIGHT)

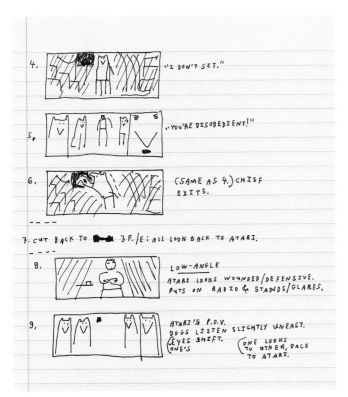

it's a really weird process—it's like a snake skin. It's just gonna sort of shed [LAUGHS]. And then no one will ever see it! But hopefully it'll still be present in the finished piece.

Audiences won't see your direct work, but it's the blueprint for everything that does end up being seen.

TOP LEFT: **Wes's early storyboard for Atari's confrontation with the pack in the bottle hovel**

Chief stands alone in the hovel, in the animatic (TOP RIGHT) and the finished film (BOTTOM).

JC: Definitely. And it's all Wes's vision. We're just helping him achieve his mission. They're sort of military missions in a way. And you've got so many different departments all kind of looking toward the animatic, so it's satisfying to know that you can help him create this tool to help with questions.

It's great that you bring up the military metaphor, because Kurosawa also said that he thought of making a movie as a battle: the director is the general, and the script is the "battle flag," the thing that everybody looks at and rallies behind. And I guess the animatic is a battle flag, too—something that inspires the whole group to march onward to the finish.

JC: Yeah, absolutely. And then they start dropping the stop-motion shots into the animatic, and it's really satisfying to see.

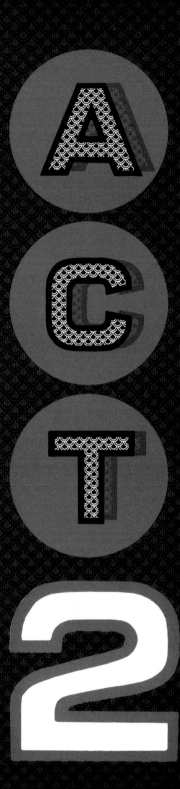

ACT 2

DESIGNING THE WORLD

PUPPETS

ODDS SEEM HIGH that the phrase "isle of dogs" first worked its way into Wes Anderson's brain while he was shooting *Fantastic Mr. Fox* in London. If not, it's a remarkable coincidence.

When Londoners hear "isle of dogs" they think of the thumblike peninsula formed by a deep southward bend in the Thames that bears that name. Three miles north of this Isle of Dogs are the Three Mills. One of London's oldest standing industrial centers, the Three Mills are now home to 3 Mills Studios, the largest film studio inside the city limits.

It's a far cry from the sun-soaked backlots and gleaming facades of a Los Angeles studio. From the outside, 3 Mills looks like part of William Blake's London, a place out of a Dickens or Gaskell novel. The sandy brick mill buildings and cobblestone streets, worn smooth from centuries of cartwheels and boot heels, have been barnacled over with trailers, tool sheds, prefab cabins on cinder block. There's a subtle melancholy stain beneath the complexion of the bricks, a testament to the poisoned atmosphere of Britain's industrial age. It's a worthy setting for a story that finds stark beauty in aging and waste, some of which has literally been scraped from 3 Mills's back alleys and worked into the sets.

In 3 Mills's central lobby, two glass cases commemorate the studio's stop-motion history. Inside the first is Tim Burton's loveable death-gray dachshund, Frankenweenie, standing on a patch of green

OPPOSITE: **The gate of 3 Mills Studios. Photo by the author; identity of accidental subject unknown**
ABOVE: **Andy Gent takes a look at some Atari faces.**

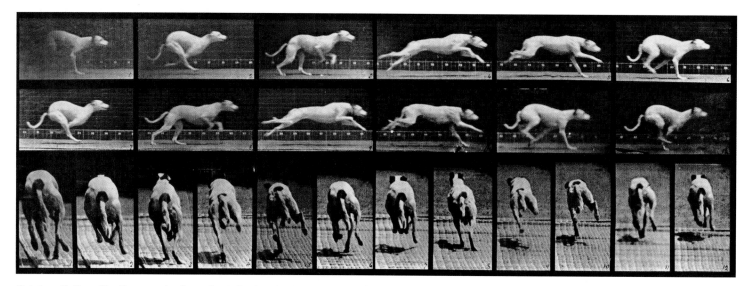

Rotatory Gallop: The Dog, a proto-cinematic study of motion by photographer Eadweard Muybridge (1830–1904). Muybridge's most well-known photo series follows the micro-movements of a horse mid-gallop, each photo in the series a piece of "stopped motion." Stop-motion filmmaking does just the opposite—where Muybridge's photos break down real motion, stop-motion builds up an illusion of motion, one frame at a time.

suburban sod. In the other, there's a big old tree rooted in a field of nubby orange terrycloth. "*Fantastic Mr. Fox*'s Tree," the plaque reads. It appears to be the one used for the scene where a squirrel foreman, voiced by Roman Coppola, barks orders to his team of contractors as they spruce up the place for the new owners.

Andy Gent, a Derbyshire-bred, London-based puppet maker, headed up the puppet departments on both these films, and is now back to oversee the *Isle of Dogs* puppet team. Andy's puppet workshop is a hop, skip, and jump away from the 3 Mills grounds, housed in another one of East London's old brick industrial buildings. Wes was able to bring back much of the same team from *Fantastic Mr. Fox* for this film, and Andy says there's more familiarity on this set than there was on *Fox*—Wes knows stop-motion better, workflows have been streamlined, relationships have been formed, experiences have been metabolized.

"Has that greater familiarity made Wes more ambitious, do you think?" I ask. "Yes," Andy responds, decisively. His eyes properly twinkle behind his browline glasses. "I've worked on big films before. But here, the numbers, the technique, the fact that everything's handmade . . . The amount of parts on this film is off the scale. These have been the quickest two years of my life."

Above Andy's computer there is a printed email from Wes:

Thank you Andy.
I'm glad you don't know what you are getting into.
This movie is going to be what you might call puppet-heavy.

Framed on the wall next to the note is one of Eadweard Muybridge's motion studies, *Rotatory Gallop: The Dog*—two dozen primitive black-and-white freeze-frames of a racing hound running at full speed. Next to that are glossy photos of Tim Burton and Ray Harryhausen. On the shelves, in easy reach, there's a thick red-spined volume of *Hokusai Manga* sitting alongside copies of *The Ultimate Guide to Dog Breeds* and *The Howell Book of Dogs*.

These last two books are red herrings, as it turns out. According to Andy, the dogs in the film weren't based on particular breeds. "It was never *a yellow Labrador* that Wes was interested in: it was *a sad dog*," Andy remembers. "The early sculpts had a character air to them, a sense of dishevelment that he liked."

Andy's department produced no concept drawings of the dogs. The puppets were only ever "sketched" in soft brown clay. The modelers would make a few dogs and show them to Wes. Wes would contemplate the sculptures and try to express which details struck him as right. The modelers would try another set of sculptures. Wes would give another round of notes.

Around the puppet workshop, these primeval sculpts are referred to as the "giacomettis," after Alberto Giacometti, the Swiss artist. "His style is

ABOVE: Early sculpts of dogs on the sculpting room shelf

BELOW: Human characters, like Atari, were first drafted in pen and ink, but, like the dogs, they didn't take their final forms until the sculptors had worked them over a few times in Plasticine. Here, an earlier, stumpier model of Atari stands beside his concept art. "That's his default position, sort of stooped down like that," Andy says. "He gets quite shouty, at times; he's a little rebellious. And he's frustrated when he can't understand what the dogs are saying to him. The shoulders have to be a certain way. That's something that we build in, which gets passed to the animators and sort of becomes a character trait. It starts with the way it's built."

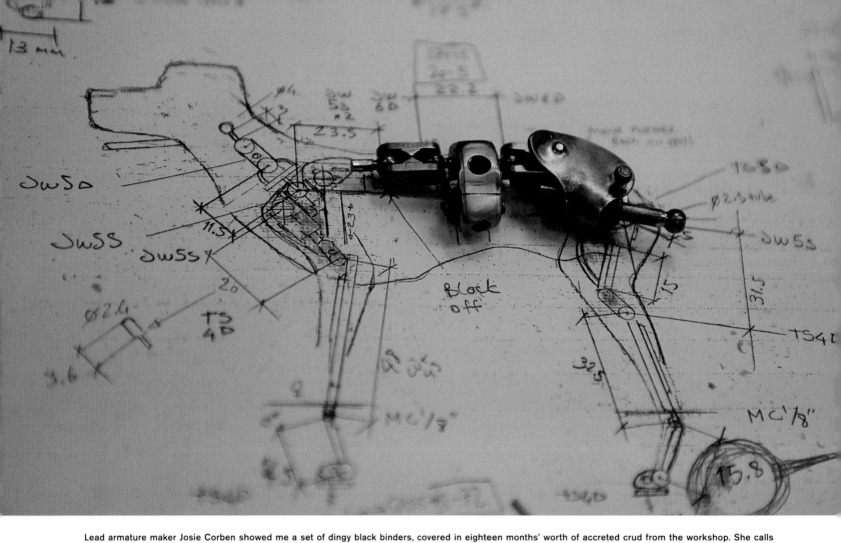

Lead armature maker Josie Corben showed me a set of dingy black binders, covered in eighteen months' worth of accreted crud from the workshop. She calls it the "bible"—filmmaker's jargon for an authoritative, comprehensive document that provides a quick, reliable reference point for multiple artists or departments. Inside the binder, sheathed in plastic sleeves, are technical drawings of each puppet, scrawled over with marginalia, addenda, errata. ABOVE is one of the bible's schematics; BELOW, a nearly finished dog armature.

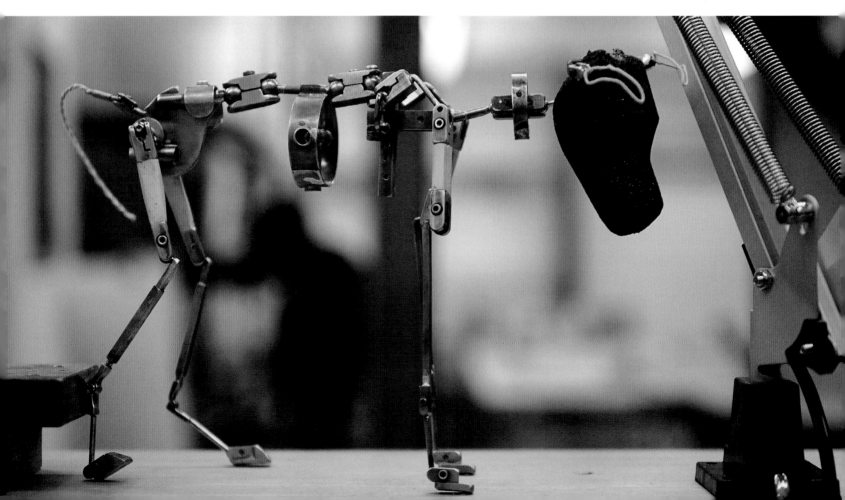

Sculptor Valma Hiblen inspects the jaw of a large-scale King puppet.

quite loose, quite rough—sort of stretched figures," Andy says. "We'd work them up really quickly, doing that sort of Giacometti-like thing, thumby and textural, working with little worms of clay."

The sculptors work next door to Andy's office, hunched over a white workbench that wraps around the room. The sculpting room doubles as a kind of natural history museum: the early giacomettis have been preserved in a place of honor, presiding over the sculptors from a high shelf that runs above the workbench. If you stand in the center of the room and follow the shelf clockwise, you can watch the giacomettis evolve. The first draft of Boss is big, bluff, broad-shouldered. A few generations later, the athletic beast has shrunk into a squat, phlegmatic mascot.

IN *FANTASTIC MR. FOX*, Fox constantly frets that he is not living like a real animal. It's almost as if he is vaguely aware that Andy Gent and the puppet modelers have half-anthropomorphized him—given him long humanoid legs, manly shoulders, opposable thumbs.

The dogs of Trash Island are not freighted with Fox's existential concerns. They do not wear cord-uroy or cashmere or camel hair. They do not have a column in the paper or a partnership in a law firm. They do not practice karate; they do not read comics. They neither cook nor sew. They're closer kin to the black wolf that Mr. Fox both admires and fears: they have the same wiry muscled limbs, the same tarry matted coat, the shrink-wrapped ribcage of an always-hungry hunter.

Deep inside each puppet is a steely underdog—a contraption of metal rods and ball joints that gives the puppet a real animal's range of motion. This skeleton is called an armature. When designing the armature, modelers need to study the script to determine what will be asked of the puppets—animators need to be sure that the puppets won't fail them, whether they're about to shoot a scene of exposive action or expressive dialogue.

Josie Corben, the head of armature for *Isle of Dogs*, describes this film's particular challenge succinctly: "The puppets had to be able to do dog things, but also Wes things." It's an action-adventure movie, but along the way, they do end up doing a lot of "chatting," she says. "This way, and that way," she adds parenthetically to make sure I got the idea, holding her fists up like dog puppets and imitating

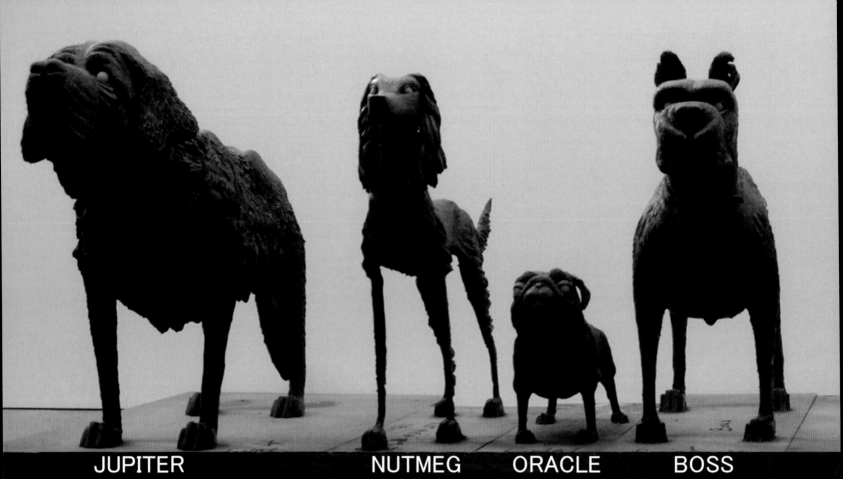

JUPITER   NUTMEG   ORACLE   BOSS

FULL DOG

BOSS   CHIEF

FULL DOG SCALE

CHIEF   KING   REX   DUKE

9 Oct 15

REX   DUKE

13 Oct 15

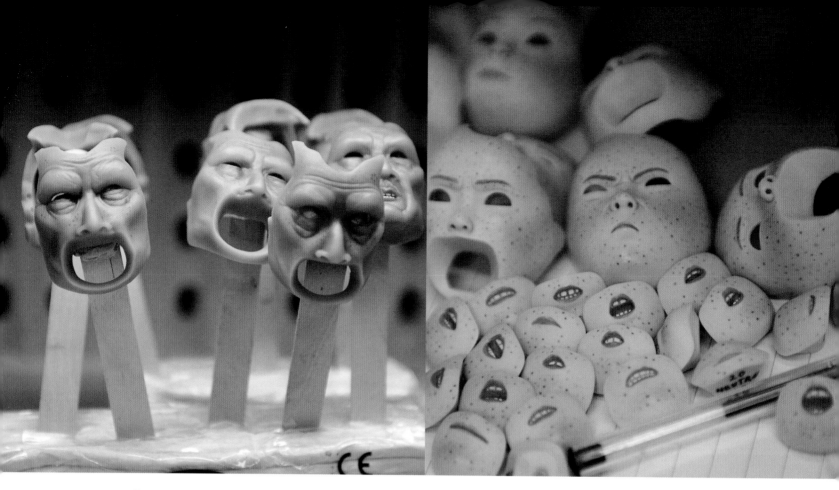

ABOVE RIGHT: Each puppet and mask is hand-painted, and painters need to maintain consistency from one face to the next. Bruises and freckles are a particular challenge. ABOVE LEFT: Kobayashi masks without their mouths. Animators will change the mouths from frame to frame to make the puppet "speak."
BELOW: A collection of partial Atari faces, each with slightly different mouths

classic Wes Anderson framings—first in a frontal shot, then in profile.

The dogs chat the same way Mr. Fox did: the animator manipulates the facial armature—a set of paddles beneath the puppet's cheeks and eyebrows—to create the expressions. The human puppets in *Fantastic Mr. Fox* worked the same way. Speech is difficult to animate believably with mechanical human faces, but there weren't very many human characters in the film, and they kept mum or mumbled through most of their scenes.

At first, the *Isle of Dogs* crew wondered if they might be able to get away with the same approach they used on *Fantastic Mr. Fox*. "Atari, initially, looked like he might be mute throughout the film," Andy recalls. "He was just going to have expression changes. Now, of course, he's a fully realized, talking little boy."

When it became clear that the citizens of Megasaki City would be doing quite a bit of chatting, too, the puppet modelers realized that mechanical faces would be too pinched and inexpressive. "The gold standard is to make the face go quickly from *oo* to *ee*," Andy says, exaggerating his facial muscles as he makes the vowel sounds. "Mechanical faces are really good, but there are points that they can't go to. But very quickly we said, 'Well, let's try replacement faces.' That, essentially, frees up that character. You can give them any expression you can sculpt."

On *Isle of Dogs*, any change in a human puppet's face—pronouncing a syllable, furrowing a brow, widening an eye—requires an entirely new face to be fabricated. The animator switches faces frame by frame. The mouth is a separate piece and can be swapped out independently.

Andy points out several Atari faces lined up on a shelf. "Originally, we were in familiar territory, with solid resin faces, but it felt a bit lifeless. So instead, we used clear resin that we pigmented to a place of translucence." This resin really does seem to glow with a human warmth when lit. The skin looks soft; lifeblood seems to beat beneath it. It provokes a protective instinct: it's hard not to feel a bit faint the first time you watch one of the face pieces being "scraped off," only to have the ghastly, droid-like inner core of the puppet's head lock eye sockets with you.

The face-replacement system is not without drawbacks. For example, Wes wanted Tracy to have freckles. Then he kept wanting her to have more. The puppet modelers talked him down to three hundred and twenty freckles. When Tracy smiles, her cheeks move, and so do her freckles. All those freckles need to appear in exactly the right place from face to face—if the faces don't match down to a fraction of a millimeter, the freckles will dance like TV static when the footage is played back. The modelers have set a "key freckle" from which to chart the other three hundred and nineteen, a pole star from which the rest of the freckle constellations can be plotted.

IN A NARROW SIDE ROOM, half the width of a walk-in closet, Alex Williams spends "all day, every day, making all the hair, for everyone," she says—wigs, mustaches, even eyebrows. In the early models, eyebrows were painted on, but Wes preferred the realism of real hair for close-ups. Real eye*lashes* were even attempted, but this became, as Andy gently puts it, "tiring on resources" during animation.

Hair, especially fur, is tricky business in stop-motion film. No matter how careful the animators are, they still have to put their fingers and thumbs all over the puppets. Every time they touch a patch of fur, the hairs will be displaced a few millimeters. This creates an effect called "boiling"—when the footage is played back, the fur appears to dance or blow throughout the shot. Wes was initially advised against using fur on *Fantastic Mr. Fox*, but he embraced the boiling look—it helped emphasize his deliberate homage to the old days of stop-motion. The world of *Isle of Dogs*, on the other hand, offers a few convenient justifications for boiling. A bit of visible skin-crawling makes the sick dogs look itchy, maybe mangy or flea-bitten. And Trash Island is a barren landscape, unprotected from the sea—a few well-placed sound effects help convince us that the boiling is just the ocean breeze tousling their fur. This time, serendipitously enough, boiling may help emphasize another homage—Kurosawa's frames are full of grasses, hair, and fabrics rippling in the wind.

In the film Rex, King, Duke, and Boss spend some time in an incinerator. The fur department had to create a special "singed" look.

As for the human puppets, their hair gets "punched in" to silicone "wig caps," which wrap all the way around the puppets' heads and faces. Alex holds up a key ring from which hang locks of every shade, perfectly ordered in a slow gradient from white to yellow to red to black—every color used in the film. Every head of hair and patch of fur, no matter the color, needs to be mottled up with hairs of contrasting colors, or it won't look realistic on screen.

Alex's workspace is covered in tools and bottles of glue. She has a small chest of plastic drawers on her workbench for needles, toothpicks, tweezers, mascara wands, and small scissors. Crammed right up behind her is a shelf on the back wall that holds bins with labels like "Cats," "Tracy #2," "Tracy Bits," "Watanabe Bits," "Domo Bits." "Bits" is a Britishism heard in every workshop, used wherever an American might expect the word "parts" or "pieces." On a miniature film, almost everything is, or is made from, bits.

"I'm making bits for the fight cloud," another modeler says. She indicates a bin full of body parts, belonging to dogs or people who've gotten the crap beat out of them in comic-strip fashion, surrounded by a round, roiling cloud of smoke and debris. These dustups are handmade and hand-animated: the cloud is made of cotton fluff, with heads, legs, fists, and other bits poking out of it.

WHEN WE TALK ABOUT the "scale" of a shot in live-action filmmaking, we're talking about the size of the figures relative to the frame. To make the subject appear bigger on screen—to go from a wide shot to a close-up, for example—you can choose any of three simple options. You can switch to a telephoto lens, or you can bring the subject closer to you, or you can move the camera closer to the subject.

In stop-motion filmmaking, there are severe limitations on every one of those options. Often, when you want a wider view, the only way to get it is

ABOVE: Modelers tried out several colors for each dog's fur. This notebook is open to a page of options for Rex.
BELOW LEFT AND MIDDLE: Modelers work in detail with each dog's fur, made from the hair of angora goats and alpacas.
BELOW RIGHT: Each hair on the Shinto Priest's head will be inserted with a needle. This puppet is about halfway through the procedure.

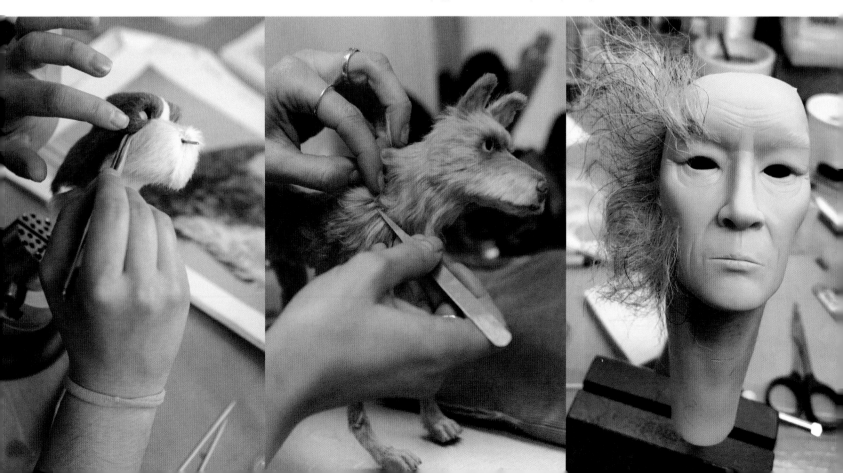

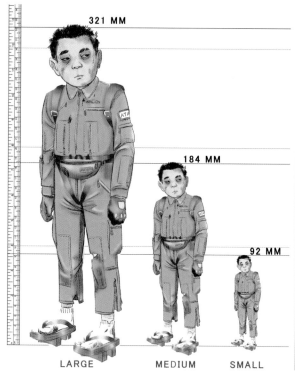

321 MM

184 MM

92 MM

LARGE   MEDIUM   SMALL

Puppets are built at three main scales (LEFT, concept drawings of Atari; RIGHT, sculpts of Rex). Some important puppets, which feature in extreme close-ups or extreme wide shots, are built at five scales.

to build versions of your sets and puppets at a smaller scale. When you want to get a closer look at something, you're often better off just building it bigger. Shot scale often has much less to do with the camera and much more to do with what's created in front of it. A surprising amount of what we would ordinarily call cinematography is accomplished by the puppet department and the art department.

On *Isle of Dogs*, puppets come in three main scales. The large-scale puppets, used in closer views, are fully articulated—they're tricked out with ball-and-socket shoulders, flexible spines, and, in the dogs' case, expressive facial armatures. Medium-scale puppets, used in wider views, are hard-bodied with moveable limbs and swiveling heads. Sometimes a cloth costume is made for medium-scale puppets, but in some cases the costume might just be painted onto the hard body. The smallest puppets tend to be softer rubber with a simple, bendable wire armature—they're used in extreme long shots. Some puppets are specially made at additional scales for particular cinematographic effects. One of the biggest "overscale" puppets was built for an extreme close-up of Spots's weaponized tooth. It's a neckless, eyeless maw—the shaggy jaws are covered in silky

white alpaca hair. The mouth is wider than some of the film's full sets.

Main characters like Kobayashi and Atari have seven duplicates made at small, medium, and large scale—the characters may need to make appearances in several scenes shooting at the same time. The film's puppet wrangler, Daisy Garside, is responsible for knowing where each duplicate of each puppet is at all times and makes sure the animators get the puppet they need.

The large-scale dogs set the scale for the entire film. All things being equal, there are advantages to making your puppets on the smaller side, but you can only make a fully expressive, all-purpose mechanical dog head so small. Atari shares most of his scenes with the dogs—their size determined his size. His size helped determine the scale of Kobayashi and the other human characters.

Even the large-scale puppets on this film are at a smaller scale than full-size Mr. Fox, in part to make the sets look bigger, more epic. At the same time, the demand for plausible realism is higher on *Isle of Dogs*. The world is meant to feel textured and tactile, but this time, Wes doesn't want anything to look charmingly hokey or homespun like an old Rankin/

ABOVE AND BELOW: To create the shot of Spots's "secret tooth," the puppet department fabricated an "overscale" mouth.
OVERLEAF: A table covered in Atari masks and sculpts

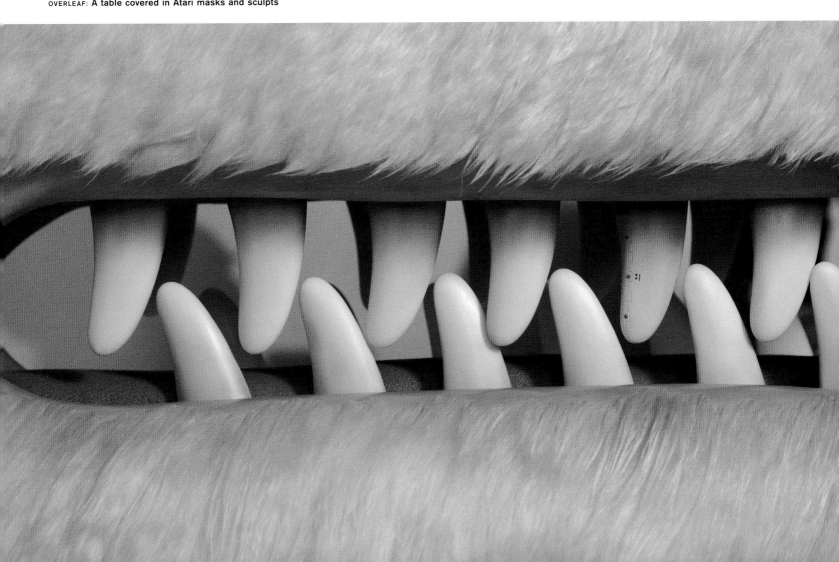

After the sculptors agree on the final look for a character or element, the finished Plasticine sculpt is cast into a mold. Pictured is a moldmaker pouring silicone into a mold—the silicone will form the flesh over an armature's skeleton. The moldmaking room is a Wes Anderon set in its own right—stacks of blocks in gray and turquoise, yellow paint cans full of filler, not a single other color in sight. Andy, cupping a mold between his hands, explained the process to me: "A hard mold, because it's a soft creature. A soft mold, if you have a hard creature."

Bass Christmas special—*Isle of Dogs* is not a Roald Dahl storybook, and the animation itself is not meant to be understood as a good-natured metacinematic joke. "If it were possible for Wes to do this live-action, maybe he would have, but it's not something he could have: it's a story about talking dogs," producer Jeremy Dawson says. "But I think none of us thinks of it as a cartoon—it's a movie."

The challenge for the modelers is to make the people and places look even more lifelike than the ones in *Fantastic Mr. Fox* but at even more vanishingly small scales. Mitch Barnes, a tall, older modeler, sits in the corner of the sculpting room, poring over some props, deeply impressed by the handiwork of his colleagues: dog collars, pairs of glasses, tiny helmets with tiny, functional buckles the size of a nail head. He holds up a pen, no bigger than a sliver of fish bone, its clip made of etched brass. "I have never seen people who can sculpt this well at this size," Mitch marvels. He looks as though he just discovered the objects under a toadstool. He shakes a paper espresso cup full of tiny walkie-talkies into his outstretched palm—at a glance, just a handful of cupcake sprinkles.

THE PUPPET WORKSHOP functions like a kitchen in a busy restaurant. A big whiteboard out front reminds the modelers of the "Upcoming Deliveries"—the "orders" the production has put in.

Today, they've ordered sushi. Oversized Tentacle, plus sections. O/S Snapper + sections. O/S Crab + sections. The seafood's going to star in a classically Andersonian overhead insert, a bird's-eye view of the chef's hands at work.

It's Josie Corben's last day on the set, and as she shows me the dog armature with her right hand, she's got her final project dangling in her left: Oversized Sushi Chef Hand, rough-edged and Crayola-peach. Andy's been walking around wiggling a long magenta tentacle, flopping it back and forth to see "how it behaves" in an animator's hand. Modelers at the workbench are taking a crack at the crabs; one asks Andy to inspect a fish skeleton he's just made which Andy, beaming, declares is "just like the real thing."

As soon as the short-order cooks at the workshop deliver these—order up—more orders come in behind them.

A live-action film follows a familiar life cycle—

Puppets are built in stages. These partially painted puppets are waiting for heads.

development, preproduction, production, postproduction. Production is the phase where crew are on their feet, sets are built and lit, cameras are up and running. By May 2017, *Isle of Dogs* has been in production for about eighteen months—the sets are spread out, by now, over three soundstages at 3 Mills Studios. *Isle of Dogs* has also been in postproduction for almost as long. Editors and visual effects artists are holed up in a computer lab in an adjacent building, churning through the footage they receive from set. And in the workshops, where sets, puppets, props, and costumes are made, preproduction has never stopped. It might be more accurate to say that they are continually reenacting the development phase—sketches and mockups are still being submitted to Wes, reviewed and annotated, sent back to the drawing board.

These phases do overlap a little in live-action filmmaking, too. On most productions, prop departments are scrambling to fill last-minute requests, and the next scene's sets are under construction while the cameras are rolling. Radical script overhauls are always possible, and enterprising editors are getting a head start on their work as soon as

footage is available. But the overall paradigm of preproduction, production, postproduction is a passable approximation of the process. At the very least, it's a good gauge of the film set's atmosphere. The high-alert anticipation of preproduction gives way to the underslept flow-state of production, which ends with the relief and refocusing of postproduction.

But in stop-motion filmmaking, the processes overlap and interrupt each other to the point that they're virtually inextricable: never separate periods of time, and barely even separate states of mind. Animation happens so slowly and invisibly that, no matter how thorough your plans were in preproduction, a lot of early, steady postproduction work is essential just to determine where you are, what you've got, and what you still need. And when whole warehouses of physical objects have to be fabricated from scratch, there's neither space nor time to wait until everything is built before you shoot. Mind-meldingly close communication is critical. Modelers have to think like animators; animators have to think like editors. The finished film has to be envisioned down to its minutest detail by the higher-ups before the modelers' work can even begin.

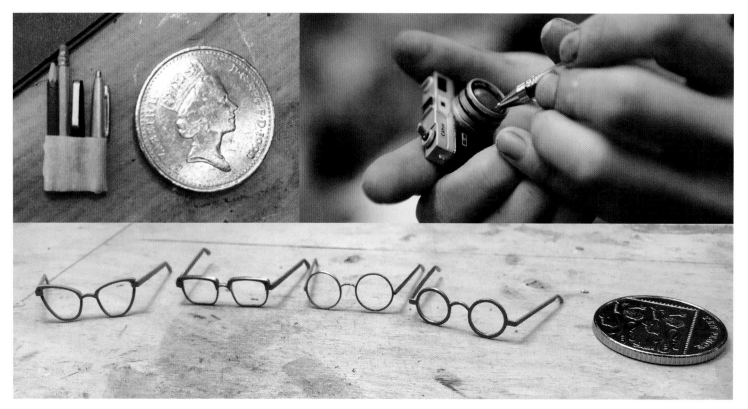

A pocket protector (TOP LEFT), miniature camera (TOP RIGHT), and glasses (ABOVE). The art department modelers design and fabricate any objects that appear on the set, but the puppet department is responsible for props—anything a character will personally handle or wear.
OPPOSITE: A large-scale sculpt of Boss sporting a miniature dog tag and collar. Note the red baseball-lace detailing.
OVERLEAF: One of the film's many "fight clouds," made from cotton wadding and puppet "bits"
PAGES 100–101: Modelers at work in the puppet workshop's armature and mold assembly room

At the same time, no live-action crew is ever so widely dispersed and alone. One day on a live-action production might involve thirty or forty people working together on a single scene on a single set, covering a few pages' worth of dialogue. A single day's shooting at 3 Mills means infinitesimal progress on thirty or forty different scenes spaced throughout the film. Each scene might be unfinished for weeks or months—still missing props, still only partly shot, still roughly cut—and then a dozen might be finished within hours of each other. It is filmmaking in massive parallel. The logistical headaches are enormous.

Spending a single week on set means seeing dozens of scenes in progress. Some characters are being shaped for the first time in the workshop; others are fully dressed and traipsing across carefully lit sets. Some sets have been broken down for good—their wreckages lying in dry dock, and their finished footage hung up as reference stills for the editors and visual effects artists. Months of the film's history are visible, tangible, in a single day, laid out in space rather than time, so that a cross section is as revealing as a longitudinal study would be for a live-action production.

Nonetheless, this book, any book, is bound to falsify this unique filmmaking process—a page-by-page reading experience can't capture the simultaneity, cycle, recapitulation that are the rules, not the exceptions, in stop-motion animation.

What it can offer are a few glimpses into the day-to-day challenges of the short-order cooks working in each department. These challenges require choices, inspire solutions. What we call a film is nothing more than the sum total of the daily solutions to daily problems.

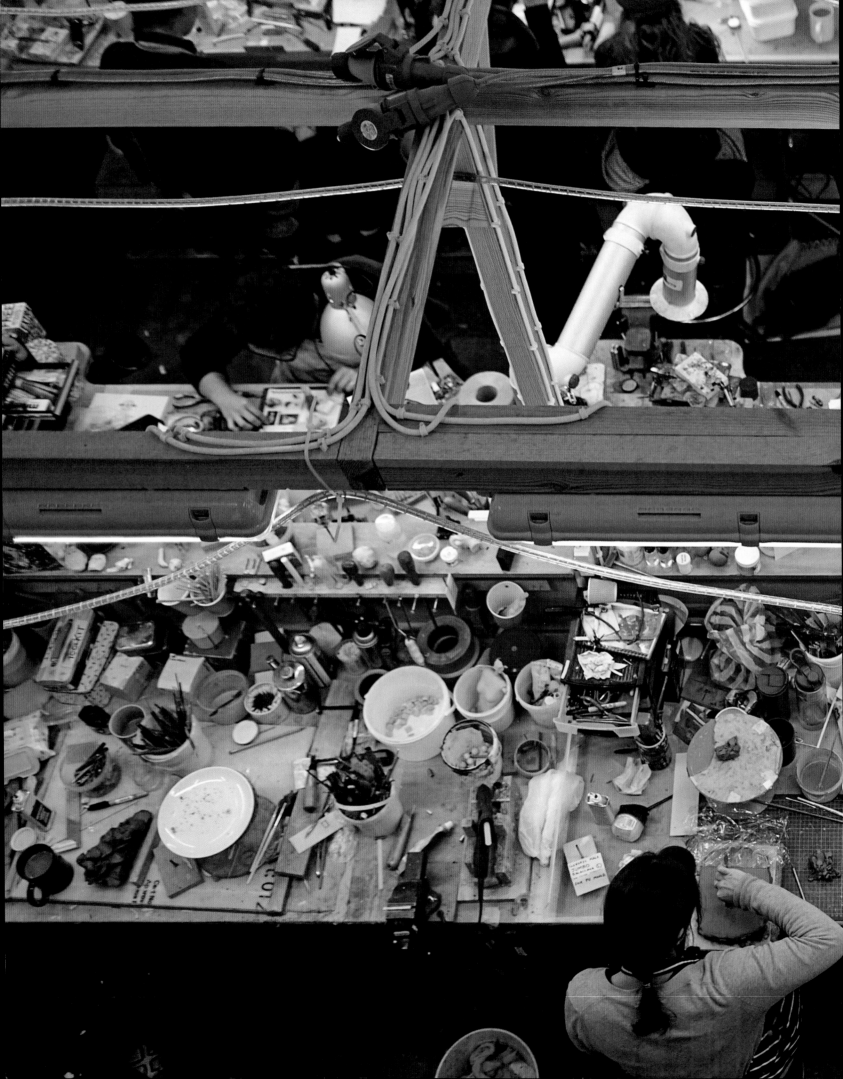

TALKING BACK

AN INTERVIEW WITH HEAD OF PUPPETS DEPARTMENT Andy Gent

ANDY GENT has been "looking after puppets" ever since he finished at university; his first job on a feature film was *Corpse Bride*. Since then he's worked on films like *Max & Co, Coraline, Fantastic Mr. Fox, Frankenweenie,* and *The Grand Budapest Hotel*—he made the puppets for the stop-motion ski chase.

Andy's office belongs equally to Charlie, a chocolate lab, who lounges calmly in the center of the room throughout our talk. Charlie came into Andy's life during the shooting of *Fantastic Mr. Fox*. He's with Andy at the workshop every day.

OPPOSITE: **Andy and Charlie**

ABOVE: **Gruff, pictured here, is one of many dogs who roam the puppet workshop during production.**

So how did you first get involved with *Isle of Dogs*?

There's that amazing moment where I get a phone call and hear, "Hi, it's Wes, Andy. We've just, you know, got this little project. Are you interested in making some puppets?" Brilliant, it sounds great. He said, "Oh, I'm going to send you a little YouTube link, and then I'll send you the script. And you must watch the YouTube link, the little video clip I'm going to send you first." And I was going, "What is that going to be? What is this first thing that I'm going to see about his idea, or his imagination, or whatever it is that's going to capture this?"

And when it arrived it was an amazing clip, a few minutes long, of traditional Japanese taiko drummers. They were so dramatic and very powerful—*boom, boom, boom, boom*—with amazing

synchronicity and raw energy. I was so charged up by the moment of this clip, and the sound, and how inspiring it was. It left me saying "I'm in. I'm in."

Whatever this is, I'm in.

I hadn't even seen the script at that point, just watched the video clip which was so amazing. I got it. You know, it was super-dramatic, it was so powerful. It just took hold of you. So that's how Wes opened it up. [LAUGHS]

You've got Charlie at the workshop with you here. Have there been other dogs around?

Oh, yes. There's been a few. Choco, Treacle, Piglet the Chihuahua mix, and Billy the sheep dog were all the regulars. Other than Charlie we had one full-time real dog in the shop called Hazel. She was a puppy when we started and was here to the last few days of the filming. Amazingly, she grew up to be pretty identical to Rex, one of our Hero Pack dogs. She is so like Rex in many ways, in shape and look and color, it's possible that people might think we based Rex on her.

What's it been like to create these dog puppets with all these real dogs around?

The only big difference between real dogs and the puppets is that the puppets can talk [LAUGHS]. I think it's very good anyway, having real dogs around in the workshop—they help keep everyone happy and less stressed. They're also amazing in this instance as reference. Dogs can look sorrowful, thoughtful, mischievous, alert, and you can always tell when they're really happy. With the puppets, you've got to try to give them this ability, especially with their faces and eyes and ears, to help them make these expressions or emotions. So, having real dogs around doing exactly that is super helpful. Sometimes we can almost tell what a real dog is trying to say, but with our puppets, they can actually say the words. It's still magic hearing them and seeing them speak every time I see it happen.

When you have imagined something from the first reading of the script to something that's then

three-dimensional, it's an amazing thing. Whether it started as description or a quick sketch, it's just magical to see it jump from the page to something physical, something that everybody else can then see and move around. Then you can imagine how it would move and walk and even what it might sound like. There isn't such a dramatic moment of realization again until they've got their skin and fur applied. Then the animators start testing, and the puppets start to wriggle their faces around, or open and close their mouths, or perhaps scratch an ear. That's when you sort of go, "Oh yeah, it's a moving dog." That's its own magical moment. The dog comes alive. And you can see its characteristics—how it drags its feet, or if it's got a limp, or if it holds its head low all the time, whatever it is.

But *then,* when they talk back to you, it takes on a whole new level. And that level of excitement is . . . it's really difficult to . . . [LAUGHS]

I imagine this is all particularly poignant for you, as someone who speaks to your own dog.

Totally. Because you talk stupid language to your own dog. But you can have a proper conversation with a *talking* dog, you know?

You seem like the person to ask about the handling of the dog-human relationship in *Isle of Dogs*.

They mention this in the film, but dogs and little boys are really connected. If you've had a dog when you were a kid, it was the best thing in the world. One of the women working here has a little baby, and she is completely gaga looking at Charlie, wanting to touch him and all that stuff. There's that connection with an animal, where the emotions run deep, and hopefully we have brought that to life in the puppets, especially with Atari and Chief and Spots.

TOP: Atari gives Chief his first hug.

SECOND AND THIRD FROM TOP: In Suzie Templeton's *Peter and the Wolf,* the Peter puppet uses only four replacement faces. "I think that's what Wes liked about *Peter and the Wolf,*" says animation director Mark Waring. "Just the way he's been posed or the way he's been photographed suggests a lot more expressions. It's all about the angle of the face, the turns."

BOTTOM: Atari wears many masks, but often the effect of the light and the pose can create multiple expressions from just one mask.

ABOVE: No real actor, living or dead, has their likeness appear onscreen in *Isle of Dogs.* But particular expressions, hair-styles, eyebrows, sometimes spark something in Wes's mind, and he shows them to Andy when they're working on a particular sculpt or a particular beat. Here's how a doubtful stare from the suggestible Inokichi (Daisuke Kato), one of the heavies from Kurosawa's *Yojimbo*, helped Andy's team envision a quick reaction shot in the Municipal Dome.

You know, I've watched the footage with a bunch of grown-ups [LAUGHS], and you'll hear them clearing their throats because you can't help . . . You do get sentimental; it's inevitable, and especially as a dog owner watching the film. It's natural, I think, for a kid to wish that their dog could talk; it's that part of your imagination kicking in.

[ANDY TURNS TO ADDRESS CHARLIE, WHO IS FAST ASLEEP] Do you know what we're talking about? Who knows.

It's quite nice—Atari and Chief obviously have those moments where, when they're talking in the film, they're clearly thinking about one another, "He has no idea what I'm talking about." Atari's talking in Japanese, Chief's talking in what we've translated as English. And the whole play of it is fun.

As I've walked through the workshop it's been funny to hear how so many of the puppets have names that aren't in the script—that you all have given them names as a sort of interdepartmental tool, and the public may never know about them.

Really, there are over eleven hundred puppets in this film so far. We've got major ones, and ones that only we'll know who are tucked away on the sides of a shot. And it's easier to remember a person by the name than "seventh person on the right in the back stage of that scene." So, they all tend to get names. And then "Other Dog" might become "Other Dog That Looks Like Charlie," which soon becomes "Charlie." In our world, anyway. We have one that we refer to as "Bryan," because he looks like Bryan

Cranston. We've got another one that we refer to as "Keanu," because he looks a little bit like Keanu Reeves.

Well, and over the course of two years, the amount of slang and shorthand that will develop—

Yeah. I'm trying to think . . . We've got "Punk Girl," which is this lady here.

Oh yeah, one of the student activists.

Yeah, very quickly you'll know them by a little nickname. After two years with them, they've become sort of personalities that you know.

Did you take anything specifically from Kurosawa films in the puppets?

The Bad Sleep Well had quite a lot of very good references, particularly for costume. And then from *Seven Samurai* you'll have bits—faces, or a headband, or an *obi* [the sash that belts a kimono]—that make you say, "Oh, yeah, that one's really nice," and we'll lift these little bits out.

Where do they end up on your people?

The one that strikes me straightaway as we have just been working on him is a character derived from *Yojimbo*. His character is very similar-looking to one of the guys in there—he was sort of, you

know, a crazy big ram of a chap. And his face is almost identical to the one that made it through the sculpting process. You'll spot him. He's got quite bushy eyebrows. And there's a moment where he glares back at camera.

One funny story: on *Fantastic Mr. Fox*, Wes took some photos at a country fair. A photo landed on the desk, and Wes said, "I really liked this guy. Could we make him?" We sculpted him, and he eventually became a character in the film. I often wonder if this random guy ever spotted himself.

That illustrates a general truth, I think—a lot of directing comes down to knowing it when you see it.

You've got it, yes. For Atari . . . Well, there's a lovely little stop-motion film shot in Poland, by Suzie Templeton: *Peter and the Wolf*. It's beautifully constructed. Wes quite liked Peter from that film, especially early on, and was often referred to for his expressions and emotions. The Peter puppet didn't talk in the film—in fact he barely opens his mouth—and he had really nice, clear eyes. And also, there was the little boy from *Angela's Ashes*, whose picture they used on the book cover . . .

Kind of knock-kneed—

You've got it. There was something about both of those that Wes really liked.

A lot of people I've talked to on set have a favorite puppet. Do you?

How many can I have?

You, of all people, have a right to more than one.

OK, all right. Well, I mean, I think Atari and Chief are my firm favorites. But I do have a soft spot for Auntie too. Chief was the first one I saw talking, so he's obviously special. Jupiter and Oracle, I'm quite fond of, you know. They have a great moment together. There's also a little group of dogs, the sheep dogs, which seem to be quite well liked, and I loved their look too. I had better stop now before the list gets out of hand.

I like the sheep dogs too.

It's funny, isn't it? There's just something that they communicate.

Charlie has, over the last ten minutes, come to sit in front of Andy, and now extends his paw gently onto Andy's knee, like a hand on a shoulder. "Why am I getting the paw?" asks Andy, but we all know why—Charlie sensed that we'd come to a natural stopping place.

ABOVE: **The sheepdog pack. Their earless leader Igor (#1) is voiced by Roman Coppola. His concerned companion (#2) is voiced by Wes.**

ABOVE: A pack of scary, indestructible alpha dogs—the Hero Pack
BELOW: Lobby cards from the international release of *Seven Samurai* show Kikuchiyo slouching out in front of the pack (LEFT) and earning his stripes in the rain-soaked final battle (RIGHT).

In Kurosawa's most famous film a small farming village is threatened by an attack by bandits. The panicking farmers ask the village elder how they should defend themselves.

"Hire samurai," he tells them. How could we ever afford to hire samurai when all we have is a little rice? That's easy, he says. "Find hungry samurai."

Properly, most of the *Seven Samurai* who come to the defense of the village are ronin, vagrant samurai who have lost their masters. To be a ronin, a samurai without a lord, was an indignity in medieval Japan. It meant going without prestige, and sometimes going without food. Many ronin resorted to banditry, joined gangs, earned their meager livings with freelance violence. By calling the film *Seven Samurai*, Kurosawa means to say that the compassion and courage of these ronin makes them true samurai. The haughty warriors who refuse the farmers' pleas early in the film aren't worthy of that name.

Six samurai answer the call. They're followed by a scruffy, moody stray. Throughout the film, the cocksure Kikuchiyo has trouble running with the pack. He pretends to have a pedigree from a noble house, but the ronin know right away that he's not one of their breed. His story takes on new pathos when we discover that he was orphaned as an infant during a brutal raid—his bark and bluster are born of insecurity and secret trauma. In the end it's his bravery, not his bloodline, that makes him the seventh samurai.

Kurosawa's masterpiece was released in America as *The Magnificent Seven* (LEFT). A 1960 remake with the same title, directed by John Sturges, moved the action to the Old West (ABOVE). Six down-on-their-luck gunfighters and one cocky wannabe agree to save a small Mexican village from a gang of bandits.

THE PUPPET THAT GOES OVER THE TOP

AN INTERVIEW WITH
COSTUME DESIGNER Maggie Haden

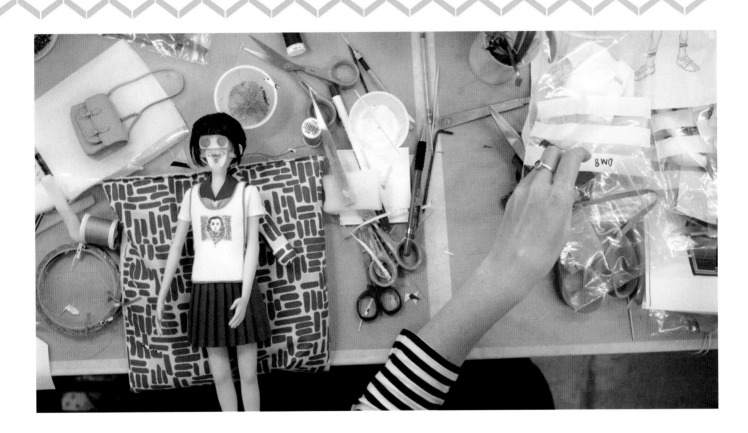

OPPOSITE: Costume designer Maggie Haden works with a puppet's prison uniform.

ABOVE: A *Daily Manifesto* activist wears a protest vest over her school colors. Female *Manifesto* staffers wear the recognizable *sailor-fuku* uniform worn by students all over Japan. Male *Manifesto* students wear the traditional *gakuran* suit—Wes has them in blue instead of the more typical black.

THE COSTUME DEPARTMENT is housed in the puppet workshop, in a windowless, low-ceilinged room. The shelving along all four walls is stacked with bolts of cloth. A big central table overflows with fabric, sewing machines, a few puppets receiving a bit of tailoring—Mayor Kobayashi in his white suit, the Shinto Priest in his billowing robes.

Costume designer Maggie Haden has been creating miniature costumes since the '90s. She talks about the trick of making tiny clothes that look full-size on screen, and also the specific challenges and rewards of working with Wes on this film.

Where do you start?

We started with the fabrics. Quite often, fabrics will give me the inspiration for how something's going to look. I would get some characters, and I just went shopping and started to develop prints so that I could go to Wes, and say, "Is this how you see this character?" That was a really good way in for me because

I'm really interested in fabrics, and what they suggest. For instance, for Kobayashi, I found some fabric that I really liked, with bamboo woven into it.

So kind of a breathable—

Yeah! And I thought, "Oh, I like this very much." Because a lot of the characters are in just plain white, which you'd think maybe doesn't give you much to work with, but in fact, you've still got texture, weave—and also, there's a million shades of white. I don't know if you've seen them, but I make these sample boards and send them to Wes, and I say, "This is what I think for his suit. This is what I think for his shirt."

Are you actually mailing the swatches, then?

Yeah. To start with, for the main characters, I would send the actual physical boards to him because Wes really likes his fabric. And he's interested to feel it, you know?

Even though we'll just be seeing it. . . . But with the close-up shots on these figures, I guess that just the naked eye might not—

Completely. I had a real shock early on. I'd bought some shirting, which I thought was really good, very fine weave. I was very excited about it. It looked fine when we were looking at laptop screens. But then when I saw it projected for the first time, it just looked like I'd gotten him in hessian [burlap] or something. You know, it was terrible. That's what upsets me, because that immediately gives the scale away. You think, "Oh, no, that's wrong. That's a model. It looks like a Barbie doll," or something like that.

So I've got this [INDICATING A MAGNIFYING TOOL], which really magnifies. And so the very first thing I do is check under here, to see what it looks like close up. Say, if a silk is brushed, then it might look a bit more like wool when it's projected that big, you know? I'm always thinking along those lines. [LAUGHS]

What is the finest-weave fabric in this film, and what is it being used for?

Professor Watanabe's shirt fabric is probably the finest fabric we used.

I wanted to ask about his costume in general. Where did the idea of a wrapped lab coat come from?

Well, the design came from Wes. But in the initial design, the kimono was wrapped the wrong way, and symbolically, wrapping it that way is only appropriate if the wearer is dead. We'd made it up and got it wrong. And because Watanabe dies in the film, at first I wondered whether the kimono was an allusion to that. But it turns out it wasn't; it was a mistake [LAUGHS]. So then we had to go back and redo it the other way.

So there's a research component to your work, even for stuff that only exists in the world of the film?

Oh, completely. Yeah, it's been really good, actually. For instance, a woodcut was given to us as a reference for the lead in the Kabuki play, the samurai boy. It's quite traditional. So I went and had a look at how samurai armor is put together, because there are kind of hard, inflexible plates, but they're put together with these beautiful colored threads which hold it all together. . . . But after I did that, which I really enjoyed [LAUGHS], I found out that they're school children, so it's meant to look like a costume for a school play.

So it was almost too good?

Yeah, yeah. . . . [LAUGHS] So that had to go, unfortunately.

To go back to the fabric question, I've been really excited because for years now, we've been playing with putting fabric through a computer printer. Because, obviously, I want miniature patterns, but they've always been a bit unstable. But we found a way of doing it.

Being able to print the fabrics suddenly opened up a lot of options because it meant that we could design fabrics to start with. Wes was really excited the first time we printed Yoko-ono's trousers because we were able to reproduce the drawing. Some characters in this film are in five scales, and it meant that we could print exactly the same fabric at those different scales, which was amazing. For instance, for two of the geishas that appear in the film, we actually designed and printed fabrics directly from reference pictures.

OPPOSITE TOP: **Fabrics for Duke's owners' kimonos**

OPPOSITE MIDDLE: **Fabric patterns preceded the costume design for Kitano, director of Kobayashi Robotics (LEFT). A costumer stretches fabric over a concept drawing of a geisha's costume (CENTER). Swatches for the costumes of the school singers (RIGHT)**

OPPOSITE BOTTOM: **Assistant-Scientist Yoko-ono's cotton print capris are decorated with organic molecules—ethane, benzene, and salicylic acid. Her hair ties, naturally, feature yttrium and oxygen. She wears a Geiger counter on her wrist to monitor her personal exposure to radiation. Character design by Félicie Haymoz**

THIS PAGE: **Kobayashi's broad, burly proportions presented a challenge for his tailors (LEFT). The Shinto Priest's look (CENTER) was inspired by Tatsuya Nakadai as Lord Hidetora Ichimonji, the King Lear character in *Ran* (RIGHT).**

OVERLEAF: **Costumers sit around a central table in the one-room costume department, surrounded by tools and boxes of fabric.**

Another thing I guess you have to consider is that these costumes have to be used by the animators, unlike a costume you'd see in a live-action film. The animators have to be able to manipulate them, but the costumes and the fabrics also have to drape a certain way that feels realistic.

That's right. Andy Gent [head of puppets department] always refers to a puppet's costume as "the puppet that goes over the top of the other puppet." I always say that when you get it right, no one notices. It's only when you get it wrong that people say, "Well, why is this stuck up at that odd angle?" For instance, this fellow is the Shinto priest. And all this excess fabric here is really difficult. But you can see how stiff it is.

Right. Because if a person were to really move their arm, that whole sheet would billow in a certain way.

Yeah, yeah. So this is all wired and foiled—you almost have to make an armature to fit underneath the costume.

The costume has its own armature, so that the animators can manipulate it independent of the puppet?

That's right. And you get some animators that really understand the fabric, and they're happy to manipulate it. It's very odd. Some animators seem to be able to kind of magically control it. [LAUGHS]

So when you're given a sketch or a brief or a reference that says, "This is what we want," it's up to you to figure out how that's going to work for other departments—not only as a costume but as a miniature costume, and then as an animated miniature costume . . . which is stuff that most people who design clothes never have to think about.

Helly McGrother, one in my team, who I've known for a long time, is a trained tailor. I said to her, "Will you attempt Kobayashi's suit?" because it's so sharp and beautifully tailored, which is very difficult to achieve on that scale.

Especially on a body that's like no human body that's ever existed before.

Oh, I know. Exactly. And it's got that really nice kind of sharp, sort of '60s or '50s—

Right, it's got that thin tie, thin lapel . . .

We had loads of film references for how he comes off with that sort of cool, sharp, slightly gangster look. We knew what we were trying to achieve. It was in the medium scale, which was the first one we'd built. But even with her training, making the suit at that scale proved to be really problematic. She got it eventually, but it took about three months, I think. I mean, the buttonhole was tiny, only stretched across two strands of the fabric, you know? That was a little painful, I think.

There are a lot of iconic white suits in Kurosawa movies—*Drunken Angel, Stray Dog, I Live in Fear*. Were you looking at any of those?

Absolutely. Wes passed along a list of films. Luckily, I knew some of them, and I sort of power-watched a few [LAUGHS]. Luckily, I'm a big fan of Japanese film anyway, so . . .

Any favorites?

Ozu. I especially love his film about the theater troupe, *Floating Weeds*. And the one where the mom and dad come back . . . *Tokyo Story*.

You were talking about the lightness of the bamboo fabric earlier . . . . What's the weather like in *Isle of Dogs*?

I've always thought, "Oh, it's hot," because everyone's in white, light fabrics. And of course, because the dogs are so furry, you get that slight boil, which Wes really likes. It just looks to me like it's windy [LAUGHS]. All the time I'm thinking, "Oh, it's really breezy. They'll be fine. They won't be too hot."

Did you have a favorite costume that you worked on?

I especially loved Atari, his suit. And I got a lovely email from Wes talking about how absurd it was; we just had to go with it. I'd misunderstood the brief, so

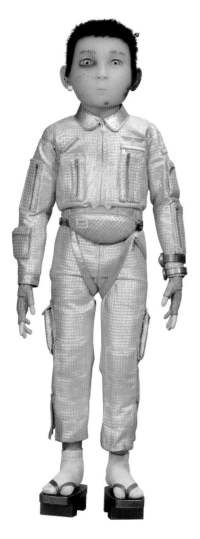

I'd gone way out there. And I think he thought, "Oh my god, what's this?" [LAUGHS] But then he really liked it.

How did you misunderstand it? Productively, I guess.

I'm sure I heard the word "silver." I'm positive I did hear that. [LAUGHS]

Really early on, maybe there was a reference to, "Oh, what we think it may be is white-silver." And I sort of translated that into, "Oh, he's wearing a space suit—of course it's silver, don't be silly." So I found all these beautiful tech fabrics, which are fairly new. I think they might have even originated in Japan, actually. They're a very, very fine weave because they're synthetic. And they're incredibly strong. So I'd found a silver tech fabric and I thought, "Oh, I love this." And I was a big Bowie fan. Wes said, "Oh, he looks a bit like Ziggy Stardust," and I'm thinking, "Yeah!" [LAUGHS]

And now that costume is actually quite iconic—I mean, it's on the poster—

I know. I know. And I love it.

I was working really closely with Collette Pidgeon, who was making the puppet props, and I said to her, "You know, I've got to put all these zips on it." And she just came up with some fantastic . . . the etched zips, which were then assembled. I

couldn't believe how beautiful they were. So that finished it for me. And then of course, we had to mock up a piece of masking tape which says "Biscuit" on it, for one of the pockets. He's got a pocket for everything.

I've been hearing people talk about which puppet they like the most. Which was your favorite? I have a good guess.

I think ultimately Atari is my favorite because I just . . . He ended up looking like I wanted him to look. I've got a lovely, lovely costume test of Atari, early on, and Wes says, "Huh, he just looks like a little person." And I thought, "That's just perfect." I do love the dogs. And I think maybe that's because I can have some distance on them. I'm still finding some of the human characters difficult to watch because I know how much pain we've been in, in here, to get them to there. [LAUGHS]

I'm looking forward to seeing the film projected. And what really, really gets me—and I love this—is that I've known most of the people we're working with for years and years. And what we make is more than the sum of our parts. I can't make these things on my own. But with everybody, you make something very special. Animators can still catch me. I'll watch something from the film, and I think, "Oh, look! Look at him!" And then remember, "No, no, it's a puppet," you know? [LAUGHS] But it just suddenly catches you, how they bring them to life. It's amazing.

Barry Jones is doing set dressing on this film. On *Mr. Fox*, I was working in the art department, and the ultimate compliment Barry can pay you is when he says, "Oh, that looks like a bought one" [LAUGHS]. And he means, like, if the characters could go out and buy something, that it would look like that. He's great, Barry. They're all great, let's face it.

THIS PAGE: **Atari in his flight suit**

OPPOSITE: **Atari hangs his flight suit over a fence while he gives Chief a bath.**

OPPOSITE FAR RIGHT: **Details from Atari's main costume, including a futuristic, metallic version of traditional *geta*. The geta is a sandal with an elevated base supported by two tall, blocky "teeth," good for navigating muddy terrain.**

OPPOSITE TOP: A geisha puppet covered in protective plastic

OPPOSITE BOTTOM: A set of puppet torsos

THIS PAGE TOP: Costumes for the Dragons, Boss's baseball team

THIS PAGE MIDDLE: The color-coordinated costumes of Duke's family

THIS PAGE BOTTOM: The villains (known to the crew as the Cabal) in costume

OPPOSITE: Compacted cars, one of the many heaps of homogeneous junk on Trash Island. In the film we first see Nutmeg brilliantly backlit at the crest of this hill. ABOVE: A collection of stacked cars, pre-compacting. In the film we see narcoleptic dogs on them as the Narrator, voiced by Courtney B. Vance, describes the symptoms of Dog-Flu.

PRODUCTION DESIGN

WHEN WE TALK ABOUT how a film looks, we often jump straight to praising its cinematography: if the film looked beautiful, it must be because it was photographed beautifully. But this raises the question: *What* was photographed beautifully? Before textures, colors, and shapes can be lovingly rendered by the camera, they first have to be sewn, painted, and placed.

On a live-action film, it can be easy to take production design for granted. On some level, we know better, but in practice, we viewers—and we critics, worst of all—still find ourselves talking about movies as if the actors just showed up on set dressed that way, as if the filmmakers shot that interior scene in a pre-furnished room, as if that wallpaper just happened to be that color.

But on a stop-motion film, the art department is less likely to be overlooked. We know that no desert or dump on Trash Island was just found that way—the set designers and set dressers placed each piece of garbage. Kobayashi didn't drive to the shoot wearing his natty white suit—the costume department cut it from whole cloth. You can't pick up a package of pill-size Puppy-Snaps at the Tesco up the street from

119

To create the trash landscapes seen in the film, set dressers glue debris onto the Styrofoam topographies created by the set construction team. ABOVE: Set dresser Cristina Acuña Solla sits on top of a platform for better access to the trash mountains she's decorating.

the studio—prop modelers had to carve each one by hand. Uni Prefecture isn't a real place you can visit and take snapshots of—production designer Paul Harrod had to make a full-immersion study of post-war Japanese design and cobble a mental picture of Megasaki City together from *tokusatsu* flicks, Ozu dramas, and photojournalism of the Anpo protests.

ISLE OF DOGS'S ART DEPARTMENT is spread out over several workshops at 3 Mills Studio. The modelers sit at long workbenches, each artist installed in their own delineated space, each space with its own towering Craftsman toolbox with racks of wide metal shelves. The workbenches are lined with gridded green cutting mats or white butcher paper; plastic bins are stocked with laminating brushes, petroleum jelly, wet wipes, scalpels. Little sounds of rubbing, tapping, and buffing fill the air.

Every scene in *Isle of Dogs* goes through the three-part "BDL" process before it's ready to be shot—"build, dress, light." The first two are the purview of the art department. "Build" happens largely in the set building workshop. At 3 Mills Studio, the workshop is housed in a big, airy, tent-like structure attached to one of the brick studio buildings. It's full of stacks of lumber and flats and regular, human-scale construction tools. This is where the bones of the sets are sawed and hammered, roughed out and painted over but left mostly undressed.

One large set here is in its early stages—blank white buttes around a wide canyon of unpainted Styrofoam. Abandoned in the canyon is the longest folding knife I've ever seen—not just a folding knife, a hunting knife, a foot-long murder weapon with a blade long enough to carve the surrounding mountain slopes with one long scrape. These Styrofoam landscapes are tested in front of a camera and sculpted to fit the framing Wes has in mind. Wes commits to the framing early, though adjustments are inevitable. This is one reason Wes's films look so good: by working out the relationship between the shot and the set early on, the crew can save the time and resources they would have spent on things that won't be in the frame anyway, and spend more on things that will. If only the left side of the mountain will be seen, only the left side of the mountain will be finished. The right side might get lopped off and repurposed on another set.

Stop-motion films have been shot on larger sets than these, and on many sets, but rarely so many of such a size. Whole locations have been dreamed up for a single image—rusted-out water towers, bamboo bridges, dunes piled high against the windward walls

ABOVE: Many of the sets are carved from white foam. Here, the hardened lava set sits half-carved.
BELOW: Set dressers tested many different materials to create the colors and textures for Trash Island's different zones. These hills are set up for a test photo.
OVERLEAF: The main art department workshop, where modelers build and paint set elements

SPRAY PAINT
BOOTH
PAINT FUMES
MAY BE PRESENT

ABOVE: The clusters of blossoms on the cherry trees were made by putting foam rubber through a blender.
BELOW: Cherry blossoms on set.

of ramshackle old factories, their steel walls creaking under the weight of the sand. These might receive three or four seconds of screen time in the middle of a montage. Art department modelers have spent weeks on these, and yet it's clearly not a waste—the very brevity of the shot plays an effective psychological trick on the viewer. Watching the film, we're made to understand that in the world of *Isle of Dogs*, there's room for vast deserts so dreary and lifeless that the camera declines to dwell on them. The montage shows only a representative sample: we imagine the miles and miles of similar wildernesses that were never filmed.

AFTER THE SETS ARE BUILT, they're ready for phase two of BDL and are sent off to be "dressed" on or near the soundstage where they're going to be shot. Just outside the soundstage is another row of workbenches, where set dressers apply some not-quite-finishing touches before the sets are sent inside. Resting near one wall of the workshop is a gloomy marsh set. The set dressers plant hummocks of moss and brown grass around gray pools of dirty plexiglass—the bushy stalks are the blond bristles of paintbrushes. Tufts of cotton are glued to the tops—"cattails" gone to seed.

Set dresser Collette Pidgeon sits at the communal workbench, ensconced among glue pots, grimy laptops, a dozen desktop cabinets of washers, screws, and nails. Today she's making cherry blossoms—the falling petals will accompany Atari's Hail-Mary haiku, which softens Kobayashi's heart at the film's climax. Collette's cut the blossoms from tissue paper with tiny scissors, and she is painting each white petal with a dab of pink nail polish. The foliage of smaller trees, destined for the background of the shot, are made from a sponge that's been shredded in a blender.

No one's consulted a big book of stop-motion materials for any of this. The sponge trees and paintbrush grass are discovered through experimentation, camera testing, and a few rounds of show-and-tell with Wes and the department heads. Stop-motion modelers are used to taking things back to the drawing board and starting fresh with each new film. No

matter how much experience these artists have (and many have quite a bit), each film's needs are different and hard to predict—Wes's playfully unorthodox films, all the more so. Many of the materials and techniques used on *Fantastic Mr. Fox* have been deliberately abandoned for *Isle of Dogs*.

For *Isle of Dogs*, even atmospheric elements—waves, clouds, smoke, fire, toxic fumes—are created in-camera with real materials. Visual effects artists will adjust their placement and opacity within the finished frame, but they're all made of physical stuff.

A water test is being shot nearby—shallow white waves glitter against a black sand shore. A mechanism beneath makes the seas roll gently. It's quite beautiful. "Plastic wrap, hair gel, and K-Y Jelly," explains first assistant director James Emmott. The production is constantly sending runners to the Tesco up the street for another twenty tubes of the stuff, he says. "Everything on this set is K-Y Jelly." Another test is happening next door: A thick cardboard tube is stuck all over with cotton balls, streaked with dirty gray and black. It rotates slowly. This is the rolling band of dark stratus clouds that tops so many outdoor shots in *Isle of Dogs*.

Nowadays, this is unusual. Lots of stop-motion films use computer-generated images to flesh out settings; studios that use this method have creative ways of integrating the two animation styles. They may, for example, shoot footage of a fabric rippling in the wind, and use that footage as a reference to animate computer-generated ocean waves, so that the waves move as though they were made of the same material as the puppets' costumes.

Such seamless integration with CG imagery is partly made possible by industry advances in puppet design and animation methods—today's best stop-motion puppetry is fully capable of rivaling computer-generated animation for hyperrealistic slickness and smoothness. Audience tastes, too, may have helped convince stop-motion studios to move in this direction. Wes's films have bucked this trend. He wants his films to feel "real," too, but in the opposite way. Where other filmmakers strive for flawlessness and weightless flow, Wes wants it frank, raw, tactile—all materials freely and honestly them-

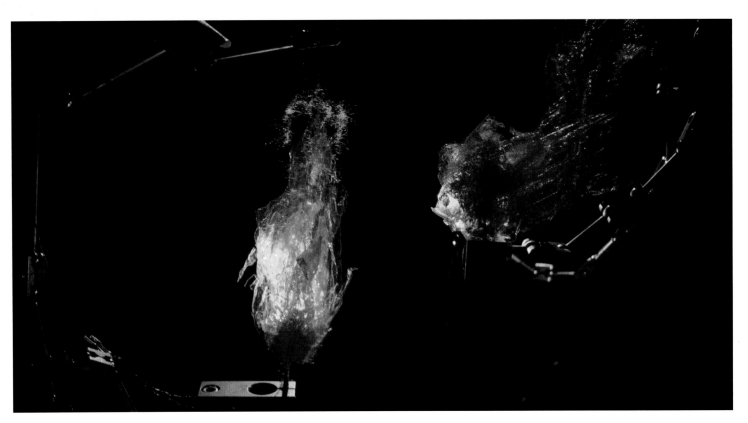
The animation department created fire effects with cellophane and cotton.

selves. He's chosen approaches to animation, composition, and lighting that openly celebrate the physicality of the production design.

Much of the *Isle of Dogs* crew have learned how to make stop-motion films in an industry that has increasingly de-emphasized and disguised some of the handmade aspects of the medium. On *Fantastic Mr. Fox*, and here again on *Isle of Dogs*, Wes has asked many of these experienced artists to forget everything they've been doing and start from scratch. He's invited them to return to stop-motion's primitive, physical roots. He's reassured them that the results will not look cheap, wrong, unprofessional. To put it that way, it may look like Wes is a whippersnapper, wasting their expertise. In fact, he depends on it. If you want to reinvent the wheel, it helps to hire a team of expert wheelwrights. It's a case where hiring old dogs is the only way to develop new tricks.

Either way, it says something that they've all come back to do it again. "It's the sort of thing that makes you feel young again," Andy Gent says. "I don't want to always be doing what I already know how to do. I love getting to feel the excitement I had when I was just starting out."

IN THE PAINT SHOP, little pieces of set dressing sit on shelves—a milky white statue "dedicated to Spots Kobayashi" waiting for a faux finish, wood panels for the Shinto shrine waiting for stain and varnish.

The wall behind them is covered from floor to ceiling with small square swatches, a rainbow of shades in every brightness and saturation, offering not a single clue to the film's primary colors at a glance.

"It would be really interesting to see what it looks like when somebody does a barcode of this film, you know?" production designer Paul Harrod muses.

I'm nonplussed for a moment—wouldn't the production designer already know?

"You know, the barcode?" he asks.

Paul's referring to a program that looks at all the frames from the beginning to the end of a film, squashes each frame into a single vertical line, and then lines them up left to right. The barcode is one of several methods of representing a film's complete color palette in a single handy infographic. Some methods are more scientific than others. Identifying a film's palette, with an algorithm or by eye, is a

ABOVE: Placid seas of plastic wrap coated in personal lubricant. The waves move gently with the motion of the rollers underneath.
BELOW: A cardboard tube covered in cotton becomes a rolling band of clouds along the top of the frame.

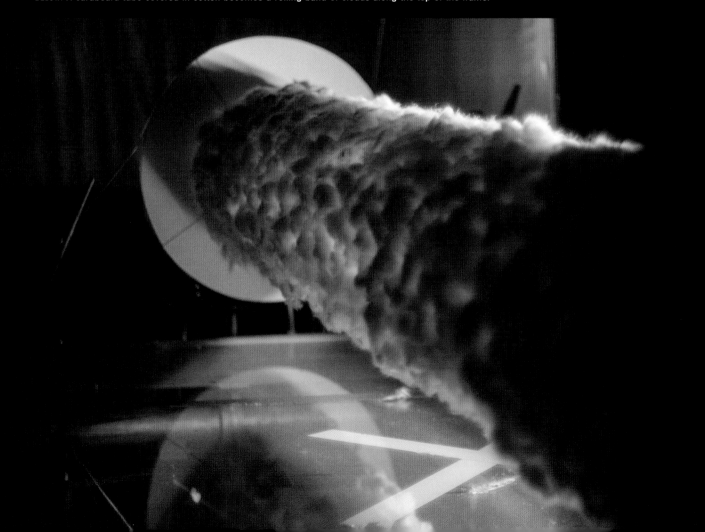

The paint shop, located in the larger art department workshop

popular pastime among film fans online, and it's quite safe to say that no filmmaker's palettes are more frequently dissected, discussed, and disseminated on social media than Wes Anderson's.

Most cinephiles know that the palette is worked out largely between a director (like Wes) and a production designer (like Paul), and part of the game is to deduce what tightly delimited six- or seven-color palette they picked before they started shooting. With Wes's films, the game seems easier than usual, and lots of people play it on Pinterest and Tumblr. For *The Life Aquatic with Steve Zissou*, everyone agrees that Wes picked yellow, red, and cerulean blue. For *The Grand Budapest Hotel*, he picked pink and purple, except in the parts that are orange and brown. *The Royal Tenenbaums* has a lot of pink, but it's a different pink. *Moonrise Kingdom* has a lot of yellow, but a different yellow. The palettes feel so specific, so consistent, so harmonious, that it's easy to assume that Wes figured them out top to bottom before the camera rolled on the first shot, maybe before he typed the first line of the screenplay.

"Yeah, you would think," Paul says. "This is the first time I've worked with him, but when I came onto this film, there was no palette. And actually, Wes purposefully wanted to avoid establishing a palette." One look at the big back wall of the paint shop, bristling with swatches, proves that he still hasn't.

When you watch a finished Wes Anderson movie, the palette appears to be a fixed law, a first commandment: it looks like Wes approves or nixes filming locations, costumes, wallpapers, or eyeshadows based on how closely they match a set of swatches he picked out in advance. The abstract precedes the concrete, we assume. But when you watch a Wes Anderson film in process, it's often the reverse—palette looks like an emergent property of a thousand small choices, a thousand points of contact between the concrete options and Wes's mind, his taste, his gut. The difference between the shade of yellow that predominates in *The Life Aquatic* versus the one that characterizes *Moonrise Kingdom* has less than you'd think to do with a predetermined color scheme and more with which couch Wes wanted to put on Hennessey's boat, which kerchiefs he liked for the Khaki Scout uniform. Even for this film, where no object or location is merely found, Wes's instincts follow, as much as they lead, the materials or the designs his crew offers up to him. Objects are picked, swatches are made—the color of this gets matched to that; that gets contrasted with this. The palette grows, refines, and defines itself as the film does.

Each swatch on the wall of the paint shop represents a particular concrete object in *Isle of Dogs*—this is the red of the lacquerwork in the Municipal Dome; this is the robin-egg blue from the mural behind Kobayashi's bathtub. The art department registers and tracks every one, makes fine distinctions between one pigment and another that would be lost on untrained eyes. Wes can tell the difference, and Wes cares about the difference. Perhaps, above all, what makes a "Wes Anderson palette" recognizable isn't the presence of any exact shade, but our recognition that each individul shade was exactly chosen.

Wes Anderson palettes certainly have something in common chromatically, too, but it's hard to put your finger on it without drifting into poetry, or even oxymoron. A faded saturation; a vintage freshness; bold tones that have been washed or dusted or misted over until they take on the patina of a reminiscence. It might be easier to say what a Wes Anderson palette is not—beholden neither to mundane reality nor a classical sense of unity nor minimalistic chic, Wes's palettes are never cold, never gritty, never dark, never bleak. What a Wes Anderson palette is, is a set of colors that are colorful.

Or at least that's what it always had been, until *Isle of Dogs*. In many scenes, Wes is working with an extraordinarily desaturated palette unprecedented in his earlier work—even, in some sequences, flirting with a black-and-white-film look, executed wholly in-camera with set design: silvered grass and rocks, dark gray clouds, white sky, a black dog, and a boy in a silver spacesuit.

"We started with a black and white set of concepts," Paul says, "and worked color into it." The most distinctive, and likely the first, were the recurring lacquer reds, seen in the long sequences in the Municipal Dome, more briefly in the Kabuki Theater, and in much of the film's typography.

Other saturated colors play regular supporting roles: a dark, flat construction yellow that leans toward tan; a brighter toxic yellow that leans toward green; a banana-peel yellow for the *Daily Manifesto* classroom; a wet, grody green brown for the abandoned testing facility. There are a few soft touches too: cornflower blue, rosy sunset pink. The pivotal scene in which Atari grooms Chief is set against a gentle, candy-colored backdrop, mountains of blue bottles in a pink twilight. Some are bolder, stranger: a purple night sky and majestic purple mountain looming over Megasaki. "Each section of the film has kind of its own palette to it—different regions, different zones," Paul says. The barcode will tell which regional palettes predominate over the others when the film is taken as a whole. Some palettes haven't been fully decided yet; some zones haven't been built.

For now, the grays and neutrals still seem to be winning over everything else. Brutalist cement grays for factories and derelict parking lots; dark charcoal grays for volcanic rock formations; a nicotine-stained white for laboratories and television broadcast studios; washed-out browns and sand-dune tans for spaghetti-western vistas and weathered driftwood shacks. Characters tend to dress in white, cream, silver, gray, and black. Dogs are dirty white, tarry black, gray, red brown, beige, and honey-colored.

Above all, behind all, stretches the soft white horizon, with the white sun glinting off white waves. Wes, like so many ink painters and calligraphers before him, has discovered the beauty of leaving most of the page blank.

ABOVE LEFT: A set dresser paints moss on the side of a wall; ABOVE RIGHT: A set dresser works on the site of Atari's plane crash; BELOW LEFT: Spot's cage lands among compacted trash cubes like these—each fit in the palm of a hand; BELOW RIGHT: Fruit baskets and bicycles for the Megasaki City set

ABOVE: A modeler paints the side of a hill on the outskirts of Megasaki; BELOW LEFT: A modeler paints a bit of overgrowth for the inside of the abandoned Kobayashi lab set; BELOW RIGHT: The tubes and towers of the gasworks, rusted over by a painter

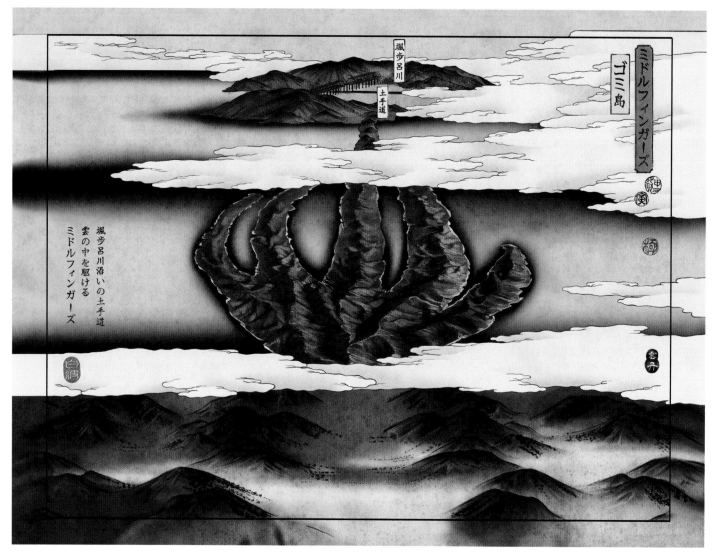

TOP: A 2-D illustration of Trash Island by Gwenn Germain, drawn in the style of an ukiyo-e print; ABOVE: *Full Moon at Kanazawa*, Hiroshige, 1857;
OPPOSITE TOP AND MIDDLE: Spots rides a trash-tram over whirlpools off the coast of Trash Island; OPPOSITE BOTTOM: *The Whirlpools of Awa*, Hiroshige, 1857

Barry Jones, lead set dresser, describes the process of creating different "zones" for Trash Island, differentiated by color and texture:

"**A**TARI'S PLANE crashes into the white zone, where there are all these white landscapes of newspaper and white trash. There are washing machines, fridges, white goods, things like that. And then he flies out of that into a much darker zone, which is the grays and the blacks, which we've made out of TV backs and car batteries. And we made bits of trash to fit in with this—wires, cables, we just mix them into it. And then there's the rusty landscapes. It's all oil, poison, and rusty metal. If you look very closely at the ground in those scenes, it's completely made of nuts, bolts, and cogs cast into diagonal tiles.

Our department is responsible for pretty much all the texture—everything that you can see. We get the sets from construction, the props from the prop shop, and then we put them together, and we make them look how Wes requires them to be. Generally we will work together with the set construction crew—we make a lot of the shapes, a lot of the hills, and we generate a lot of the trash.

The sets are made of bits of foam, and the textures are dressed on top of that. So if we need to change something, we can just literally carve or reshape the foam very quickly, which keeps things moving. And a lot of the trash we use is actually off-cuts from set construction. We reuse things that come from all the other departments as well. You know, all the packaging that comes in—if something looks a bit unusual, we take it and use it. Even the rusty walkways at the studio, you can go under them and find all the little bits of flaky old iron that's come off. We recycle everything all around."

OPPOSITE: An overhead view of the set for an aerial shot of Trash Island, with cotton clouds above a painted sea.

ABOVE: The dirt roads, heaps of trash, and tangles of scrap metal in *Dodes'ka-den* were often dyed with a spray gun or colored powder.

BELOW: A hillock in *Isle of Dogs*, seemingly inspired by the imaginary train's route in *Dodes'ka-den*

Between land and sky, there are six "layers" visible in this shot of the dogs watching Atari's takeoff from afar.

BELOW: **The black beach set—steely water under stormy skies. This set is the site of the first confrontation between the pack and the dogcatchers.**

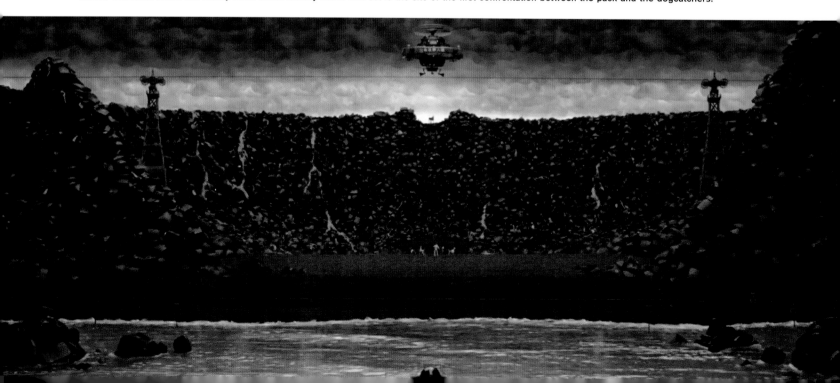

PERFECT CLUTTER

AN INTERVIEW WITH
PRODUCTION DESIGNER Paul Harrod

OPPOSITE: Paul Harrod consults on a maquette setup. Maquettes are test versions of sets and puppets that are cut from foam, so that the camera and art departments can see exactly where things should go before they start prepping the real materials.

ABOVE: Control rooms in Ishiro Honda's *Godzilla* (LEFT) and *Isle of Dogs* (RIGHT). Control rooms are recurring settings in *tokusatsu* films. Short for *tokushu satsuei,* meaning "special filming" or "special effects," tokusatsu came to refer to a genre of effects-heavy films and television shows that first appeared in Japan's postwar period. As a description of a technique and a tonal approach rather than a subject, tokusatsu embraces a variety of futuristic, sci-fi, fantasy, adventure, horror, crime, secret-agent, and disaster plots. Superheroes, robots, monsters, aliens—all are fair game, sometimes all at once.

Kaiju (giant monsters, literally "strange beasts" in Japanese) frequently star and guest-star in tokusatsu stories; Godzilla is the most famous, and *Godzilla* is generally considered the first film in the *kaiju* subgenre.

PAUL HARROD started his career doing makeup effects for sci-fi movies, but he found himself attracted to stop-motion because of the scope of the work the designer gets to do: "It became very seductive, the idea that you could generate the world that the characters inhabit, top to bottom." He's worked in stop-motion since the '80s. A film buff as well as a filmmaker, Paul pulled from a wide range of inspirations to design the world of *Isle of Dogs*.

So this film is credited to two production designers: Adam Stockhausen, who's been working with Wes ever since he was an art director on *The Darjeeling Limited*, and you. This is your first Wes Anderson gig.

Yeah, Adam worked on this project for a long time, and it definitely laid the foundation for some of our big set pieces for the first half of the film. I got involved in a lot of that stuff, too, but he really figured out many of our key pieces. My job has been to handle a lot of the second half of the film but also to fill in these little gaps between the big set pieces for the first half. And even that aspect of the film has gone through several evolutions. I came on at the phase when we actually moved into 3 Mills almost two years ago, when Adam went on to his next project.

I've been told that you're the biggest cinephile on set, so I'm eager to hear what you were watching to prepare for this project.

Well, when I first got here . . . I mean, I didn't have a lot of prep time. It's sort of a funny story. In 2015 I was at Burning Man, and it was the first year I'd been there that you could really get signal on your phone. And I was just checking the weather, and I noticed there was an email from someone I'd never heard of, and my friend Nelson Lowry's name was mentioned in the subject line.

Nelson Lowry was the production designer on *Fantastic Mr. Fox*. He did *Kubo and the Two Strings*, and he and I go way back. I saw his name and I said, "Oh, I'll check this out." I saw Adam Stockhausen's name, and it was just like, "Huh. I

think these people have something to do with Wes Anderson" [LAUGHS]. The next day I was hitching a ride out of Black Rock City to the Reno airport, flying back so I could look at the animatic, because I didn't have enough of a signal at Burning Man to look at anything.

Running from Burning Man.

Less than a week later I was on a plane to London. So I get here, and that was the first thing I did—just try to immerse myself in as many Japanese films made in the '60s as I could. And I discovered a whole bunch of really interesting filmmakers whose work I had never seen before, like Ko Nakahira. Have you seen Nakahira's *Crazed Fruit*? It's just incredible.

I haven't. Did any *Crazed Fruit* make its way into *Isle of Dogs*?

Yes, yes! In fact, there are a couple of scenes in a phone booth, and I was just like, "That's a really interesting-looking phone booth. I've never seen a phone booth like that before." And that phone booth does appear in the background of one or two of our sets, as a bit of trash.

But of course, you've got to build all this stuff anyway, so you might as well have fun with it.

Yeah, exactly. As Wes and I worked on this, we were drawing a lot from film history, especially in terms of our approach to color. Of course, early on, we were looking at a lot of film noir, black-and-white films. And a lot of the themes of the film echo the themes in Kurosawa's films.

Especially the Kurosawa noirs, it seems like.

Exactly. Things in *The Bad Sleep Well* and *High and Low* in particular, those two films, for a couple of reasons. And I've definitely borrowed a few things from *Drunken Angel*, too, here.

But the look—the idea of the film is that it takes place in the future. The opening line is, "The Japanese archipelago, 20 years in the future." But twenty years in what future? It's basically twenty years in the future from about 1964, 1965. So that's where another element comes in from Japanese cinema, which is the Ishiro Honda—

The *Godzilla* films?

Godzilla, sure, but we've definitely referenced some of the lesser-known Japanese science fiction films,

too, that supposedly take place in a kind of future setting, films like *Gorath* and *Monster Zero* and things like that. Almost all of our televisions are taken from *kaiju* movies, because they always have scenes with somebody looking at a television set on the wall. And the widescreen, color, contemporary midcentury-modern look is drawn heavily from those films, and from Seijun Suzuki's films . . . But architecturally, I would say Ozu is the biggest influence.

He's one of the most architecturally minded filmmakers we've ever had.

Yes. And I'm not the only person who has noticed a distinct connection between Wes's work and Ozu's. He and I have talked about it. And that level of pre-cision, that perfect framing, the use of symmetry, the very, very structured placement of characters, it's very ceremonial.

Where the set's kind of perfectly dressed for the frame . . .

Yeah. And I've always been pretty passionate about Ozu. And you know, I think Wes really likes Ozu's approach to clutter.

It's also really interesting, I think, that Wes, as a filmmaker who's known for this kind of neatness and precision, and this perfect arrangement of things, decided to set two-thirds of his film on a trash heap. I remember presenting Wes with some images from *Dodes'ka-den*. Because in *Dodes'ka-den*, too, it's almost perfect—the architecture of trash.

Another trash world that came to mind when I looked at your sets was the one in Tarkovsky's *Stalker*, which, perhaps like *Isle of Dogs*, is just as interested in giving you a world to sense and explore as it is in telling a story, I think.

Actually, it's funny you mention that. The different sections of this film take place in different kinds of trash, much in the way that *Stalker* did. You definitely go through phases—"OK, now we're in the hospital, with the syringes on the ground, and now we're in . . . " I definitely thought a lot about *Stalker* when we were doing the animal testing plant.

And for us to be seeing vestiges of Tarkovsky on certain things here . . . I know that's not exactly what this film is trying to signal to the viewer, but it's interesting to hear that that was on your mind, as a way to direct you to the look and feel of something, even if the end product has less to do with that reference.

Yeah, yeah. I would also say that for me, a big influence was *Fellini Satyricon* too. There is a scene

ABOVE LEFT: After his crash, Atari finds himself in an alien landscape.

ABOVE RIGHT: An astronaut from Honda's *Invasion of Astro-Monster*, also known as *Godzilla vs. Monster Zero*. The film was one of Paul Harrod's references.

A case could be made that *Isle of Dogs*'s genre is closer to *tokusatsu* than anything else—it's got a high-concept story, a futuristic setting, tongue-in-cheek humor, television monitors, snap zooms, criminal conspiracies, and robots. And as with tokusatsu films, the appeal of watching *Isle of Dogs* is inseparable from a curiosity about its medium and methods. Like tokusatsu, it invites the viewer to speculate about the technical tricks that made it possible.

OPPOSITE: Inside the hovel the dogs are silhouetted against the brightly colored bottle walls.

in *Satyricon* where there's a sky, and there are these sort of roiling clouds at the roof of the sky. Some of the stuff that we've been doing on *Isle of Dogs* actually reminded me a bit of that. And I don't think that was necessarily an intentional reference to *Satyricon* . . .

But some things just stick with you.

Yes. There's a great interview that I read with Fellini about it, and the interviewer was asking, you know, "Why did you choose to have such-and-such kind of element, and such a radical palette, on a film about Roman history?" And he said, "It's not a film about Roman history."

"It's a science fiction film."

Yes. "It's a science fiction film."

And so is *Isle of Dogs*, vis-a-vis Japanese history, in a certain sense.

Yeah, yeah, exactly. And that's one of the things that really makes it very different from *Fantastic Mr. Fox*. *Fantastic Mr. Fox* is a fable. This is, in the end, pretty much a science fiction film.

But it's interesting to hear you say that you were drawing from Tarkovsky and Fellini; I hadn't heard them come up on this set yet. Kurosawa's obviously the go-to for most of this film.

Thematically, yes. Not necessarily in terms of visual structure, though. I don't think Kurosawa's editorial or shooting structure is informing the film as much as his themes.

I'd been noticing a lot of these sort of Kurosawa-esque close-foreground, deep-background shots.

Well actually, you know, it was pretty interesting, because a lot of that . . . A lot of that comes from Welles. For those kinds of framings, we've referred to Welles, and Gregg Toland, as much as . . .

There's the explicit *Citizen Kane* references . . .

Exactly. And Kubrick is a huge visual influence. I was happy that we did manage to get our one Ken Adam set.

Oh, the *Strangelove* . . . ?

The *Strangelove*-ian circle. You know, Ken Adam, as a production designer, has probably been the biggest influence on me. And since he passed away during the production of this film, to be able to add that little homage to him . . . that seemed very poignant. But yeah, we've definitely looked at several of his sets. There's been some *2001* referenced, there's been . . .

For the labs, with the knobs everywhere?

Yeah. A lot of the lab, in the fact that it's very, very white—that was definitely an homage to Kubrick. The cabal scene is a bit of a tip of the hat to *The Killing*, too—the planning stuff, the cones of light and all of that.

The less subtle reference in the cabal scene, I guess, is Blofeld, from the Bond films.

Well, yeah, all the cats, of course. Kobayashi's monochrome suit and his cat are definitely inspired by that.

The other day I watched *You Only Live Twice*, because that's the first time we see Blofeld's face, and I was interested to see how they handled—or didn't handle—the Japanese setting. And Roald Dahl wrote the script!

I have to say, *You Only Live Twice* is the Bond film that I am the most conflicted about. Because Ken Adam was the production designer on that, and it's got, I think, the single most amazing set ever built for any film. Every time I see that volcano set on a big screen, it's just amazing. A totally effective use of forced perspective on it. There are all kinds of scenes in that film where there's just throwaway sets, a hallway that somebody will walk through, that takes up five seconds of the film, and you're just thinking, "That set is beautiful . . . !"

Very much like this film . . .

Yeah, yeah.

It's actually great to hear a production designer's perspective on Bond films, because that's probably one of the series' greatest strengths.

Oh absolutely, absolutely. The work that Ken Adam and Peter Lamont did for those films are one of the things that really elevate them. I think at the time, you know, *You Only Live Twice* was one of the more luscious-looking films around. But it's got the most ludicrous plot. I've watched it so many times, and it's just like, "Ah, this is so frustrating"—the ridiculous script, and . . .

Sean Connery gets that wildly offensive "Japanese" makeover, because he has to get married for some reason . . .

Yeah. Why—*why*?

Well, blame it on Dahl, I guess. And that's an example of a film that, for its time, was probably doing what was considered a lot of research on its setting. I imagine that sort of thing falls largely to your department on *Isle of Dogs*, and that you're doing a lot of research to get things right.

Oh, quite a bit, yeah. I've always had a love of Japanese art, Japanese cinema, but I knew right from the beginning that I had to get some advisors on this film. Hiring Erica Dorn as our graphic designer was really, really a coup. She's been great. And then Chinami [Narikawa, graphics and visual effects] came on, and between the two of them, they have been really, really valuable in terms of helping us know when we're doing something wrong.

So they've been consulting on more than just graphics?

Oh, quite a bit more. In fact, there was about a month where Chinami was still in Japan, while she was working out her visa. And she just did a ton of research for me. I would sort of say, "OK, find me as many pictures of Japanese telephones from this period." And she had a grandmother that she could talk to about a lot of this stuff, who could sort of give her a sense of real history. It was really invaluable for research. A lot of it was just providing images, but she would also write these really long breakdowns of the history and traditions of various practices.

For instance, in the Municipal Dome, we have an usher. And we thought, it just can't be the usual usher with a fez that would be in any other theater in the 1930s or something like that. We decided to research, you know, ushers in Japan . . . ? It turned out that it wasn't a very common role. But they had these various people that *could* be ushers.

And so Chinami did a lot of the research on things like that. All kinds of little details. It was really, really useful, and I learned so much, and I just sort of have relied on them throughout for fact-checking and accuracy. Erica's lived here for years, but her mother's Japanese and her father's French. So she's very worldly. And that has also been very helpful, because you have somebody who doesn't just know Japanese culture but also knows how Westerners and Europeans are going to perceive it.

ABOVE LEFT: The cat-loving Ernst Stavro Blofeld, a recurring Bond villain, first shows his face in *You Only Live Twice*. Blofeld was one of the inspirations for the cat-loving Mayor Kobayashi in *Isle of Dogs*.

ABOVE RIGHT: Andrei Tarkovsky's *Stalker* was filmed in and around a disused hydroelectric power station in Estonia. Today, haikyo explorers in Russia call themselves "stalkers," after the cautious professional trespassers in the original novel and the film.

BELOW: The War Room, Ken Adam's iconic set from Kubrick's *Dr. Strangelove* (LEFT). Paul Harrod's *Strangelove* homage in *Isle of Dogs*'s control room (RIGHT).

OPPOSITE TOP: The abandoned Kobayashi Pharmaceutical Factory is one of the production's most impressive sets.

OPPOSITE BOTTOM: The cathedral-like interior of the abandoned Kobayashi Animal-Testing Laboratory

YASUJIRO OZU

WHILE we're talking about Japanese cinema and Wes Anderson, as *Isle of Dogs* encourages us to do, it's impossible not to mention the work of Yasujiro Ozu, to whom Wes is frequently compared. Ozu was, alongside Kurosawa and Mizoguchi, one of Japan's most venerable directors and, alongside Wes Anderson, one of world cinema's most determined marchers to the beat of his own film-grammatical drum.

Wes and Ozu both follow a self-designed and self-imposed set of rules for composition and editing that look like no one else's. Coincidentally, their rules happen to look a little like each other's. The two directors have a number of other shared sensibilities. There's the deadpan tone and comic timing, the bittersweet treatments of family dysfunction, the wistful elegies for times passing by and worlds growing old. There's the tendency to treat the shot as a charmingly framed picture—a well-kept, four-sided world, which characters freely traverse to and fro—instead of a casually roving eye whose job is to merely follow the hero, keep him in frame, and capture his actions.

Perhaps above all, there's the love for precisely framed architecture and beautifully dressed clutter. Their painstaking, down-to-the-millimeter approaches to art direction probably have even more in common than their distinctive, and not dissimilar, camera-work and editing styles.

While Kurosawa and Mizoguchi delved into the social and political problems of Japan's feudal past and its postwar present, Ozu played a less ambitious role: official historian of the Japanese family's troubled passage into modernity. In *Good Morning*, Ozu chronicles the intrusion of the television set into the Japanese living room. Two young brothers have sumo on the brain; they take a vow of silence to force their father into buying them a TV so they can watch the wrestling matches. Like many Ozu films, it's a loose remake of one of his earlier ones, 1932's *I Was Born, But . . .* , a black-and-white silent comedy. Color gave Ozu new opportunities to impeccably design each frame. Sound afforded him new opportunities to make fart jokes.

As much as Wes Anderson and Ozu have always had in common, *Isle of Dogs* may represent the first of Wes's films where designs and compositions are directly inspired by Ozu's. Most of these are, naturally, in the few scenes of *Isle of Dogs* that take place in the home, a setting Ozu's films rarely ventured from.

TOP: Duke's family gathered to watch TV in their living room.

ABOVE: Ozu's *Good Morning*. Paul Harrod kept these shots as references for the interiors in *Isle of Dogs*.

OPPOSITE TOP: Rex relaxes in the library of his master's school.

OPPOSITE MIDDLE: King's family, transfixed by the news on TV

OPPOSITE BOTTOM: A "cluttered" street view: Boss's baseball team visits an outdoor ramen vendor

HAIKYO

URBAN exploration, or urbex for short, is the name for the contemporary trend of visiting abandoned and neglected sites. Urban explorers risk injury, and sometimes prosecution, to bring back beautiful photographs of the ruins—poignant tributes to mankind's follies and aspirations.

In Japan, these abandoned places are known as *haikyo*. Japan's postwar building boom, followed a couple decades later by the bursting of the real estate bubble, resulted in urbex opportunities that are famous around the world. Some haikyo are the results of natural disasters; in other cases, earthquakes and typhoons have accelerated the decay of structures that were already abandoned.

One of the biggest haikyo is nicknamed Gunkanjima, "Battleship Island,"

because of its shiplike silhouette. Located off the southwest coast of Japan, the island was home to a coal mine and some five thousand residents, packed onto only fifteen and a half acres. A public pool, movie theater, and pachinko parlor were built to entertain the miners and their families. When the mine closed in 1974, the island was deserted.

The Outer Cuticles in *Isle of Dogs* have several haikyo, relics of industrial activity that came to a halt sometime before the film begins. Kobayashi's abandoned pharmaceutical factory has been reclaimed by the dogs who once suffered there. The golf course and samurai-themed amusement park perhaps would have been built for Kobayashi's employees and their families.

A roller coaster at the abandoned Kobayashi Park

Kobayashi Park sign, inspired by Japan's Nara Dreamland sign

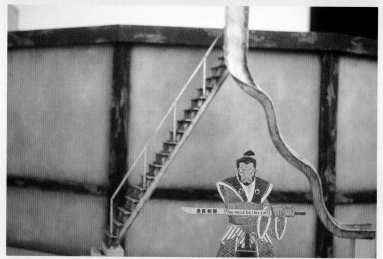

The rusty pagoda slide at Kobayashi Park

Nara Dreamland, Japan's answer to Disneyland, was built in 1961 at the height of the postwar boom. Attendance dwindled over the decades, and the park, already starting to fall apart, finally closed in 2006. For ten years, the park was a mecca for haikyoists. A housing company bought the site and began demolition in 2016. Some of the last photos of Nara Dreamland, mid-demolition, look like shots of the dumps of Trash Island: the pulled-apart pieces of the theme park are sorted into homogeneous mounds of plastic and pipe. Photos by Jordy Meow.

OPPOSITE: **The Hero Pack travels through several haikyo on Trash Island during the "I Won't Hurt You" montage. The crew refers to this sequence as "22 Views of Trash Island."**

(Daily-Manifesto)

市長養子のアタリさん 犬のため戦う

(Mayor's Ward Fights for Dogs)

交換留学生トレイシー・ウオーカーさんによる記事

(A Five-Part Article by Foreign-Exchange Student Tracy Walker)

Photo: M.T.F. Dog-Catcher's Division surveillance unit.

Mayoral Ward Atari Kobayashi violently employs state-provisioned bamboo self-defense sling-shot against official Municipal Task Force rescue-drone yesterday afternoon on Rubbish Beach/Trash Island.

市長の養子である小林アタリ君は昨夜午後、ゴミ島にある汚染ビーチにて国家所有物である自己防衛の竹製パチンコを市長直属タスクフォース救出ドローンに向けて攻撃的に発砲した。アタリさんは、自身の保護者である汚職にまみれた小林市長に対抗すべく、勇敢にも小型プロペラ機をジャックし、彼のボディーガード犬スポッツコバヤシを連れ戻す試みに出た。しかしながらサッポロ上空においてエンジントラブルに見舞われ、止むを得ずゴミ島に緊急着地したと思われる。彼の安否の確認はまだ取れていない。

写真：市長直属タスクフォース、ドッグキャッチャー監視部隊

公文書の黒塗り違法

芽崎市の情報公開巡る問題、確定判決へ

鉄道模型コンテスト

初の快挙、芽崎高校生徒3賞受賞

学生の身近な地域貢献

査員からは称賛の声

細部にこだわった苦労の成果

新校長が語る

明るい学園建設に努力

市役所前で「ゴミ島条例」反対デモ

動物虐待の容疑者

無念の初戦敗退

妻鹿崎高卓球部、準決勝出場決定（3ページ）茶道部、お茶会開催中（4ページ）生徒、来年度文化祭テーマ発表（7ページ）学食新メニュー投票（9ページ）

PLANET ANDERSON

AN INTERVIEW WITH
LEAD GRAPHIC DESIGNER Erica Dorn

A **FILM'S GRAPHICS DEPARTMENT** is responsible for designing everything that would have to be graphic-designed in the real world—labels, logos, icons, posters, book covers, newspapers. It also creates anything that's written or marked by hand—scribbled on a note-card, scrawled on a wall, or sketched in the sand.

OPPOSITE: Atari makes the front page of the *Daily Manifesto*. Text written by Wes, translated and formatted by Erica Dorn.

ABOVE: Labels for beer, sake, and dog treats in the world of *Isle of Dogs*. Most of the brand names are nods to the film's influences. There's a beer named after Hokusai and sakes with canine-inspired names: Hachiko (after Japan's famous faithful dog), Chuken (literally "faithful dog"), and Kemba no Kokoro (literally, "the heart of dogs and horses," an idiom for describing a loyal person).

I spoke with Erica Dorn about her work on the film as a graphic designer and also about the work she's done to help consult on Japanese language and culture for the film. Erica grew up in Japan; she is Japanese and French, and she speaks each language fluently.

In his other films, Wes has shown a great affection for notes, signs, book jackets, things of that sort, and he's always made very specific choices for typography, drawing a lot from midcentury design. What's it like doing Japanese typography for a film like this? Is there a specific tone that you're after or a particular design style you're drawing from?

Although the film is set in an ambiguous "future," many of the references in the film are actually from a more nostalgic period of Japan. We were very much influenced, especially for interior and background details, by Japanese cinema from the '50s and '60s. To supplement this we also built an archive of graphics, including maps, tickets, posters, packaging, book covers, and other ephemera, from the second half of the Showa period.

As you might imagine, there are not as many fonts available in Japanese as there are in English because of the sheer amount of characters that each font needs. You need to design at least a thousand kanji characters to make a basic font. So sometimes it's just easier to draw or design the characters that you need for that particular graphic. Especially if Wes has picked a reference from the Showa period. After a few months you start to work out that there is a certain typographic style that Wes is drawn to, even within the hand-lettering and hand-made typography.

Most of the text I've seen has been sans serif.

I think there's one instance where we've used a serif in the whole film—maybe. Even instances where it would be more common to have a serif font or a calligraphic font, Wes has often defaulted back to the sans serif—often choosing a simple, blocky, angular, geometric kind of style. It's from the time when, you know, magazine headlines and things like that were often hand-drawn, and we try and keep that feeling as much as possible. It's very neat and tidy but still kind of handmade.

What would you hope that people might learn about the graphics work on this film?

I hope they notice the handmade aspect of it, you know? Because we do a lot of things by hand, even if we sometimes finish them off digitally. Like these dog woodblock portraits were all carved by hand, by our in-house illustrator Molly Rosenblatt.

Oh, so those are actually real woodblock prints?

Yeah. She carved them, printed them, and colored them by hand. . . . She's got the blocks over there, if you want to look at them. There's more than thirty— Wes decided that any photograph, he wanted it to be represented as a woodblock print.

But seeing it that small, I think most people would assume that that was computer drawn or pen drawn. I don't think people will know that that's carved—[ERICA GROANS AND LAUGHS] I don't mean that in a bad way! But now they'll know because we're going to put it in the book. Those really were full-size woodblocks.

Someone taking behind-the-scenes photos came around as she was hand-printing them, and he said, "Why don't you just do that digitally?" And we said, "Well, you could say that for the whole film. . . ." But I think the real beauty of this film is in the craftsmanship.

I've heard from several people that it would be important to talk to you because your job is more than just graphics. As I understand, your role has expanded to helping the art department with all kinds of design questions.

Yes. But I think that's mostly because I'm on site, and that makes it easy. Things happen very fast, and in situations where the animator is on standby about to launch the shot it's easier for them to ask me, "Is this right?" than to contact an official consultant, since I grew up in Japan. So did Chinami [Narikawa], our assistant graphic designer. She also gets her fair share of cultural-accuracy questions.

How does that usually go?

I think it's been more about making an informed decision rather than, necessarily, going with whatever's more accurate or more common in Japan. Sometimes Chinami or I will say, "Well, this is not very common."

OPPOSITE TOP: Woodblock
prints of the Hero Pack dogs

OPPOSITE BOTTOM: Duke's
woodblock, hand-carved by
the graphics team

ABOVE: Megasaki—the old city
in the foreground dwarfed by
the modern skyline

But that is kind of the beauty of setting the film in a made-up city, in a made-up kind of timeframe, as well, because you get a certain amount of artistic license, I feel.

I think when you have a director like Wes, who has a strong artistic vision, it feels like there are two forces at play. . . . We're trying to make a film that feels authentically Japanese, but at the same time we are making a film that's authentically Wes Anderson. So when there is a bit of a clash, then sometimes it falls one way, sometimes it falls the other. But I think that usually Wes's vision and what he wants to say is a little bit stronger, sometimes, than anything else. The world of the film is kind of like an alternate reality. So it looks and feels like Japan, but maybe it's a slightly dreamier version, or a slightly more "Wes Anderson version."

In the same way that *Grand Budapest* is set in the Eastern Europe of Wes World, this is almost the Japan as it would appear in Planet Anderson, which is sort of a parallel version—?

[LAUGHS] Yeah, that's a nice way to think about it. To me the *Isle of Dogs* world feels oddly familiar but also nostalgic, like the Japan of my childhood. I've been to a lot of abandoned theme parks like the one on Trash Island, which was a common sight at the end of the economic bubble in the '90s. And there's an industrial section of the highway between my house and Osaka International Airport that looks exactly like one of the shots from the Middle Fingers montage. And downtown Megasaki feels very similar to some parts of downtown Osaka.

Some details are different, too, but personally I know that Wes has a lot of love and respect for Japan, and I think as long as people kind of know going in that this is sort of "Japan on Planet

Anderson," as you put it, then it becomes a really, really stunning film.

Lots of Wes's films have ambiguous settings—I'm thinking especially of *The Royal Tenenbaums*—where it seems to be partly the past and partly the present. Or rather, it seems like the past has persisted into the present. And in this case, partly into the future: It seems to me that the simultaneity of the past, present, and future might be even more pronounced in *Isle of Dogs* than it sometimes is in Wes's films. Like Atari's spacesuit, where he's wearing these silver metallic *geta*. I wondered if that's what Wes is up to, and if that's something you could see clearer than I can in the little details, since you grew up there.

To me it feels like the sort of costume you'd find on a manga character, so in a way, it's kind of fitting. Also, the blending of old things and new things is a very common thing in Japan, and I think we're very used to seeing a seventeenth-century temple next to a skyscraper, you know?

The opening shot of Megasaki City quite literally foregrounds that.

Exactly. It allows you to make a kind of mosaic of aesthetics, and it allows Wes to handpick the references that he wants to use. There are scenes on Trash Island where it does feel very stark, and minimalist, and wabi-sabi. And then you switch over to the city, which is very maximalist, and very dense, and full of information and signage, and every surface is covered. And those are definitely two things that both appear in the Japanese aesthetic sensibility but in different places. And you have the same experience when you travel through Japan, and you walk through a really busy alley and then

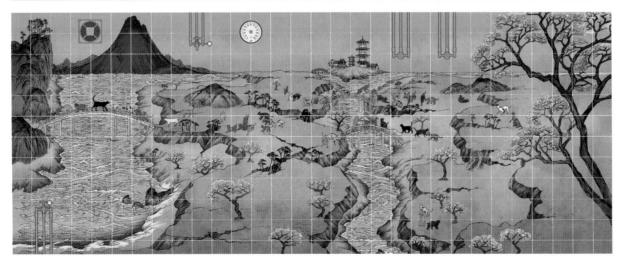

ABOVE: The rich classical style of painting that we call Yamato-e (literally, "Japanese picture") developed during the courtly Heian period (794–1185), considered the golden age of Japanese art and literature. Artists continued to paint variations on Yamato-e even after newer styles of ink painting and woodblock printing became fashionable. "Scenes in and around the capitol" (*rakuchu rakugaizu*) were a popular theme for screen paintings. The graphics department used this screen, dating from the seventeenth century, as a visual reference.

MIDDLE: A screen painting from the beginning of the film, depicting the time "before the age of obedience"

BELOW: The mural behind Kobayashi's tub

OPPOSITE TOP LEFT: The actor Ichikawa Sadanji II as the warrior Marubashi Chuya in the Kabuki play *Keian Taiheiki*. Painted by Toyohara Kunichika (1835–1900), collected in an album of thirty-two triptychs of polychrome woodblock prints

OPPOSITE TOP RIGHT: The graphics department's mockup for the school's Boy Samurai poster, based on Kunichika's painting

OPPOSITE BOTTOM: The final design for the Boy Samurai poster as it appears in the film

There are four ways of writing in Japanese—kanji are Chinese characters, imported to Japan in the first millennium. Each one represents a word, rather than a sound. Writing in kanji alone can't capture all the intricacies of Japanese grammar, so hiragana, a cursive script, fills in the missing words and sounds that kanji can't render.

Katakana is another script—*kata* means "fragment." The script, originally developed by Buddhist monks, is made up of abbreviated elements of Chinese characters. Among other things katakana is used for writing scientific terms, as well as words and names of foreign origin—a bit like the English convention of putting foreign words in italics. Romaji is the Japanese name for the Latin alphabet, which is also sometimes used.

Erica Dorn explains how she combined the characters for *mega* and *saki* into one character, unique to *Isle of Dogs*: "This is mega written vertically as two characters, *me* and *ga*:

"Here is the new combined character we invented:

"This wasn't a huge leap because kanji characters are often made up of combinations of parts like this.

This is Megasaki, using the character for *saki* as it appears in Nagasaki or Kawasaki, for example:

into a really quiet, peaceful garden all of a sudden. So that kind of switching back and forth is, I think, a really nice representation of Japan, in a way.

What has it been like working with Wes? Has he come in with a set of things he has loved that he wants to appear in the film? Or is that more coming up through your departments to him?

I think in the beginning he started with a big archive of things that he loves. But we've also collected a lot of things along the way. In terms of graphics we're looking at a lot of actual printed material and packaging from the '50s and '60s. We would also draw a lot of background details, like wallpaper patterns and bookshelves, from Ozu films and other films from that period.

The most recent big thing I finished was the triptych for the Kabuki Theater scene. There's the "Kabuki Hallway," which is a set that appears before the theater and serves as kind of an introduction to what is happening in the theater. So we have this large bulletin board with a giant poster of the play. It's the "Boy Samurai," sort of based on woodblock prints that were historically created for Kabuki theater. They're always in threes, and they have the names of the actors in them, on rectangular tags.

But that, again, was put through a very Wes filter, so there's some flaming, chunky lettering on it, and it's—

Almost a B-movie poster?

Yes, or a comic book cover, like *Shonen Jump*. You wouldn't mistake it for a real Utagawa print, but you would definitely recognize the influence.

Talk about these murals that you're working on here.

This is the mural Jupiter uses, in the tugboat sequence, to tell the story of the aboriginal dogs. The original reference for this was a big Yamato-e screen—lots of gold leaf and architectural details. But in our version it is scratched, presumably by dogs, into the rusty wall of the tugboat.

It's got that thing that many Yamato-e paintings have: using clouds as dividers between little subscenes.

Yes. And the camera does move into each of the subscenes at some point. So it was making all of that work together. The whole time I thought I was just doing a rough sketch to get the layout right—but it turned out that it was this rough version Wes actually wanted to use!

Going back to what you said about Utagawa prints a moment ago, you mentioned "recognizing the influence." When the film is released in Japan, do you think there any important things Japanese audiences are going to catch that American audiences might miss?

I often get asked how the film will be received in Japan. Maybe it will feel like that there's more to understand, if you're a Japanese speaker, in terms of background dialogue or graphics. I don't think it will necessarily change your understanding of what's going on in the film, but there might be little things that you notice. For example, the official date, written in Japanese on ID cards and newspapers, is "20 Years in the Future."

The character for Megasaki, that's another thing about this sort of alternative reality. In this world, there's a kanji character that represents the word *mega,* which is basically something we had to create because Wes wanted there to be a single character

ABOVE: Woodblock print book illustration by Kobayashi Eitaku, from an 1886 English-language retelling, *Momataro, or Little Peachling.* Momotaro, a boy born from a peach, is a fearless adventurer from a Japanese folk tale. Under his leadership, a quarrelsome animal band (a dog, a monkey, and a pheasant) put aside their differences and agree to sail to Onigashima, the Isle of Demons. The ogres underestimate the little team and are easily defeated in a battle.

"I genuinely don't know if Wes was aware of this fable, or if the parallels are pure coincidence," Erica explains. The Japanese title of *Isle of Dogs* is 犬ヶ島, *Inugashima,* and shares two of the three Japanese characters used to spell Onigashima, 鬼ヶ島. The second character, ヶ, is "a little old-fashioned, and you don't see it much in daily use anymore except in proper nouns like place names," Erica says. "But it's that folkloric feeling that made it feel like the right translation for this film."

RIGHT: For a critic, the temptation is always to "crack" the coded reference, but a reader should take this with a grain of salt. I had started to speculate that this rainbow stripe pattern—seen on the theme park's marquees, flags, and trash bags (TOP)—was a nod to the court fool Kyoami's sleeves in Kurosawa's *Ran* (MIDDLE). As it turned out, the graphics department's reference files contain only an old ad for Fruit Stripe gum (BOTTOM).

for mega. *Saki* is a character that exists—as in Nagasaki, for example. But mega is not a character in Japanese. You would write it as *me* and *ga.*

In katakana?

In katakana, yes. But Wes didn't visually like the look of that, and he didn't want to use different characters for mega that meant other things. Like, *me* could be the character for "female" or "love" or "eye"; *ga* could be the character for "bud." Lots of things can be read as *ga;* lots of things can be read as *me.* But he wanted the meaning, as well as the sound, all to be incorporated. In the end, we decided to put the kana characters together into one kanji. But it kind of works, visually, because that's how kanji are made, anyway—they're made up of lots of little parts. I think that's one of the cool things that came out of this film. But only a Japanese speaker would notice that.

I think the theme, also, is very Japanese—this kind of relationship between these five dogs and this boy that are on an impossible mission. There's something very *Seven Samurai* about it, you know?

I was just thinking earlier about how lots of the old classics of Japanese cinema tend to be about families: fewer of them are romances, compared to maybe American films of the same period. The central drama tends to be familial—like in Ozu films, where it's very much about parents and children. And this film seems to be kind of familial, too—dealing with the dog-human relationship, but there's also that parent-child relationship with Kobayashi and Atari.

Yes, and I think the familial theme is also present in a lot of Wes's previous films. One of the most moving scenes in this film, for me, is the one where Spots resigns his position as Atari's bodyguard-dog and appoints Chief in his place. I don't know why, but I still tear up even though I've seen it several times! Sometimes the most important family is not the one you're born into, but the one you acquire through shared life experiences.

Trash Bag Graphics

Pale hessian sack
Hand-drawn black stars

White plastic sacks
Black diagonal stripes

White plastic sacks
Red, yellow, green, orange stripes
(for use in amusement parks only)

YIPES! STRIPES!

CHERRY LEMON LIME MIXED-FRUIT ORANGE

NEW

BEECH-NUT GUM
FRUIT STRIPE
FIVE FLAVORS

UKIYO-E

UKIYO-E woodblock prints, treasured today by historians, mooned over by European impressionists, and enshrined among high art in museums, were originally a shrewd mass-market product that supplied a public demand. The early prints were keepsakes and sneak peeks of life in the pleasure quarters and theater districts of the Edo period, life in the so-called *ukiyo*. The term had been an old religious cliché: "the transient world." Some punster switched out the character *uki*, "transient," for another character with the same pronunciation but a different meaning: "floating." Thus, "the floating world"—a heady whirl of gambling, girl-watching, and tea-drinking, a round-the-clock idyll of flirtation and scintillating wit, a perpetual bacchanal safe from the rigid public morality preached by the military government.

In the latter days of ukiyo-e interest in the inner sancta of the pleasure quarters gave way to curiosity about the landscapes that lay outside Edo. This led to a special genre of landscape prints, developed by two of the last and greatest of the ukiyo-e artists. The eccentric Hokusai, self-described as an "old man mad about painting," started painting at the age of six and kept at it until he died at eighty-eight. In 1832 he began his famous series *Thirty-six Views of Mount Fuji*. Meanwhile, Hiroshige, Hokusai's contemplative younger rival in the landscape genre, was on the road to the emperor's court in Kyoto with an official delegation from the shogunate's seat in Edo. Hiroshige painted all the stops along the highway in his *Fifty-three Stations of the Tokaido*, released in 1833.

Arguably, Hokusai won the contest in the long run. His works are more widely known around the world today—none more than *The Great Wave off Kanagawa* from his *Mount Fuji* series,

a picture so recognizable it gives even the *Mona Lisa* a run for its money. But Hiroshige was just as much of a sensation when ukiyo-e prints reached Europe in the nineteenth century. His impressionistic approach to color inspired the palettes of French artists like Monet, Pissarro, Degas, Gauguin, and, more recently, Gwenn Germain, the 2-D animator for *Isle of Dogs*.

ABOVE: *Hiroshige knew what all landscape painters know—the blue sky is darker above, and it lightens toward the horizon. But he usually represented it with a pleasing abstraction—a single fat band of pink, orange, or Prussian blue painted straight across the very top of the painting. Some of Hiroshige's skies are gray or even black.* "It's sort of the Japanese answer to the vignette," Paul Harrod observes. "They're not really vignetted, but they're framed by darkness." *A lot of shots in* Isle of Dogs *follow the same principle, even the ones that aren't hand-drawn—the dark land at bottom, the dark clouds hugging the very top of the frame, and in between a tall block of empty white sky.*
LEFT: Under the Wave off Kanagawa, *by Hokusai, c. 1830–1832*
BELOW: *Dogs riding the waves to Trash Island*

ABOVE: Seven-ri Beach, Province of Soshu, *by Hiroshige, date unknown*
BELOW: *The coast of Trash Island*

ABOVE: Oi Station, *by Hiroshige, c. 1835*
BELOW: *One of the pictures of "virtuous dogs." Professor Watanabe uses these to illustrate his speech at the start of the film.*

ABOVE LEFT: *An old man and his faithful dog*
ABOVE RIGHT: Shop with Famous Arimatsu Shibori Cloth, *by Hiroshige, 1855*

2-D ANIMATION

As a story of protest, political intrigue, and media hysteria, Isle of Dogs includes lots of news footage and journalistic photography. One of the film's conceits is to represent in-world photography with a different style of animation: a 2-D, hand-drawn look, influenced by Japanese ukiyo-e woodblock prints.

The artist heading up the small 2-D department is Gwenn Germain, a French animator fresh out of university—he's just twenty-five years old at the time of our interview. Wes scouted him after producer Jeremy Dawson came across one of Germain's student films. Gwenn describes his process for arriving at Isle of Dogs's 2-D approach:

"I THINK it's never been done like this—in which a 2-D animation department has to work closely with a stop-motion department. So our 2-D animation borrows some techniques from stop motion. The faces, for example: There are sudden, big changes from frame to frame, so that it looks like how the puppets' faces switch out.

At first, our solution was to use rotoscope to make the 2-D animation match the stop motion, because there are some shots in which these two mediums appear simultaneously or in fast succession. But in the end, Wes thought it was more important for the 2-D to be its own thing and not an exact copy of the stop-motion.

We still had to come up with something close to the stop-motion style—but also close to the ukiyo-e style and close to what Wes liked . . . and, also, to the style I can do. [LAUGHS]

At first, Wes wanted to have something really close to Hayao Miyazaki and Isao Takahata's films at Studio Ghibli. I think I was hired based on this; Wes had seen my short film, which is also influenced by Japanese manga.

I like that all Japanese animation goes straight to the point and is subtle at the same time. The Disney school, for example, is very, very broad—there's a lot more gesture and a lot more movement. And in Ghibli films, I like the colors; there's a lot of work done on the choice of colors, expression through color. This is, I think, the thing that I'm

best at doing: choosing colors, understanding how colors work together.

At first, Ghibli was the reference for the 2-D animation in Isle of Dogs. You can still see the Ghibli influence on this palette. But then, when Wes and I started, he changed his mind. Wes wanted to take the animation in the direction of this woodblock and ukiyo-e influence. And I like the ukiyo-e colors; it gave me a lot to draw from. The

traditional ukiyo-e printing technique makes it so that there are more muted tones, which we have in a lot of our designs, but also really bright and saturated colors—this became my palette and guide. So for example, we have a shot of a brick mansion, which is bright, bright red, with pinks and other bright colors.

And this is the most difficult part of the color for this film. In a Ghibli film, the color is homogeneous throughout. You can have a lot of colors in one shot, but it's homogeneous. In ukiyo-e, a picture can have all desaturated colors, and then just one color is a very dark saturated blue. So in the animated scenes, we wanted to play with this, because it's the code of the ukiyo-e. So, usually, I've been starting with a pastel palette, and then I choose which colors to play with in the saturated areas.

Wes is also someone who plays a lot with composition. And he's broken every rule of composition. This is the same in ukiyo-e. So I think this is why he likes it. He likes the flatness in ukiyo-e style; he likes that when you have something close, it's on the bottom of the image. This is not my specialty, because when you like Ghibli, you like the depth, the perspective. So we had to understand what you can do with this ukiyo-e style, and with my style. We had to find some blend. On the brick mansion, for example, you see the area in front—no perspective on it. There is just a fake perspective. It's theatrical. Wes is very theatrical. And the shot he prefers, it's when there is no perspective at all—everything just flat."

Tokyo's Imperial Hotel, designed by American architect Frank Lloyd Wright (RIGHT) *and the mayoral-household as it appears in the 2-D animation* (ABOVE)

IMPERIAL HOTEL· TOKYO· JAPAN·   ルテホ國帝京東

ABOVE: *Frames from* Celles et Ceux Des Cimes et Cieux, *Gwenn Germain's Miyazaki-inspired short film that first caught the attention of producer Jeremy Dawson*

ABOVE: *A 2-D frame of the train accident that left Atari an orphan. Though Wes and Gwenn moved on from the Studio Ghibli look for most 2-D images, this one still owes a lot to Miyazaki.*

ABOVE: View of the Kabuki Theaters at Sakai-cho on Opening Day of the New Season, *by Hiroshige, c. 1838*

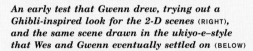

An early test that Gwenn drew, trying out a Ghibli-inspired look for the 2-D scenes (RIGHT), *and the same scene drawn in the ukiyo-e–style that Wes and Gwenn eventually settled on* (BELOW)

OPPOSITE: Animator Rachel Larsen works on one of the Interpreter's scenes.
ABOVE: Signs outside each unit tell passers-by all they need to know: which scene is underway, and which animator, assistant director, lighting cameraman, and motion-control operator is assigned to it, and whether the set is "hot"—that is, in the midst of being shot and not to be touched.

ANIMATION

A **STUDIO SOUNDSTAGE** is a big box that keeps out the light and noise of the real world—a black bubble in reality where a new world can be born. The newly shaped world of Uni Prefecture spreads across three soundstages at 3 Mills. Each soundstage seems about the size of a school gymnasium, but it's difficult to say, because each has been subsectioned into still more black boxes, substages, bubbled off from the others. The walls between are ad hoc wooden flats, painted in thick light-eating black. Nothing spills out; nothing spills in.

Each of these wood-walled cubicles is a "unit." The term refers to a subdivision of a film production with its own crew, operating independently of other subdivisions, other crews. On a live-action film, the most important footage is shot by what's called the first or main unit, with a second unit gathering supplementary footage. On *Isle of Dogs,* there are forty-odd units shooting at once.

Around 3 Mills, the word "unit" is usually used to refer to the cubicle itself. For a few days or weeks, the unit houses a set, and is assigned its own small crew: assistant director, set dresser, rigger, camera assistant, lighting cameraman.

Assigning an animator to a scene is a particularly crucial decision. It's called "casting," as if the animators were actors—and, in a sense, they are. Animators are the ones who move the puppet, frame by frame, and each of those small nudges and tweaks adds up to a "performance" that is no less emotive, and no less distinctive, than the voice track provided by Jeff Goldblum or Bob Balaban. Animators have their own signature styles, and they have different strengths—some are better at big setups, some are better at highly technical scenes, some are better at small emotional moments. The idea is to keep everyone working on the kinds of scenes they do best.

It takes a unit's whole crew to get a set built, installed, dressed, lit, and in focus, but when it comes time to shoot the scene, the animator is left to work alone, largely uninterrupted for long stretches.

The soundstage is quiet. There's no rule about being quiet, and it doesn't affect the shot one bit—no one's recording any sound. But everyone's mindful of the animators' concentration, unconsciously

Animator Marjolaine Parot makes Spots, Atari, and Chief "swim."

listening for their silent movements behind the black-curtained doorways. The animators' solitude is punctured only by the short cough of a walkie-talkie in the hall, or the tinny whisper of music from the earbuds of the animator next door.

The animator operates the camera by means of the "tower," a kind of standing desk, housing a computer and topped with a monitor. The camera is plugged into the computer. The animator can see the shot on the monitor, and can capture a frame with a keystroke without touching the camera. Animators' days are spent gently tapping the puppet, turning, and tapping the key; turn, tap, turn, tap, turn, tap. Hours go by. Time is ambiguous in here. The artificial darkness promotes the same unself-consciousness as the witching-hour writing desk or painter's easel. Even if it weren't necessary from a photographic standpoint, I have to wonder if the darkness would be worth cultivating just to keep the animators productive. A hard day's work generates a few seconds of footage at best—to face such an infinitesimal task, without being opiated by this pre-dawn feeling, would probably sap any sane person of motivation. Too strong a sense of man-made clock-time would probably just confuse them. They somehow have to get into the headspace of a tortoise or a

sequoia tree. They have to be able to see a turn of the head, a lifting of the paw, or the spreading of a grin protracted across an entire afternoon.

CLIPPED TO EACH UNIT'S curtained doorway is a "do not disturb" signal: a small red light, the sort you might see on the back of a bicycle. When it's on, a shot is in progress. In this unit, it's off, and James Emmott, first assistant director, pulls the curtain back and ushers me inside.

The little room is bright with the sour-apple glare that bounces from a long sheet of green screen draped along one wall. All the lights are lit, the camera on, the tower unattended, and no one in sight. Scanning the room from right to left, our eyes finally adjust to the sight of a tall figure sprawled in a shaded corner. Jason Stalman is kicked back in a bucket chair, all big beard and ball cap, bare feet up, doodling on a ukulele in his lap.

"This is where we find our lead animator," James notes drily.

Jason hitches up his shorts and slips his feet back into his Birkenstocks. *"Bone-idle!"* he crows. "Couldn't be lazier."

Nutmeg lolls indifferently on a table, on the far side of the room from Jason's man cave. They needed

ABOVE: Animator Kecy Salangad works the crowd at the Municipal Dome.
BELOW: These puppets were built to fill out crowd scenes. The crew calls them "happy clappers." Many are constructed without legs.

Key animator Steve Warne works on Atari's landing. His parachute, which will flutter and fall in the finished shot, stands frozen between frames.

a break from one another. "She's a show dog," Jason apologizes. She's not like the Hero Pack or Gondo's tribe or the random Trash Island mutts with their matted hair, rugged bones, and weary forbearance. Nutmeg's glossy tresses are unforgiving, easily smudged or mussed. Her delicate physical mannerisms require extra finesse. Jason sets down his ukulele and resumes the all-day deep-tissue massage. Today, frame by frame, Jason is slowly wringing a wry reaction out of her. Offscreen in the reverse shot, Chief is half-confessing his feelings: "Sometimes I lose my temper" is the line for today.

When it comes to armatures, animators all have their own preferences. Some like the joints limbered up; others like a bit of stiff resistance. The puppet workshop does its best to tune the armatures to the animators' specifications.

Nutmeg has a green T-shaped bar coming out of the back of her head, the same shade of green as the screen. It gives the animator leverage; Jason shows me how adjusting the bar allows him to turn Nut-

meg's head without disturbing her coiffure. Another green T-bar extends from her lower back. The bars will be removed, along with the screen, by the visual effects artists during postproduction.

On the wall is a small printout of the storyboard frame for the day. What I expected to see was a wall plastered with rows and rows of pages, breaking down a single movement into dozens of freeze-frames—something very much like Eadweard Muybridge's *Rotatory Gallop: The Dog* hanging in Andy's office. That's what I imagine I'd need if I were in Jason's shoes. But the animators don't need that, or don't need it anymore. There's actually nothing to tell them how a puppet should be postured for any given frame. It's up to them. *They* don't even know how they know what should come next, Jason admits. Here, at the heart of this obsessively planned production, where even chance itself is anticipated, scheduled, and organized, is a dude in board shorts just winging it by sheer finger-instinct, and everyone else just has to trust that his mojo will hold out.

Lead Animator Jason Stalman takes Nutmeg for a walk.

Animators will sometimes study footage of animal and human bodies before they get to work. If they can't find footage of an action they need, they'll record themselves or a buddy aping the motion—one animator couldn't find footage of a dog limping, so he shot himself. Animators call these "LAVs," or live-action videos. Some hard-to-place performances make more sense when you see who's behind them. (The wolf in *Fantastic Mr. Fox*, for example, is Bill Murray—he provided the reference footage for the perfectly-paced fist-pump scene that always makes me weirdly verklempt.)

Wes makes these videos, too, and zaps them over to the animator if it's easier to show something than try to explain it. You could practically cut full-length alternate versions of *Fantastic Mr. Fox* and *Isle of Dogs* out of the grainy videos of Wes delivering the lines at the proper tempo, craning his body into the proper postures, making the deliberate but understated gestures he wants.

A second of animation, like a second of stan-dard live-action film, is made up of twenty-four still pictures. Back when all movies were shot on spools of celluloid, you'd need a special motor that could advance and expose a single frame of the film strip. A program called Dragonframe, installed on the tower's computer, allows the animator to use a digital still camera the same way. Each newly captured frame is lined up after the last one, so that the footage acts like a single smooth strip of celluloid rather than a stack of separate photographs. The whole sequence is ready for immediate playback and can be sent to the editing room as a single video file.

That doesn't mean it's always reasonable to ask the animators to break down a puppet's motion into twenty-four distinct postures for each second of screen time. That's called animating "on ones"—one frame per position, twenty-four positions per second. It's lifelike, ultrasmooth, and, in the long run, terribly costly. It tends to be suitable for those few action-heavy scenes that depend on lifelike, ultrasmooth

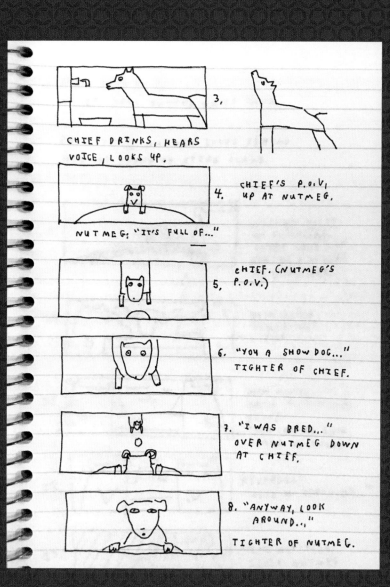

3.

CHIEF DRINKS, HEARS
VOICE, LOOKS UP.

4. CHIEF'S P.O.V.
UP AT NUTMEG.

NUTMEG: "IT'S FULL OF..."

5. CHIEF. (NUTMEG'S
P.O.V.)

6. "YOU A SHOW DOG..."
TIGHTER OF CHIEF.

7. "I WAS BRED..."
OVER NUTMEG DOWN
AT CHIEF.

8. "ANYWAY, LOOK
AROUND..."
TIGHTER OF NUTMEG.

Wes's early storyboard of Chief and Nutmeg's
first meeting (ABOVE) and corresponding
shots from the finished film (RIGHT)

TOP LEFT: A puppet reporter snaps a picture, while animator Rachel Larsen works on the protest outside the Municipal Dome; TOP RIGHT: Puppets wait obediently between scenes; BOTTOM LEFT: An animator adjusting candle flames at the vigil for Atari and Spots; BOTTOM RIGHT: Key animator Matias Liebrecht shares a high-five with Chief.

motion for their very intelligibility. But it would be wasted on the many scenes of "chatting," as Josie in the puppets department called it, and other "Wes things" the dogs do.

For most scenes, motion is plenty believable if it's animated "on twos." The animator positions the puppet, shoots two identical frames—tap, tap—and moves the puppet to its next position. There are only twelve distinct postures per second of screen time. Audiences don't notice the difference, and it takes less of a toll on the production in money, man hours, and morale. *Fantastic Mr. Fox* was largely shot on twos.

Until the advent of computer animation, hardly any films were ever animated entirely on ones. And Wes actually tends to prefer the vintage look of

shooting on twos—the staccato stagger-step has a pleasing falseness. It has that classic snap, crackle, and pop that he likes. It "feels more like animation"—much as shooting twenty-four frames per second "feels more like cinema" to most of us, even though little prevents us, in this day and age, from shooting more than twenty-four frames per second and creating extremely smooth motion.

But even animating a shot on twos can take days, or even weeks. And when it's done, something might be wrong with it—it might not jibe with the shots that come before or after, the tempo might be off, or the character's energy might be wrong for the dramatic beat. It's hard to know until you see it, but Wes needs to see it before the animator loses whole days doing it.

Fox and Wolf, proud to be wild animals, salute one another in *Fantastic Mr. Fox.*

This is where "blocking" comes in. In theater and film, blocking means telling the actors how, when, and where to move, what marks to hit. It's a stop-start process with lots of stumbling-through until the director and actors feel that it's working and decide to set it in stone. Blocking in stop-motion isn't totally unlike blocking in live-action: roughing out the actor's movements and seeing how it comes across. Live-action filmmakers don't bother to shoot the blocking process, but on a film like *Isle of Dogs*, of course, a puppet like Nutmeg can't "move" without pictures being taken. Still, no one wastes time shooting the blocking too well. It's about speed and broad strokes; perfection comes later.

Depending on the scene, blocking means animating "on fours" or "on sixes." It looks rough and jumpy but gets the job done—Wes can watch it and give meaningful notes. Ideally, when it comes time to animate the real shot, they can get it in a single try.

After a scene has already been through blocking and the animator feels confident about the shot, he or she will take the first frame of the sequence—the "launch frame"—and send it over to Wes. If Wes thinks that everything in the launch frame looks good, the animator can begin shooting the scene in earnest. There may be reshoots down the line if something in the animation isn't working. But once the launch is cleared, the animator proceeds as if this is the real deal, the only "take."

THE PUPPETS ARE DURABLE, but a single hair out of place, a single threadbare patch of silk, a smudged shoe, or a smutty cheek will cause a continuity error. This is where the Puppet Hospital comes in—an outpost of the Puppet Workshop that serves a similar purpose to the hair-and-makeup trailer on a live-action shoot, where actors check in from time to time for maintenance so that their look matches from one shot to the next. The puppet, manhandled by animators, is run to the hospital between scenes for spot-cleaning and sprucing up. On *Isle of Dogs*, each "puppet actor" has a host of doubles in various scales, some of whom are being shot simultaneously on different sets. Each has to match the others or continuity will be spoiled when it comes time to edit these different shots together.

In one corner of the hospital, a puppet physician is replenishing the fur on Spots's throat with fine-

Key animator Chuck Duke works with robot-dogs at the causeway battle, a scene full of complex animated pyrotechnics.

pointed tweezers, plucking tiny tufts from a swatch of white fabric and tucking them under his chin. The dogs' heads, necks, and jaws receive the brunt of the animator's prodding, and their beards become patchy.

This afternoon, Mayor Kobayashi is here for one of his frequent checkups. One of the hospital staff is pressing the mayor's suit with a tiny iron. It's objectively adorable. It's also deadly serious. There are high-dollar repercussions for any oversights: precious seconds might need to be reanimated, setting the production hours or days behind schedule. Every

artist who works with puppets on this production seems to be able to shift focus back and forth between two frames of mind, seeing both the adorability and the urgency of the task—whatever helps them stay motivated.

DOLLYWAGGLING
AN INTERVIEW WITH
LEAD ANIMATOR Jason Stalman

J **ASON STALMAN** is one of three lead animators on *Isle of Dogs*—a role he earned after his strong work as a key animator on *Fantastic Mr. Fox*. He's also worked on Tim Burton's *Corpse Bride* and for Laika Studios on *ParaNorman*, *The Boxtrolls*, and *Kubo and the Two Strings*. He took a break from his work at 3 Mills to talk about England's stop-motion history, the inner life of an animator, and his perspective on Wes as a stop-motion director.

OPPOSITE: Jason Stalman ruffles Rex's fur. Puppet fur naturally "boils" when the animators move the puppets between shots, but the animators need to intentionally muss the fur during scenes of stillness—otherwise the dogs will appear strangely lifeless when they're not moving.

ABOVE: Jason animates Rex's mouth.

You're the first animator I've spoken to on this set. What's that all about, I guess?

Wow! [PUTS ON A MOCK-PRETENTIOUS VOICE] "Creating the illusion of life . . . [LAUGHS] Frame by frame."

"You see, the word 'animate' is . . ."

"Comes from the Latin . . ." Yeah. Let's not do that [LAUGHS]. The first question you always get asked is, "How did you end up doing it?" And I have absolutely no answer for that question. I guess we just grew up in England with a big tradition of stop-motion animation here. All the kids' TV stuff I grew up with, a mere twenty years ago . . . no, much longer ago. [LAUGHS]

We'll print "twenty years ago."

Maybe "fifteen years ago," then. But in the United States, I think stop-motion was used more as a sort of special effect, where the monster would be animated. Whereas in England, the whole program is made in that technique. You know, kids' TV shows were made in stop-motion.

Was it cheaper than other options, do you think?

I don't think it's ever cheaper. I think it's just a tradition of old men down the garden shed puttering around and fiddling with these things, you know? *Bagpuss* and *Clangers* and . . .

I've definitely never heard of any of these.

Well, they're really famous in England, by a guy called Oliver Postgate, and I just was obsessed with this world that he'd created. It was based on inanimate objects coming to life, with toys. It was well before *Toy Story*. It was the most charming, beautiful thing. And it was completely naïve, and they wrote all the music for it, and I loved that . . . I loved that they did everything. I loved that they wrote the story, made the puppets, designed it, and you could create this whole world, and put music to it too. Which I guess is exactly what Wes is constantly doing.

So you're almost saying that stop-motion has kind of arisen from the British *volksgeist*, or something—that there's something in the sensibility of this country that gives rise to that? To the puttering?

For me, that's what my memories are. But obviously, you know, we are an island. There are other places—there's a lot of stop-motion animation from all over Europe. I'm a big fan of Jan Švankmajer. And the more you get into it, the more you end up seeing that there's so many people across the globe using this bizarre technique.

Yeah. I'd had heard that Wes was even thinking of shooting this is in Central Europe, just to sort of be in the Švankmajer spirit . . .

In the feeling of it, I can imagine. That creepy, cursed, weird vibe that we're all after . . . [LAUGHS]

By settling here, though, he's still in a country that has this history, and this sort of guild of craftspeople who do this stuff.

Definitely. I think there's an amazing history of those crafts here in England. Not just in stop-motion, in every kind. I think it's something that we celebrate here and are trying to keep those things alive. I can't explain why. It's not something that I'm getting proud and patriotic about. I'm not a psychiatrist, psychologist, or historian, but, you know . . . It's definitely there.

Speaking of childhood memories of stop-motion, Wes has spoken of his own love for the Rankin/Bass Christmas specials.

So they stay with you, these things, right? And you have a nostalgia for them.

Well, as far as *Isle of Dogs* goes, if you're expecting it to be a Rankin/Bass Christmas special, it seems like there's a fair amount of blood. The puppets are injured a lot of the time— bruises and cuts, ribs sticking out.

Yeah, definitely, there is darkness. You know, people used to say that you could tell a hard, dark, gritty story quite well with animation, either 2-D or 3-D, because you have that removed distance from it—it's not reality. It is animated. So you could say certain things, or challenge certain things with this medium that allows a safe distance for the audience.

I've been noticing these connections to a lot of English stories and themes in *Isle of Dogs*. As a person who grew up in

TOP LEFT: The puppet stars of Oliver Postgate and Peter Firmin's *Clangers* (1969–1972) who are space creatures of a sort.

TOP RIGHT: Henry Selick's *James and the Giant Peach*, like Wes's *Fantastic Mr. Fox*, is a stop-motion adaptation of a children's book by Roald Dahl. Stop-motion is perhaps the ideal medium for Dahl's slightly twisted stories.

ABOVE LEFT: The eponymous puppet star of Postgate and Firmin's *Bagpuss*, a British children's stop-motion television show from 1974

ABOVE RIGHT: The grotesque puppets and begrimed sets of *Street of Crocodiles*, the best-known stop-motion short by identical twins Stephen and Timothy Quay. The delicate subtlety of the Quay Brothers' technique creates a beautifully poignant, mournful mood that a still frame fails to fully capture.

TOP LEFT: Ladislas Starevich's *The Mascot* is about a toy puppy willing to go to hell and back to bring his young master an orange. Starevich was one of the first stop-motion animators, and he worked from the 1910s through the 1960s.

TOP RIGHT: In Jan Švankmajer's short film *Darkness, Light, Darkness* large human body parts vie for space in a small room. Švankmajer's surreal films mix stop-motion, live-action, and live puppetry for an effect that's as wry as it is macabre.

ABOVE LEFT: The gothic charms of Henry Selick's *The Nightmare Before Christmas*, produced and conceived by Tim Burton, have made it a favorite of misfit teens since it premiered in 1993.

ABOVE RIGHT: Tim Burton's *Corpse Bride*, a film both sweet and spooky. Jason Stalman was one of the animators.

England, do you feel a bit of that particularly English sense of the macabre in this story—Roald Dahl, Richard Adams?

Right. I guess *James and the Giant Peach* was stop-motion that kind of clung to my brain. There always seems to be a theme of some kind of *odd* . . . ness, in these English stop-motion things. I don't know. There's something that's very unreal, dealing with these very *real* things, right? Very real subjects. And I guess the cool thing is, you're going through the imagination. So you're using what kids do—how they function in the world. They use their imaginations mostly. They're lost in their imaginations, they're storytelling.

I think that's what animation *is*. It's a very good storytelling medium, right? When you're playing with your toys when you're a kid, you're animating, you're bringing your Barbie and your Ken or whatever to life, and you give a narrative and a story. And this is what we're doing. And I think that kids can also explore very difficult, deep questions with themselves by acting those things out and playing. That's what playing is, isn't it? It's figuring out those problems with the world . . .

And so your job is to be that kid? . . . You're the one on set who actually gets to play with these toys.

Oh sure, we call it "dollywaggling" [LAUGHS]. That's the term that was coined years ago by a friend of mine. That's what we are. Dollywagglers.

Just doing it very carefully.

Very careful dollywagglers, yeah. Very *slow* dollywagglers. You know, that's the thing that I don't think any animator enjoys. I think we love the idea of it, and we love the hands-on, we love the puppet, and we love the creation of that, and we love the result—that odd, edgy vibe you get from stop-motion. But the *process* of doing it, I don't think you'd find one animator who says, "I really love animating," because it's horrible [LAUGHS]. Everyone goes, "Oh, you must be really patient." Like, no. I'm not patient. Not at all. I can't believe I do this. I kind of keep wracking my brains for something else to do, but I've become really good at this one specialty . . .

I had prepped all kinds of highbrow questions about the animator's mind, and what kind of temperament you need to have for this. And you're telling me that, in fact, none of you have the temperament . . .

We're all the same as everyone else. We're all mental. [LAUGHS]

But you think you actually don't have the temperament to be doing this kind of work?

Well, you have to go to a special place. I think a lot of animators are grumpy. We're seen as really grumpy, and there's this whole diva thing. And it's not. It's just . . . *You* stare at a puppet for ten hours and move it from there to there and see how you feel with someone going, [KNOCKS ON THE TABLE] "Hi, do you need anything?" No! Piss off, just leave me alone! You just want to kill someone. It's ridiculous. Right now, I'm doing this shot where this blossom's blowing in, and it's landing on Nutmeg, and it's blowing and fluttering on her . . . [A FLOWER FROM A NEARBY TREE FLOATS OVER AND LANDS ON THE TABLE] Like—exactly. See? God has provided. [LAUGHS]

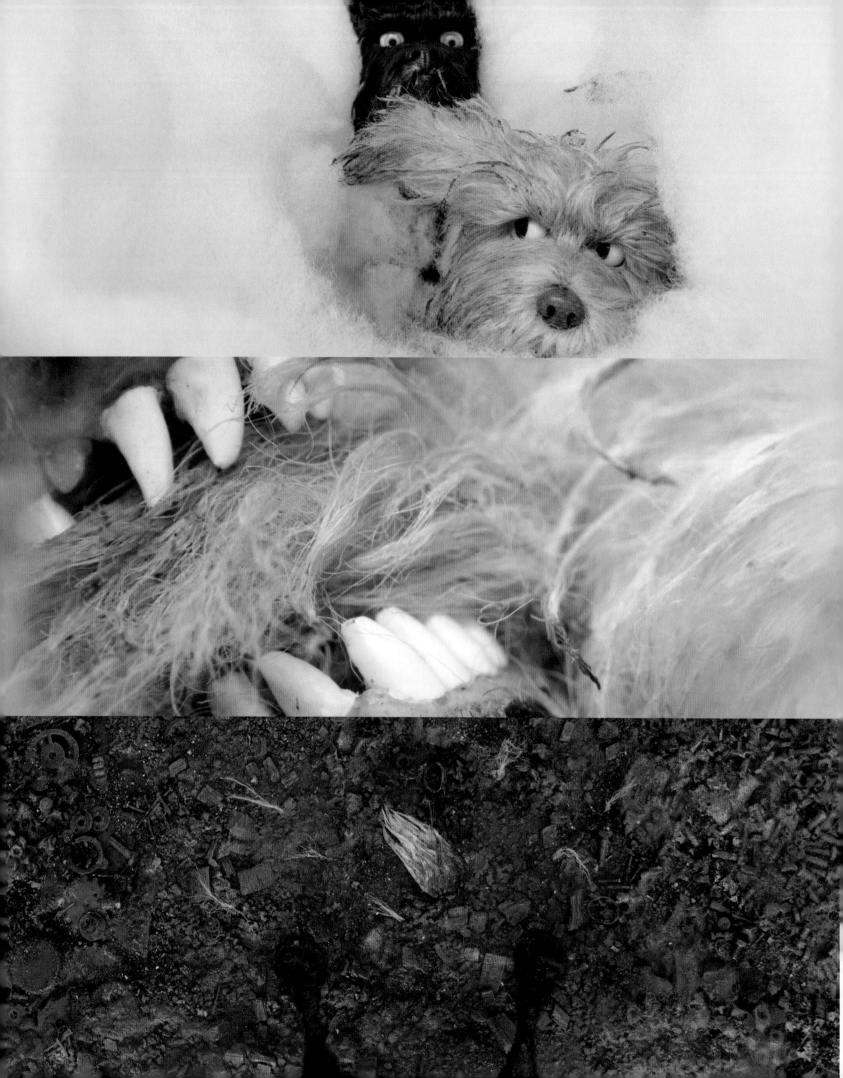

And so, yeah, it's just stupid. I'm using a tiny pair of tweezers to plant these flowers in her fur, and then the petals have to *dance* in the *wind*.

I've heard from the puppet department that they're designing things and altering things based on what the animators need— but the puppets have to be handled by multiple animators, and they have to incorporate lots of different feedback.

And it can drive them crazy because one asks for this, and then they've got to work backward because the next person that comes along wants the opposite of what they've just spent a day doing. And that's just the nature of the beast.

And especially with the way that Wes works, I'm beginning to sort of see that it's a nice, organic evolution. As you're unfolding the animation, he can see what you're doing, slowly, and he can change his mind, and it will drive people crazy. But it's not like he's being fickle. He's just looking at it going, "I know what's going to work so much better." So then you've got to cut back, or you've got to start again, or you've got to change something mid-shot or whatever. It can be challenging because it's such a tricky and time-consuming process. It takes so long to do that you're driving yourself crazy doing it. And to do it twice is really hideous.

But at the same time, you want to give Wes what he wants, and you want it to be the best. So it's big-deep-breath, pull-your-big-boy-pants-up time, and you do it again and you get it right, and you always—every single time, everyone always has to stand back and go, "Damn it, he was right!" And that's kind of cool.

I really liked working on *Fox*, and I love working on this because I like that he's just got such an eye, and a vision, and knows what's working on this, and that you can't always see it until you see it done.

One thing that's been surprising to a layperson like me is just how much of stop-motion animation is about the knowledge in the animator's hands and head. It's not laid out for you—you're not metaphorically rotoscoping-over some preestablished

sequence of frames. You guys are in there literally just feeling out what the next frame needs to be.

Yeah. Just years of doing it. I think you get a feel for it . . . It's a weird thing. The other day I was animating on the puppets, and my hands were on the puppet, and then I looked away to look at the monitor. And before I'd look back at the puppet, my hands were exactly on this tiny little thing in the right way, just moving the eyes. And I spooked myself. You know? [LAUGHS] I had this muscle memory. You're just in the zone.

I kind of describe it as sculpting the performance. That's how I think of it. Because it's there in a three-dimensional space. I've always loved sculpting and clay-making when I was a kid, and Plasticine and that kind of thing. Feeling the form in space.

So I think something in me naturally lends itself very well to doing animation, and feeling that negative space, and how this thing sits in space, and how I really want to nail just that little tiny movement. Doing the small stuff's the hard thing; doing the big broad stuff, that's kind of easy. It's a bit like riding your bicycle slowly. It's much easier to ride it fast.

OPPOSITE: **The Hero Pack's scrap with the sheep dogs. Chief goes for the ear.**

TOP: **In *Isle of Dogs*'s penulti-mate scene, a blossom lands on Chief's nose.**

VOICES
AN INTERVIEW WITH
LEAD ANIMATOR Kim Keukeleire

OPPOSITE AND ABOVE: **Kim Keukeleire at work in the greenscreen glow**

O ONE HAS ACTUALLY ever seen Kim animate," joked associate producer Ben Adler when he introduced lead animator Kim Keukeleire. First assistant director James Emmott corroborated this: "She's very fast."

Born in Seoul but raised in Brussels, Kim came to stop-motion "just by accident, in art school in Brussels." She chose it because "you could do everything—photography, sculpture, drawing." She applied three times for what she casually refers to as "the chicken job"—a position as an animator on Aardman Animation's *Chicken Run*—before finally getting it, and her career took off from there.

Kim confesses that she didn't know Wes Anderson by name before she heard about a job opening on *Fantastic Mr. Fox*, but she was thrilled once she looked him up and recognized his films. Her experience as a key animator on *Fox* was positive (of note: she lists the time she kissed George Clooney under the "other experiences" section of her online CV), and she's happy to be working with the old team again on *Isle of Dogs*.

For someone watching this film, which scenes have your fingerprints on them?

I did a lot of the scenes with Spots—I liked the scene in the hospital. I love doing Spots. And Jupiter, also—I think there weren't many other animators who did scenes with Jupiter. I loved doing a little with Oracle, of course, also. The shot I did is only a very small one, but Tilda Swinton, she's got a great a voice. I really enjoy it when the voices are so great. And I really enjoyed doing Scrap. I think he's probably my favorite just because I think the voice is so, so funny.

Jason was saying you have great comic timing, and that you get cast in comic scenes.

Oh really? I don't—[LAUGHS] Sometimes you don't realize what you're doing. Maybe that's how other people see my work.

How do you see your work?

I don't know. You know, it's really difficult to tell because you keep doubting yourself [LAUGHS]. You're always worried about whether it's good enough. And you don't see it the way other people see it, I'm sure. I would never be able to tell what I'm doing differently—what my fingerprint is. But I can recognize the fingerprints of other animators. I think it's like recognizing your voice—your voice, in your head, it's very different from your voice in a recording.

But you can recognize other animators' work. Can you give us a couple examples of another animators' scenes that really struck you?

I really like Danail [Kraev]'s work. He makes me get goosebumps sometimes. He made that lovely scene where they're on the raft, with the puppies. And, also, I love the sequence of washing Chief and discovering he's white. That's also Danail.

Jason mentioned he's had a hard time getting a bird's-eye view on this project because, with the way he works, he's not been able to watch a lot of footage outside his own scenes, but it sounds like you've seen a lot.

Yeah, yeah, I'm watching footage all the time. Everything. I think it's really interesting to see what everyone is doing, even if it's not my sequence. I know that Jason has a different approach. But my approach is that I like seeing everything there is. I just really enjoy watching the movie.

Also, I like seeing all of Wes's notes on the other sequences, just to understand better what he's thinking, what he likes, and what he doesn't like, so that I can get as close as possible to what he wants in my sequence. Because he's got some really precise ideas.

You can see that on the—[LAUGHS] sometimes you look at the LAV [live-action video] of Wes doing the scene, and you think, "Mm, he's got some subtleties in

this LAV that you have to be careful to catch." Like all his movies, it's a little bit deadpan. And you have to think of how to show that—the stillness, the subtleties.

Human characters in this film, especially, are really hard because they have replacement faces, and you have to work with those, and Wes has some really precise mouths he likes. It's a lot of different faces before you get to the right face.

Are the animators the ones choosing which face to use in a given frame?

No, that's chosen by Wes. But then they have to work with that because if you're the one animating, you need to make sure it comes at the right moment. And the expression sometimes unfolds really slowly. It's hard because, when you're animating, that's where you put all the subtleties—the tiny, tiny little move of the eyes or the mouth, and you cannot do that if it's a mask. But people are really getting things out of it—the puppets all look great, I think. But it's amazing how many human puppets there are. I didn't realize there would be so many humans in this film, in the beginning.

So Wes is really giving you direction on this, but you have to perform it, like an actor—you're just given basic blocking.

Yeah, exactly. But it's true that—well, I'm a shit actor. [LAUGHS] I cannot perform. But I think it's probably more like an internal performing. Also, I think the voice helps you animate. That's a lot of it, for me, I think. The voice track carries you, and it gives you a lot of inspiration. When you have to work with a shit voice—like on a children's TV series, if it's really cheap—it's really painful, sometimes, to work with.

Fantastic Mr. Fox **was known in the United States for having a uniquely good voice track—not just because of the way actors recorded together, but also because they were just great actors who took it really seriously. Not all animated films get that.**

Yeah, what a pleasure to work on a great voice! It's amazing. I loved the Mr. Fox and Mrs. Fox voices.

And you've talked about subtlety, in the movements, but that's in the voices too. I think a lot of the time, with animated films, the voice actors are asked to go big.

ABOVE: Oracle is shocked to learn what may become of the dogs on Trash Island.

OPPOSITE TOP: Atari on set, meeting Peppermint's puppies

OPPOSITE BOTTOM: A frame from the film of Peppermint and her pups

Yeah, yeah, I think that's what I love about this project. With Wes, there's no overacting. And you recognize that he's not doing any clichés. He's got his own personal things that he always likes to do. But it's never big, American—well, I would say American . . . [LAUGHS]

You can say that, we know.

The American clichés of, like, so much of the CG animation that you see. I hate that, actually. I cannot animate like that [LAUGHS]. There are a lot of comic moments in this film. But not because it's slapstick, like in so many animated films. It's more like the way they're talking, when they're all together. It's the rhythms of it. When the pack is together, they sound like a bunch of old ladies.

Have you gotten to do many of those Hero Pack scenes?

No, I've done one scene where they're talking a bit, but so far, I haven't done that many scenes with the group. I've worked on the scene where the dogs are all on the tugboat—but they don't talk, mostly they listen.

It's funny that you're describing puppets as listening; I imagine Wes's animated films probably feature more puppet-listening than some.

Yeah, probably [LAUGHS]. And also, again, with the two languages—Atari doesn't understand anything they're saying, which is really funny. I find it really interesting, the use of Japanese, the use of two languages. The fact that we never understand, really, exactly what they're saying in Japanese, and that in the film, the dogs are translated in English. I thought that was really great. Because it goes really far, actually—even the puppies, they scream like babies. Which is a bit weird, really.

It's unsettling.

Yeah, it's a bit unsettling [LAUGHS]. But then it's completely true to himself, and to what he's doing. I can't really tell yet how it's going to all fit and go, but every sequence I see that is finished, I say, "Wow, that's great. That's really working." He's quite clever. We all know that.

CINEMATOGRAPHY

THE **MUNICIPAL DOME** on Re-election Night: a small-scale Kobayashi speechifies on a lustrous hardwood stage. Behind him, a black-and-white poster of the mayor's glowering mug soars several stories high. It's one of the many details designed to link Kobayashi with Kane, and it's one of the many scenes where Wes has imitated Welles's compositions.

Up in the box seats to stage left, Wes has positioned a puppet film crew, documenting Kobayashi's speech for posterity. The puppet filmmakers aren't on set at the moment, but they've left their gear behind in the theater: the familiar stack of steel-cornered white trunk cases that come with a rented Panavision camera package. Next to the cases is a tiny Fresnel lamp on a silver C-stand, the light's face ringed by four black barndoors the size of flower petals. And there's a black rubber-coated cable, yarn-thin, with its slack properly coiled; the plug snakes away to an outlet somewhere in the Municipal Dome's mezzanine.

It's lunchtime at 3 Mills Studios, and the *Isle of Dogs* crew has left its own lights and cables, identical but a good sixteen times larger, in much the same state. It's warm in the studio. The sets are all lit with full-scale professional film lights—most of them no more than 650 watts, but they're far brighter than anything in the ordinary home. In each unit, an animator works all day with these lights looking over her shoulder, breathing down her neck. Together, their tungsten filaments burn with the heat of a dozen Easy-Bake Ovens.

Keeping the lights on at all times, whether the filmmakers are on set or off, helps keep the temp-

An extreme long shot (TOP LEFT) and an iconic publicity still (DETAIL, ABOVE LEFT) from the political rally scene in **Citizen Kane**, with corresponding shots from **Isle of Dogs** (TOP RIGHT, ABOVE RIGHT). BELOW, an early draft of Kobayashi's campaign poster by the graphics department, even more explicitly Kane-inspired than the one that appears in the film

erature steady. A shift in temperature can cause the wooden sets to expand or contract by a fraction of an inch, which could ruin the shot. Once again, the critical thing is absolute stillness, absolute congruence from tap to tap to tap.

The lights are planted close to the edges of the table that supports the set. The animator, moving between the puppets and the tower, maneuvers through a jungle of steel trees. Sturdy C-stands, splay-rooted and thick-trunked, extend their cantilevered arms over the set and interpose their broad rectangular leaves—translucent white "silks" to diffuse a ray of light, black "flags" to block it, "nets" of stretchy tulle to dim it.

Trying to get a better view of Mayor Kobayashi, moving sidelong through this steel thicket, my left foot taps the leg of a light stand. I feel phantom tingles in my foot for the rest of the day, wondering whether I shifted the light by a few degrees and what butterfly effects might have rippled forth: how many hours of shooting might have been ruined, how expensive a reshoot could be.

ABOVE: The Tristan Oliver look, as seen in 2000's *Chicken Run* (TOP), 2005's *Wallace & Gromit: The Curse of the Were-Rabbit* (MIDDLE), and 2012's *ParaNorman* (BOTTOM)

TRISTAN OLIVER, the director of photography, is responsible for planning each scene's lighting setup, with the help of gaffer Toby Farrar and the crew of lighting technicians, called "sparks" for short.

Draping his long arms across the jutting light stands, Tristan eyes the wide white sky that hangs above a black sand beach. The sky spreads above nearly every Trash Island set—a diffusing silk, stretched over a steel frame, each one twelve or twenty feet across. Soft white light falls gently from this artificial cloud cover, wrapping softly, shadowlessly, around the dogs below.

Left to his own devices and given his druthers, Tristan favors hard, raking light from the side or the back. He likes patches of pitch-black shadow, dark faces caressed by a new-moon sliver of backlight, eye sockets swimming in a ghoulish campfire underglow. His usual style is on full display in *Chicken Run*: long shadows stretching across silver-blue midnight barnyards, scenes of conspiratorial clucking lit from below by orange embers.

It's not so much that Wes's tastes are different from Tristan's; it's that Wes's needs are different from those of most directors. Tristan understands this, and he is having to think in the particular way that Wes does about art direction, and about how to use light in a way that showcases Wes's signature designs. When you've perfectly decorated every composition from edge to edge, there's usually not a lot of room for chiaroscuro. When you've got the perfect counterpoise between the chartreuse of a lampshade at frame left and the turquoise of an ottoman at frame right, you might not want a huge shadow cutting across the wall and turning half the colors into mud.

You can see this lighting-for-color principle at work in the Megasaki High School classroom, in Atari's hospital room, and in the many wide-open spaces under white cloud cover. At the same time, *Isle of Dogs* does contain a surprising number of low-key shots—the photographer's term for compositions that embrace darkness and leave large areas of the screen in shadow. There are the cavernous interiors: the gaping ruins of old factories, where green-gray sunlight barely penetrates tall, grimed windowpanes, or the vast auditorium sets, where red lacquer walls catch the firefly reflections of stage lights and paper lanterns. And there are the night exteriors: strangers exchanging glances, trading understated film noir one-liners, in the hot pools of light cast by street lamps. These are some of Wes Anderson's most lugubrious scenes to date. It might be because he's working with Tristan and wants to make use of his talents. It might be because he's working with a palette so desaturated that it's rarely in danger of being washed out any further. Or it might just be the only logical look for the story—this is, after all, a tale of black deeds, moral rot, murder most foul, finally brought under the bright, unforgiving light of truth, justice, and student journalism.

A wide view of a Trash Island set,
showing a typical lighting plan for a
Trash Island day scene

A high-contrast, low-key shot that Tristan surely enjoyed lighting. Oracle, Jupiter, and Nutmeg

THE MODELERS, builders, and set dressers, banging out hundreds of puppets and hundreds of sets, continue to marvel at the vast scale of the film's world. Tristan looks around and lowers his voice. "I don't know why they think that," he confesses. Each set is a smaller world than he's used to. He explains *Chicken Run*'s huge barnyard sets, each one an arena for dozens of complex camera setups, movements, lighting schemes.

But it's not hard to account for the different perspectives. It has to do with the way Wes frames a shot.

Wes's distinctive approach to framing needs little introduction here: it's already been explained by critics and scholars, illustrated by video essayists, imitated by countless film students, and parodied by waggish YouTubers. If you've seen a Wes Anderson movie, you probably already recognize it, remember it, could demonstrate what it looks like with a few hand gestures.

What we think of as the classic Wes Anderson shot feels frank, feels flat. It's frontal, or it's profile, often centered, often symmetrical, and so is the next one, and the next one, and the next one. If you're a filmmaker, you'll say that Wes keeps putting his tripod on or very near the axis of action, and when it's not on the axis, it's usually exactly ninety degrees from it. If you work in theater, you might use the word "proscenium" to describe certain Wes Anderson framings. If you are respected film theorist David

Bordwell writing an essay for *The Wes Anderson Collection: The Grand Budapest Hotel*, you might, borrowing a term from art theorist Heinrich Wölfflin, call Wes's approach to composition a "planimetric" style, and you might astutely summarize the way he chooses his camera angles as a "compass-point" style. If you're most people, you probably just call it "Wes Anderson style."

Whatever you call it, this style has significant implications when you're shooting a stop-motion movie. Some are pitfalls, but many are perks. Rather than swinging your camera around a motel, or a moving train, or the Mediterranean, until you land at a ninety-degree angle to something you can set-dress until it feels passably Andersonian, you can just build the shot you've got in your head—not the whole world you see in your head, but the exact four-edged picture you want to show on screen. There's no sense in spending time and money building anything that isn't going to be in the frame. In a film like *Chicken Run*, the average shot is just one of several possible views of a set—each one a small, limited slice of a large, continuous space, which the camera can explore from many angles, almost as if it were a real room or a real barnyard. But in *Isle of Dogs*, most sets were built with a particular planimetric view in mind.

Lots of sets aren't good for anything else. One reason the world of *Isle of Dogs* looks so big for its

ABOVE: Illustrator Molly Rosenblatt waits in a darkened unit. The light behind her is aimed at a big foam "bounce board"—the reflected beam of light is broader and softer than it would be if the light were pointed straight at the puppets. BELOW: A hot light on Chief makes his hairs stand out.

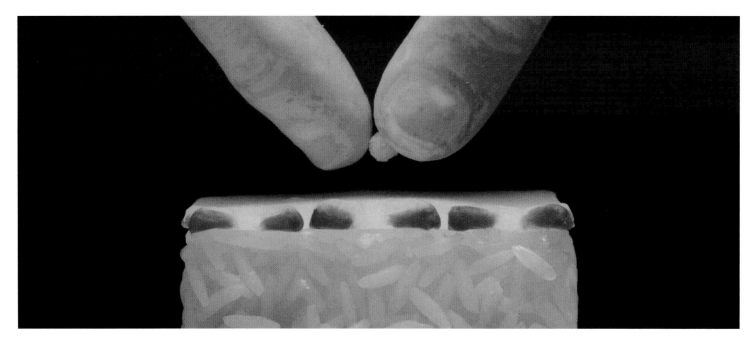

When you see an image with shallow depth of field, your brain often concludes that the object must be "small" or "close up." It's the way the object would look if you held it up six inches in front of your eye. (Proximity of the object to the lens, whether it's the lens of a camera or the lens of your eyeball, decreases depth of field.) In this critical shot of the poisoned wasabi, shallow depth of field was exactly what Wes and Tristan were after.

budget is that many sets use forced perspective: Objects in the foreground loom larger than life; objects in the background are scaled down to make them look far away. A set that might be only, say, four feet square looks the same to the camera as an expensive, twenty-foot-deep vista that hogs two whole units.

A street protest scene, for example, has been set up with full-scale puppets in its foreground, mid-size puppets in the mid-ground, and small-scale puppets in the background. The street slopes away from the camera, each skyscraper smaller than the one a few inches in front of it. It's a set built for one particular camera angle and one particular lens—seeing the set from any other viewpoint would spoil the illusion of a towering metropolis.

EVERYONE KNOWS Wes's films look a lot more like each other than they look like anything else. At a glance, this can obscure the fact that Wes's directorial voice has varied and evolved over the years. He does try new things with each new film, and, as a cinephile, he's constantly challenging himself to imitate the old masters and master their old tricks

If you talk to anyone on the crew, you keep hearing the same names: Welles, Frankenheimer, Kubrick, and, of course, Kurosawa. These directors have been on Wes's mind, and they all have some-

thing in common: a cinematographic technique that Wes wants to make a stylistic keynote for *Isle of Dogs*. What's ironic is that stop-motion filmmaking is perhaps the most inopportune place for him to try it.

The overgrown golf course is one of Wes's simplest and cleverest sets, full of visual puns and subtle references. It's also the stage for one of *Isle of Dogs*'s pervasive, time-consuming, and, if it works, almost sure to be ignored camera tricks: the illusion of "pan-focus" cinematography.

The Hero Pack sits patiently on a white-skied set, their heads popping through the silver grass, some near, some far off. It's a consciously Kurosawa-style composition: blocking big groups was one of Kurosawa's many specialties. Wes has always been good at group shots, too, but he's making a special effort to stack the figures even deeper as a nod to Kurosawa's sensibilities.

Kurosawa (like Welles, Frankenheimer, Kubrick, and many other greats) liked playing with pan-focus or "deep-focus" cinematography. There were earlier efforts to achieve pan-focus shots, but the technique was famously pioneered and popularized by cinematographer Gregg Toland for Orson Welles's *Citizen Kane*, released in 1941, which relied on pan-focus more than any film before. Toland's innovations

The deep-focus shot of Atari and the Hero Pack in the grass (ABOVE), described in the text, and the reverse angle of the same shot: Jupiter and Oracle emerge from the silver grass (BELOW).

allowed Welles to stage his actors in the deep foreground and deep background and keep everyone in focus at the same time. To accomplish this, you need to understand, and then circumvent, certain laws of optics. To do that, you need the right equipment. You need fairly short-focal-length, wide-angle lenses, or else you need a fairly light-sensitive film stock or very brightly lit sets—something that will allow you to close down the iris of the lens until the aperture is a very small hole. Toland relied on a combination

of all three: wide-angle lenses, sensitive film stock, and bright lights. Kurosawa and his cinematographers often pulled it off with very long telephoto lenses, compensating for the lens length by using extremely bright lighting.

The goal in pan-focus cinematography is to maximally increase "depth of field," or DOF, the photographer's term for the range of distances that appear in focus before and behind the person or object you've set your focus on. To say you've

ABOVE AND OPPOSITE: **The Science Lab set was photographed in several "passes," with different lights on and off for each photo.**

achieved "pan-focus" (where everything in the shot appears to be in focus, from the farthest objects to the closest) is another way of saying that the shot has extraordinarily deep DOF.

Unfortunately for the *Isle of Dogs* crew, there's one more factor that affects a shot's DOF: the proximity of the subjects to the lens. This presents a problem when you have to shoot miniature actors instead of real ones. If you pick up your phone and open the camera app, you can see the trouble for yourself. Your phone has a very wide-angle lens, and if you're outdoors, or in a brightly lit room, the camera has no trouble keeping your girlfriend in focus in the foreground and that scruffy barista in focus in the background. But get down level with the table, and try to get a big close-up of your espresso cup in the foreground with your girlfriend's quiche Lorraine in the background: You'll notice that your espresso is in crisp focus, the quiche a little fuzzy, the barista almost indiscernible.

The closer the in-focus object is to the lens, the shallower the depth of field gets. And of course, the smaller something is (an espresso cup, a slice of

quiche, a ten-inch-tall boy in a spacesuit looking for his lost dog), the closer you have to put the camera to it in the first place.

The result is that, in fact, most shots in *Isle of Dogs* are bedeviled by shallow focus, shallow depth of field. This constrains Wes's ability to imitate Kurosawa's group shots. Thankfully, there is a time-intensive but very effective workaround, which is used in one way or another on most shots in *Isle of Dogs*: the use of "passes." To shoot a pass of a scene, the animator isolates a particular set of puppets or objects, animates the shot from start to finish, then starts over with a new pass and animates a different set of puppets. There may be two passes; there may be ten. The passes are composited together into a single image by the visual effects team.

If you're using passes to simulate a pan-focus shot, as the crew is doing for the golf course scene, you have to take a new pass for each layer of depth. Focus on Chief in the foreground, then animate his actions: tap, tap, tap, tap until you complete one pass. Adjust the lens: pull the focus to Rex, farther off in the mid-ground, and animate his actions, tap, tap,

TOP: One of Wes's group compositions from *Moonrise Kingdom*: the Khaki Scouts discover that Shakusky has flown the coop.

ABOVE LEFT: Kurosawa appreciated the intrinsic comedy of large groups reacting in unison, and he found creative ways to fit all the faces into the frame. These detectives move as one in this shot from *High and Low*.

complete a second pass. Pull the focus to King, tap, tap, complete a third pass. Send all the passes up to the VFX lab, where they'll combine the passes and likely add even more elements sent over from other units—shots of water, smoke, drones, trams, or city skylines.

LORD FALKLAND once said, "When it is not necessary to make a decision, it is necessary *not* to make a decision." Shooting passes is sometimes useful when it is important for Wes *not* to make a decision until he can see how the shot plays.

The mod and modular Science Lab set is a wall of bulging boxes and panels. Its numerous computer panels are studded with tiny diodes, glowing buttons, backlit keyboards. The back of the set, unseen by the camera, is a bushy tangle of wires. "Thousands, pouring out like spaghetti," Tristan Oliver notes. "Every single lighting fixture is individually wired."

In the final shot, the lights will twinkle. The exact twinkling pattern is too complex to try to figure out here in the animation process. The easiest way, believe it or not, is to take multiple passes of each framing with the lights on and off in different configurations.

These passes happen a little differently: there's no need to back up and take the scene from the top each time. Move the puppets to a new position. Take a picture. Flip a light switch. Take another picture. Flip another light switch. Take another picture. And so on. Then it's up to Wes and the postproduction crew to decide how the keys and screens will flicker in the finished shot. In a film where Wes wants

almost every effect to happen in-camera, everyone wants to avoid a situation where artificial "light sources" have to be created using computer effects. Shooting multiple passes allows the filmmakers to make final adjustments to lighting, focus, and the timing of puppets' movements. "I can't think of a single shot that doesn't have at least three passes on it for some reason or other, just to give him that choice at the end," Tristan says.

"CAN WE MAKE IT MORE LIKE THIS?" a note from Wes says on the initial sketches for the TV Studio scene. He's attached an image of the particolored curtains that Johnny Carson stepped through every evening. The upholstery of the boxy mod seating is another homage to *The Tonight Show*: blocks of color plaited like a first-grader's paper placemat. Carson's geometric carpet has arrived, too, likely by way of *Twin Peaks*'s Black Lodge, its meandering bars of orange and green wool regimented into strict zigzags.

The TV Studio scene calls for a long tracking shot—the camera's supposed to crab-walk horizontally a good three or four feet, moving past the monitors, cables, and light boards of the TV control room to settle on the colorful talk-show set. Animating a tracking shot requires a high degree of precision. If the camera positions aren't perfectly spaced, the shot will appear to stagger and lurch. For a simple camera movement, or one that's allowed to look herky-jerky, a talented animator could plunk the camera down again and again by hand, but that won't work for a long, smooth motion like this. To make matters worse, the shot calls for a focus pull: The focus ring

Orson Welles and Gregg Toland used wide-angle lenses in *Citizen Kane*'s pan-focus shots (OPPOSITE BOTTOM LEFT). In the 1960s, Kurosawa started to favor longer lenses but still wanted the pan-focus effect. In order to have his cake and eat it too, he called for brighter—and hotter—lighting.

According to the crew members interviewed in the Kurosawa documentary series *It Is Wonderful to Create*, the temperature on the soundstage sometimes rose to 120

degrees Fahrenheit. This interior scene from *The Bad Sleep Well* (OPPOSITE MIDDLE RIGHT) required lots of takes. Kurosawa kept insisting that Takeshi Kato (screen right), then a rookie actor, wasn't getting his character's physicality right. According to Kato, the guys in the lighting crew were roasting sweet potatoes on the heat radiating from the lamps. Kamatari Fujiwara (screen center) started visibly smoking. Tatsuya Mihashi, another actor in the

film, watched Fujiwara step outside between takes—he was wringing buckets of sweat from his handkerchief.

Stop-motion filmmakers have it easier—in addition to adding light, they can also adjust the shutter speed and take a long exposure. They don't need to approach the heat levels Kurosawa's crew withered under. But there are still limits to how far they can stop down the iris, which is where "passes" come in.

Like *Isle of Dogs*, *Citizen Kane*

is chock-full of compositing tricks that make optically impossible shots possible. The shot of Kane finishing Leland's opera review (OPPOSITE BOTTOM RIGHT) is actually two shots (two "passes," we could say) taken from the same angle, with the focus set at different depths. One pass focuses on Kane in the foreground. The other pass focuses on Leland in the midground with Bernstein, silhouetted in the door, still sharply defined in the deep background.

ABOVE: Wes and the art department paid tribute to the midcentury greats when they decorated the TV studio set: tulip side table and television screen modeled after Eero Saarinen's 1958 Pedestal Collection; armchairs adapted from the Gentilina model by André Vandenbeuck and reupholstered by whoever did Johnny Carson's, with white antimacassars to keep the Brylcreem off the chairbacks; the News Anchor's smirk and upswept hair inspired by a rakish photo of young Kurosawa.
BELOW: The camera will track across this set with the help of motion control technology, or MoCo.
OVERLEAF: Atari will appear in the background of this shot of the golf course set. A small patch of grass is positioned between the camera and the dogs to add foreground detail. The grass is made from the upturned bristles of a push broom, spray-painted silver.

will have to be nudged a few degrees for each new frame, so that the TV crew is in focus when the shot starts, and the News Anchor is in focus when the shot ends.

Hitting all these marks perfectly would be impossible for mortal man. Enter MoCo, or "motion control" technology. It's a robot, basically: MoCo devices allow animators to chart camera positions and focus marks with the help of a computer, and then make mechanically assisted movements between these positions. Perfect every time, and perfectly repeatable.

This scene's MoCo machine is a smooth metal track over a long, threaded bar. The camera's mount is threaded onto the bar like a nut on a bolt. The camera can slide along the bar from precise position to precise position. The whole thing is wired into the tower.

The puppets haven't arrived on set, but the crew is using the MoCo machine to "plate" the shot. Plating means capturing a clean, blank first pass of the puppet-free set, and it gives the VFX artists a useful empty layer, which comes in handy when they're compositing other pieces or digitally erasing supports or other junk. The crew is going to have to hit each position exactly when they take the second pass. With MoCo, it's no sweat.

My foot catches the leg of a light stand again but lands with a surprisingly solid *thunk*. I look down and notice that the leg has been protected by two chunks of wood, set at right angles and fixed to the floor. The crew calls these "kick plates"—I look around the soundstage and notice that most lights have them. The ones that don't have been securely hot-glued to the floor—easy for the professionals to tear up when the scene is finished, but impervious to the wayward sneakers of the uninitiated.

IN PRAISE OF SHADOWS
AN INTERVIEW WITH
DIRECTOR OF PHOTOGRAPHY Tristan Oliver

T **RISTAN OLIVER** has had a storied career in British stop-motion: He worked on two of the original Wallace and Gromit shorts, and worked as the director of photography (DP) on Aardman's *Chicken Run, Wallace & Gromit: The Curse of the Were-Rabbit*, and Laika's *ParaNorman*. He was Wes's DP on *Fantastic Mr. Fox* and is back for *Isle of Dogs* on the strength of Wes's writing: "When he first sent me the script, I read it in one sitting, and I said to my girlfriend, 'That's one of the best scripts I've ever read.' And I read a lot." In Tristan's brief reprieve from set duties, he sat down to talk shop about lighting, lenses, focus, and the evolution of the art form.

OPPOSITE: Tristan adjusts a light.

ABOVE: Atari and the pack lined up for a shot. A small "bounce" reflects light to their faces.

What does a day look like for you, on something with this many units?

It's busy. But I'm kind of used to it. I mean, this is my sixth stop-frame feature—not shorts but proper features. And in fact, this is slightly smaller than what I was running at Laika, where I was running a fifty-six-unit stage. This is low-forties. There is a saturation point mentally, completely. I think this is just about handleable.

I'm also very hands-on with a lot of stuff. So of those forty-odd units, I'm typically running between thirteen and sixteen because I enjoy the physical process of lighting, and it's also important for me that other people see that I do that.

So you're not just supervising—you're in there?

By no means am I just supervising. I see pretty much every frame that comes off the floor, with reference to how it looks photographically. So I've got three other guys lighting for me who I've worked with a lot over the years, so I know them and trust them.

They're the LCs [lighting cameramen].

They're the LCs, exactly. And James [Lewis, LC] was with me on *Fantastic Mr. Fox*, so he's kind of like my right hand in that respect. I see everything they do, and I'll give them notes before we start, and I'll make sure we're on the right page in terms of what the palette is, what the time of day is, you know, where the key light[1] is. And often with Wes, nowhere. There is no key light. So it's my responsibility to keep it looking coherent.

So how is a director of photography's job different on a stop-motion film versus a live-action film?

There are a lot of things to consider, comparing the photographing of small things with the photographing of life-size things. Forget the art, but the general physics of lens mathematics and things like that. Focus is intensely difficult. And I still get a sense from Wes that he wishes he could have the focus that he gets in live-action. But in live-action, his nearest thing is four or five feet away. And so, you've got from four or five feet to infinity[2] at a reasonable stop[3] on your camera. Whereas we have an inch of depth of field.[4]

I was looking at the camera on the black beach set and saw the aperture set at f/16. Is that typical for you guys?

That's where we start, yeah. Because he'll always ask for a bit more. So the only way he can get more is if we start at f/16, and then he gets f/22. But that has implications in terms of how the lens performs.
    The lenses are optimized for between, sort of, f/4 and f/8, and everything else is not quite what it should be. And also, because of the sheer number of lenses we use—we've got maybe two hundred lenses on this job. We need a library for every camera, essentially. So we cannot spend the kind of money I would like on lenses. I'm not holding two sets of Cooke[5] series 5 primes[6] on this job. I'm holding one hundred and eighty Nikon manual lenses, which were manufactured sometime in the past forty years.

Yeah. It looks a little vintage-y.

Yeah. It looks vintage-y, not just for that reason. I mean, it has that kind of feel to it. But those lenses were never meant to do anything other than take a picture of Christmas here, and a birthday here, and the beach here. And even professionally, maybe a guy scoring a goal. [LAUGHS]

You're asking them to go above and beyond . . .

Exactly. And you're asking the camera to do something that it was never intended to do. Cameras are getting better and better, but with every new feature, we have to sit down and do an extensive testing process on what is out there in terms of digital cameras because these cameras are not designed to take a coherent strip of images that run together.

Walking around set, it looks like you're shooting with common-or-garden Canon DSLRs[7]—is that the case?

They're common-or-garden in one respect, but in another respect, they're not. It's the 1DX—these are pro-end cameras. We have full-frame raw data to work with. And it's certainly a massive step up from the 5D, which had sort of become the industry standard. It's actually a great camera for what it was designed to do, but it's completely unsuitable for shooting animation for all kinds of reasons, including the stability of the chip under temperature fluctuation. The 1DX is fabulously stable.

So these cameras are all rigged up to a tower.

Dragonframe, yeah. That's the single biggest change to our lives over the last ten years, I think. It's a fantastic piece of kit. We've kind of been waiting for it for twenty years, if not thirty. Back in the day, we were running a system off Commodore gaming computers.

Dragonframe does sound a bit like a Commodore game.

It does. The great thing about Dragonframe is that it's incredibly responsive. It's incredibly user-friendly. I've got full manual control over the camera from the tower, absolutely. So I can change pretty much everything.

ABOVE: It's not unusual for crews to name their gear—it's the best way to keep identical pieces of equipment straight from each other. Names are easier to remember than numbers, and a clever theme is good for morale. This Canon 1DX has been named for director Takeshi Kitano. On set I also noticed DSLRs named for (Teinosuke) Kinugasa and (Kei) Kumai.

OPPOSITE: Rex faces the camera, his fur softly backlit.

Except the vintage primes, presumably . . .

No—but in terms of the camera control, I can control the shutter speed,[8] color temperature,[9] ISO,[10] you know, all that stuff is all there. And I've got it there, so I don't have to go into the camera and look at some display . . .

And you don't have to touch it, either . . .

Exactly.

There's a technique that came into vogue a few years ago, "miniature faking," where you can trick out cameras with tilt shift lenses and make it look like all the people and buildings are a few inches tall—like in the regatta scene from *The Social Network* or in the opening credits to *Sherlock.* It seems like here, you're doing the opposite—you're "large-faking," in a sense. What sort of things do you have to do to keep it from looking like you're shooting a bunch of puppets?

That's a very good question, and it's a question that we asked ourselves a very long time ago. And there's no real answer to it. But I think a lot of the advances in terms of camera movement are just to take you away from the sense of watching animation. For me, an animated film shouldn't be about animation. You should go and see it and say, "That

was a really great movie. . . . Oh, by the way, it was animated."

And I don't make any concessions photographically, or lighting-wise, to that. Though the lighting look Wes prefers is something flatter and softer than I'd normally do.

There's a lot of those big silks—[TRISTAN GRIMACES] You don't want to talk about it?

Probably not. [LAUGHS]

Is it about trying to get the design—?

Yeah, completely. My feeling with him is that what he's really after is a big picture book, you know? And you open it, and you go, "Wow, look at that." And you peruse it, and then you turn the page, and there's another lovely picture, and it doesn't necessarily have anything to do with the picture you just looked at.

On set, we always talk about that scene in *Moonrise Kingdom*, where Edward Norton bends down and gets into this tiny little tent from the outside, and then you see him stand up inside this huge tent, full height, and you never question the fact that the tent has quadrupled in size. But it kind of works.

You accept the Wes version of reality.

I think you do.

Can you talk about lighting for fur, and also lighting for this translucent resin that they're working with for skin?

Fur, in and of itself, isn't difficult. It's an issue when you want a very flat look. Hair has a certain refractive quality, no manner how flat you light it; it's slightly incandescent because it's got that very high, very defined radius to it. It splits the light. So we've softened beyond soft, sometimes.

So besides the usual Wes Anderson reasons, you're pushing the light in that softer and softer direction because of the intricacy of these textures?

Yeah. And then sometimes Wes will want a really hot backlight, but then you end up with this fringe around the dogs.

Quite often, we shoot multiple passes on stuff, just to cover ourselves. So we would probably then shoot a green screen behind that puppet, with the backlight off, so that if we need to reduce that glow, we've actually got a non-glow version that we can dial down, in case Wes says, "Oh, that's a bit bright."

In terms of skin texture, I mean, translucency is brilliant because it gives a kind of more natural, subsurface scatter—the light is coming through as well as bouncing off. Clay is a very dense material. When we were making the *Wallace and Gromit* movies, Gromit the dog was an absolute bloody nightmare because he's almost white. And he would just clip out[11] sometimes. He'd be the brightest thing in the scene, and it was really difficult. So you know, silicone is actually quite a nice material to work with.

There are a lot of practicals[12] on some of these sets. I was looking at the Kabuki Theater, for example . . . those little lanterns seem like they're actually throwing quite a bit of light.

Yeah, they are. And in the last three or four years, LEDs have become color-accurate. But we've got a lot of tungsten fixtures as well because there's something about a small tungsten bulb that has a sense of glow and reality to it. So in the Municipal Dome, the big red lacquer theater, all those lanterns around the edge of the balconies are tungsten filaments. They're actually car brake bulbs.

What else are you lighting that scene with? Are people in the boxes actually being lit by the practicals for the most part?

Yeah, there's not much in there, actually. It's pretty low-key.[13] But there's a few bits and pieces. The idea is to make that sense of high lacquer red work in there. And so, you have to keep your angles of incidence[14] sorted out, so that you never see the source reflected in the shiny things. If you get your light in the wrong place, you of course see a hot spot. So everything's constantly being bent 'round, to make sure it doesn't do that.

There's a great passage in Jun'ichiro Tanizaki's *In Praise of Shadows*, where he talks about how lacquer was never meant to be seen in a museum, and it was never meant to be seen in daylight. He argues that these black lacquer boxes with gold dust, for example, were always intended for shadowy rooms in teahouses where just a corner of it will pop. The Municipal Dome set definitely feels like that when you're on it—there's a shadowiness to it, but subtle glimmers where the light strikes the lacquer.

Exactly. And we fight the flat look with that, as well. There's another little scene where each of the cabal members is in front of this incredibly elaborate lacquered panel, this amazing sort of high, almost sort of manga-style thing, super detailed. And the art department went through iteration after iteration of lacquering because Wes just wants a completely flat look, so there are no highlights on them at all. They might as well be printed on matte paper. [LAUGHS] There's no indication that they have any reflectance at all.

You have to just sense that the lacquer is there . . . [LAUGHS]

Yeah. But the process has been gone through. It's like the back of a statue. You never see it, but you know it's been carved.

There's such a contrast between interiors and exteriors on this film, it seems. Between the Trash Island look versus the nighttime interiors—

I think the interiors, you have to think of them as little jewel boxes, really. And Wes will invest a huge amount of time in the dressing—the wallpaper, the carpet, the light switch, even. I feel he's very happy in that zone. There's less fettling with the outdoor scenes which is probably fortunate, given how big they are.

ABOVE: Conrad Hall's cinematography is an artistic touchstone for Tristan Oliver. *Fantastic Mr. Fox* featured some Hall-inspired lighting effects, as seen in this comparison between *Fantastic Mr. Fox* and *Road to Perdition*.

OPPOSITE TOP: The Kabuki performance scene features several practicals—footlights on the stage, paper lanterns above.

OPPOSITE MIDDLE: Paper lantern practicals in the shot of the baseball team at the ramen shop.

OPPOSITE BOTTOM: A tiny lantern with a tiny bulb serves as a practical in this shot of Atari and Chief.

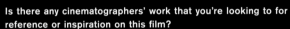

Is there any cinematographers' work that you're looking to for reference or inspiration on this film?

There's plenty of live-action DPs that I greatly admire. I very rarely take reference from other animated movies because, as I say, I don't want to make any concessions to the fact that these movies are animated. I always liked Conrad Hall—*Road to Perdition*, for example. I think he's an absolute genius. And Roger Deakins, I think, is fantastic.

Wes is really fond of *The Godfather*, and he's very fond of Kubrick. There's a lot of Kubrick everywhere, I think. Big, flat white spaces.

But sometimes he does let me do a quite dramatic-looking sequence. In *Fantastic Mr. Fox*, in the sewer, I was able to just kind of throw texture in there, and key lights and hard shadows and all that great stuff.

That does have kind of a *Road to Perdition* feel down there.

Good. Thank you very much. And on this, there's this enormous tracking shot where the two dogs go around the animal testing plant. It's over a minute long, and we're still shooting it, and it just goes from fabulous, ruined environment to fabulous, ruined environment. We just kind of bolted the sets on, and it just got longer and longer. And Wes just stopped sending me notes. I'm like, "Maybe this is it. Maybe this is the one he gives me!" [LAUGHS]

NOTES

1   *Key light:* the primary source of illumination for a scene.
    The placement of the key light is often motivated by the
    presence of some bright light source in the world of the
    story—a streetlamp, a television screen, the sun. The method
    that cinematographers call "three-point lighting" begins
    by determining the angle of the key light, and then plac-
    ing the "fill light" (to lighten the areas left in shadow by
    the key light) and "backlight" (a light that strikes the back
    of a character or object and helps separate them from the
    background). In many of Wes's shots, such as the overcast
    scenes on Trash Island, light seems to come evenly from all
    directions at once, or radiates from so many small points
    that distinguishing one of them as the key light becomes a
    bit of a false exercise.

2   Tristan is describing the depth of field. When you're focused
    on an object four or five feet from the camera, in the situ-
    ation he has in mind, the depth of field continues to an
    infinite distance in the background when the iris is set at a
    fairly typical stop (see below).

3   *Stop:* refers to a setting of the "aperture" (literally, the open-
    ing), the hole through which light passes into the body of
    the camera. The diameter of the aperture is controlled by a
    dilating metal structure inside the lens: the "iris." The iris in
    a camera lens is not dissimilar from the iris in the human
    eye; the aperture is sort of like the lens's pupil.
        The iris allows a photographer to adjust the brightness
    of the shot, but it also helps determine the shot's depth of
    field. The openness or closedness of the aperture can be
    described in stops or "f-stops," a set of ratios that fall along
    a fixed scale. f/2 describes a fairly wide-open aperture,
    which produces a shallower DOF. f/11 describes a more
    tightly closed aperture, which produces a deeper DOF.
    Changing from a higher to a lower f-stop number is called
    "opening up." Changing from a lower to a higher f-stop num-
    ber is called "stopping down."

4   *Depth of field:* When a lens focuses on an object, there will
    be some areas in front of and behind that object that also
    appear to be in sharp focus. The range that appears to be
    in focus is called the depth of field (DOF). There are optical
    laws governing the depth and shallowness of a shot's DOF:
        Proximity: When the object in focus is closer to the
    lens, the depth of field (DOF) is shallower. When the object
    in focus is further from the lens, the depth of field (DOF) is
    deeper.
        Lens length: When the lens is longer (has a longer
    "focal length," and shoots a narrower, zoomed-in view), the
    DOF is shallower. When the lens is wider (has a shorter
    "focal length" and shoots a wider, zoomed-out view), the
    DOF is deeper.
        Aperture: When the iris is more open, the DOF is shal-
    lower. When the iris is more tightly closed, the DOF is deeper.
        Any of these three factors can be adjusted to compen-
    sate for the others. A long lens means shallower DOF, but if
    the iris is very tightly closed, the effect can be counteracted.
    Here, Tristan notes that if an object (an actor, for example) is
    four or five feet from the camera, it's not hard to get a deep
    DOF, but when you're shooting puppets that are very close
    to the lens the DOF is often only an inch deep.

5   *Cooke:* Cooke Optics is a venerable British lens manufac-
    turer. Cooke lenses are sort of the Rolls-Royces of the film
    world—prestigious, precision-made, and pricey. Cinematogra-
    phers sometimes speak of the highly prized "Cooke look."

Chief stares down the barrel
of a 28mm prime

6   *Primes:* A prime lens is the opposite of a zoom lens. You can't change the length of a prime lens—it can't "zoom in." Prime lenses tend to perform much better than zoom lenses, but you have to swap out one lens for another whenever you want to go from, say, a wide-angle view to a telephoto view. This means you need a whole set of primes where you'd only need one zoom lens. Every make and model of prime lens has its own "look," and if you want all the shots of your film to match, you need to use a matching set of primes by the same manufacturer. And if you have forty cameras going, you're going to need more than one of each model. That comes out to a lot of lenses.

7   *DSLR:* DSLR stands for digital single-lens reflex, which is to say, a professional still-photography camera with inter-changeable lenses and a digital sensor. Canon and Nikon are popular brands. Professional photographers typically use high-end models, but there are affordable DSLR models for home use and point-and-shoot situations. The early twenty-first century ultra-low-budget independent filmmaking industry was built on the back of the DSLR, which can shoot high-definition video through high-quality lenses and costs less than most decent video cameras. And a DSLR can take still photos that are much higher resolution than that. Stop-motion filmmakers can achieve extremely high-resolution footage with a DSLR—footage that, if they were shooting live-action, they could only rival with a much more expensive high-end digital cinema camera.

8   *Shutter speed:* a measurement of the amount of time the camera's shutter is open—that is, how long the sensor is exposed to light, measured in fractions of a second.

9   *Color Temperature:* In this case, Tristan is using the term to refer to what's also called the white balance. Daylight, lamplight, and fluorescent light are different colors; setting the white balance means telling the camera to interpret a certain color of light as "white."

10   *ISO:* Originally, the ISO number specified the light sensitivity of different kinds of celluloid film. Now, ISO is an adjustable setting that determines the light sensitivity of the DSLR's digital sensor.

11   *Clip:* Any signal that exceeds the medium's ability to record it accurately can be said to "clip." Areas of an image that are too bright to be accurately reproduced by the camera's film or digital sensor will appear as solid white; the details of shape and texture will be lost. Bright areas that are starting to approach the point of clipping are described as "hot." A hot spot is not always a bad thing, if it's part of the look the cinematographer is after, but they're usually areas that need close monitoring.

12   *Practicals:* lights that are part of the set but also provide illumination for the shot.

13   *Low-key:* A term used in painting, still photography and cinema, with a number of slightly different definitions. In a low-key image, large areas of the composition have been left in darkness. In this case, Tristan is saying that the shot is lit with few lights, that he's eschewed some of the usual light sources that would be expected in three-point lighting, and that he's allowed the whole shot to be rather shadowy and low-toned, with few highlights and only subtle, partial illumination of the figures.

14   *Angle of incidence:* physics term for the angle of the incoming beam of light that strikes the object; a matter of concern for cinematographers, along with the angle of reflec-tion, which describes the direction of the outgoing beam that bounces off the object.

A PLEASANT SHOCK

AN INTERVIEW WITH SENIOR
VISUAL EFFECTS SUPERVISOR Tim Ledbury

TIM LEDBURY has been doing visual effects for feature films since *Harry Potter and the Prisoner of Azkaban*, working both in live-action and stop-motion films. He led the VFX department on *Fantastic Mr. Fox*. As the VFX supervisor on *Isle of Dogs*, Tim knows more than just about anyone about how the final shots will look. The fact that he can't declare anything for sure about the film's look is proof that, at this stage in the process, no one can.

OPPOSITE: Department heads watch footage in the production's main meeting room. The room was designed by Ab Rogers in keeping with the film's color palette and using wall-to-wall carpet that matches the red of the Municipal Dome.

ABOVE: Still frames from shots in progress, printed and mounted in the production's meeting room. Tim Ledbury, senior visual effects supervisor, gestures to these during our interview to point out things that will change when VFX starts work on the shots.

It's been emphasized to me many times that everything in this film is made physically. But here you are, the visual effects supervisor. What is it that you do as VFX on a film like this?

Oh, you've found me out now [LAUGHS]. Well, if you're doing standard sort of Hollywood fare, you're generating a lot of stuff in VFX. Wes likes to manipulate the frame quite a lot, but he wants to use real elements. In a way, it's actually harder than CG because CG you can completely control, whereas here, you have to get the elements on set to combine them together. So it's more of an old-fashioned sort of challenge, rather than generating things in the computer, which Wes hates.

So, you're not generating anything?

We manipulate. Might do the odd thing here and there, if it really comes to it. I mean, we did do some CG on *Fantastic Mr. Fox*, but that was emergency stuff, very minimal. It's more manipulating things. You might take a real set, stretch it a bit, and duplicate it. So that is technically CG, but really, you're just manipulating real things.

A lot of shots that started with the white sky look quite different now. Some of the ones on Trash Island have a ruined city in the background, or dark clouds on top, or trash trams moving around.

One shot, we put a river behind with barges on and a city in the background.

These layers are going to make the world feel fuller?

With some of these stark shots, you know, it's not going to take much. For instance, some of them will have a hill in the background and tiny little trash tram towers out of focus. And Wes wants all these hills to stack up so they form a block, but you see the depth of them, and he wants it hazed back. As soon as you put that in, it doesn't feel like the world is dropping off the end of the table. A lot of the interiors tend to stay the same, but exteriors will be changed quite a lot.

For the interiors—for the Municipal Dome scenes, for example—the raw footage I've seen is more true to how it's going to look in the end?

We'll put in atmosphere and misting. To make it look bigger. And again, subtle. It's supposed to give that hint of cigarette smoke, just to give that sort of haze, as you get in those big spaces. I mean, some of the sequences will stay quite stark. Some of these shots will have quite dramatic, colorful skies, but predominantly, the main pass of the animation is shot against white. It might be white, bright clouds, and that means we can stick in the cotton ball clouds later on.

We also do what we call "checkerboarding." Checkerboarding is, from a stop-motion point of view, if you need to do different lighting states, we'll slide in a green screen behind the puppet, take a frame, and that gives us the option to change the sky later.

There are also different lighting passes. For instance, when they're in the trash tram, traveling along, we shoot lighting passes, and then we can

ABOVE: A small-scale Rex puppet leaps with the help of a rig. The VFX department will remove it from the finished shot.

BELOW: Atari's plane takes off. The finished shot has been composited together from several elements: Mountains, towers, and fog were all separate layers.

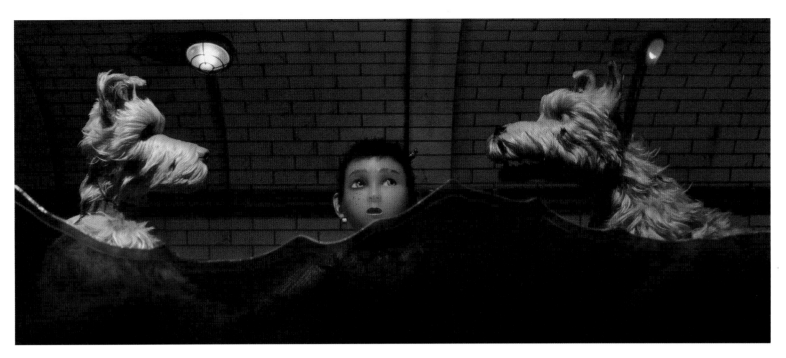

time them with things passing, when we shoot elements of towns and things like that. That's one of the advantages stop-motion over live-action gives us.

And beyond all that creative stuff, you have just the plain clean-up alone. The characters are running along with great big metal rigs sticking out of their backs. And cleaning up the mouth plugs can take, you know, three or four weeks on some of the characters—especially Tracy. She's a very talkative character. So there's a lot of resources going into, basically, getting the shot to look like nothing's happened. It's less glamorous, but it's a little bit of work.

Can you talk a bit about how the overall color palette of the film is starting to look in postproduction?

ABOVE: The trio bobbing along in the finished shot, rigs removed and a layer of "water" added.

BELOW: Spots, Atari, and Chief "float" with the help of rigs.

From a palette point of view, you know, Wes wants this quite white, stark feeling. So there's the shock of the white, and then it's punctuated with these quite colorful shots in the middle journey of the film. And the nighttime may or may not be purple or blue or black. Don't know yet.

It's still evolving?

I think it's almost a slow-motion version of what it must be like shooting live-action with Wes. In terms of choice of color palettes and things like that, he has a fairly strong idea. Generally, if he says one idea, and then he deviates away from it, you can almost know he's going to go back to it, because that was his first instinct. I mean, we went through many, many versions of skies on *Fox*. We did seventeen versions. But it does tend to go back to a similar sort of idea in the end. And in the end, it kind of looks like how the animatic's drawn. Sometimes he just wants to explore something. For instance, I'm saying a sky is going to be colorful, but it might not be. [LAUGHS]

I've wondered whether there might be some of those phantasmagoric matte-painting skies that you see in some of these classics of Japanese cinema, like *Kwaidan* and *Kagemusha*.

We did explore the idea of painted skies with him, but he was more interested in all of these plain skies, or with cotton balls in there. I mean, that could change. But I tried that; I did a whole document with the very things you're talking about. We even explored the idea of doing glass matte painting. But he wanted a physical model.

So you've actually seen much more footage than most folks on this set have—

Well, I have to see everything.

Right, yeah. [LAUGHS]

But I kind of like the idea that people haven't, because then, when they go away for a few months and come back, it's more of a pleasant . . . a pleasant shock.

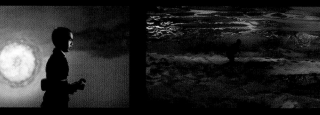

ABOVE: Early in the development stage, Wes recommended that his department heads watch *The Ballad of Narayama* (TOP). Like *Isle of Dogs*, it's a story of forced abandonment. In a small village a local tradition demands that old folk go off to die on a remote mountain. An elderly woman and her adult son reluctantly prepare for her journey. Made entirely inside the studio, with lush painted backdrops, Keisuke Kinoshita's film feels like a fable, stage play, or storybook. Exuberant color goes hand in hand with horrifying stories in many other great films of Japanese cinema history. Similar painted skies appear in Masaki Kobayashi's anthology of ghost stories, *Kwaidan* (SECOND FROM TOP). Kurosawa played with stylized skies in late films like *Dodes'ka-den* (THIRD FROM TOP, LEFT), *Kagemusha* (THIRD FROM TOP, RIGHT), and *Madadayo* (ABOVE).

LEFT: The dogs of the Hero Pack are introduced.

OPPOSITE: A golden sky over Trash Island. In an earlier version of this scene, the sky was white and the mound of trash appeared as a dark silhouette (TOP). Atari lands on Trash Island, with silvery clouds above and a silvery sea below (MIDDLE). Atari and Chief run below ominous orange clouds at the causeway (BOTTOM).

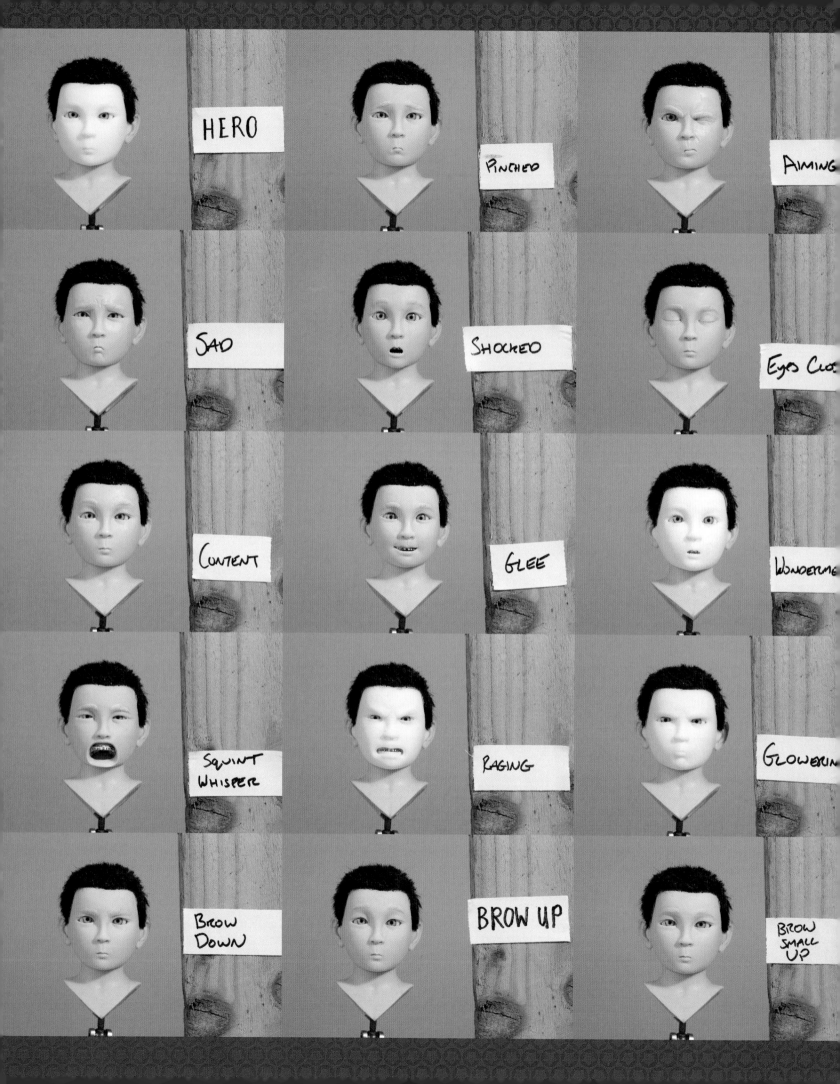

STRUCTURED PLAY

AN INTERVIEW WITH
ANIMATION DIRECTOR Mark Waring

A **KEY ASPECT** of animation director Mark Waring's job is to keep the puppets' performances consistent across a team of twenty-five animators. He worked as a supervising animator on *Fantastic Mr. Fox* and now finds himself with an even bigger responsibility on *Isle of Dogs*. "My job is to collect all of those thoughts and ideas Wes has expressed and make that one coherent vision that gets put through the animation team," Mark says. "By now, it's almost like I have an inner Wes." Mark gave me his thoughts on the film's editing process, Wes's directing style, and what *Isle of Dogs* will be like as a finished film.

How did you go about setting the animation style?

At the very start I had initial conversations with Wes about how to establish a look. He was very insistent about trying to keep a handmade feel. He made it clear that you would have to see the craft. For the replacement face masks and replacement mouths that he wanted to have a go with, he definitely wanted a sense that they didn't have super-smooth changes. From the outset, we wanted something that was literally a pop from one face to another, something to help you recognize the handmade-ness of the process. Another key criteria was that he wanted to see the crawl in the fur of the animals.

There are certain moments where you look at what he's doing and think, "Why are you doing that? Why are you making that continuity completely jump?" And then you go, "Oh, of course, he's doing it deliberately." He is trying to create something new and different and he's doing that all the time.

I think on a live-action film, people always wonder how much of what makes it into the film is intentional, and how much just happened that way. But with a timeframe that's this long, and happening this incrementally—you're saying that if we notice something, it's almost certainly on purpose. That very few things could be merely an oversight on a timeframe of, like, a whole month for a shot.

Oh, yeah. Every single tiny detail has got Wes's fingerprints all over it. You know, for example, take that bottle of water, the color of that top, how many little ridges are on it. All the details have been ticked off. There's nothing there by chance. It's absolutely Wes.

I suppose you've been introduced to the database?

Tell us about it.

Mark whips out a tablet and opens a program that he says contains "the whole film," sorted by shot, containing everything that's been shot so far with animatic frames standing in for what hasn't. In the program, every note that Wes has made on a given shot is attached to it and displayed below it.*

Mark clicks on a shot at random. For this one shot, Mark scrolls through several screens of notes, all responses to questions that have been asked. "So that nothing gets lost in the system. We have a trackable record of every single conversation we've had with him." There are notes on lighting, art direction, animation, camera.

I think that's probably why he's done another one of these films. . . . He has absolute total control over absolutely everything. I remember thinking after *Fox* that he would do another one because he's almost found his ideal medium. It's all about the detail. And when he's on a live-action shoot . . .

There are acts of God.

Yeah. If it's raining we can't get that shot, we've got to do something else. Here, he's got control over everything, every single tiny detail. What's not to like? He's got it all. So of course, he's going to do another one.

And I think that's because he feels comfortable in this world. Which means he can experiment with stuff. Again, he's almost trying to build in those deliberately wrong things. You might not notice that at all. But then if you do notice it, you go, "That's interesting. You could have avoided that quite easily, but you haven't . . ." He's playing within that structure.

I think that's an underappreciated and too often maligned key quality of a director—the ability to keep playing. That they actually have to build a system that will allow them to do that, even if it does sometimes make other people's jobs harder. But preserving that ability to play, and building a structure that will allow you to do that—if no one does that, the film won't work. You need the player-in-chief, kind of.

Yeah. That's it. The rules are there, and he's made very, very strict rules for himself that he doesn't break, unless it's absolutely necessary. And then if

ABOVE: Atari emerges from the bottle hovel set.

OPPOSITE: Mark Waring works with set dressers Collette Pidgeon and Jo McDonald on

it's almost like an impossible thing, he'll say, "Just do it, you can make it work."

Yeah. When you say rules, we're talking about the sort of strict frontal shots, things like that?

Yeah, all that sort of stuff, because it is limiting. But it's a structure that he's placed there himself. So to then see him play within that structure, it's interesting to sort of see how far he lets himself go with that.

Right, because a game is nothing but a set of rules. Rules make a game. And you can't play a game if there are no rules to constrain your behavior—creating rules can give you creative voltage.

Yes, because sometimes it'll spark up something where you think, "Wow, how do we do this? How can we make that work?" Everything is about problem-solving. You know, the day-to-day issue for everybody is basically this puzzle.

Wes sometimes deliberately sort of tests you. Like, "I know that's difficult. I know that's going to be really hard. But you're going to do it."

And he does always listen at the end, it seems . . . ?

Oh, absolutely. It's not like he compromises, but there are certain things he will listen to, and say, "Actually, you know what?" Like Tristan, for instance, will say, "I just cannot physically get focus that close to the lens on this lens. I just physically

can't do that." And then Wes will go, "OK, all right, well, we'll try and find another solution." But he'll try and get as close as he can to that, you know, by pushing people just to try that little bit more.

Actually, he sometimes goes further than you would go, and further than *he* would go. Say, a puppet is in a certain position. And he'll say, "No, no, take it further." Like, "Take it off frame." You know it's not going to work then. *He* knows it's not going to work. But at least he knows that, now, that's too far.

Theater directors do this too. "Play it too big and let me see what that looks like, and then I'll know what the right place is." Calibrating, I guess.

Exactly. It's always about giving him options, like maybe giving him three things. One's ridiculous, one's not enough, and one you think is about right.

I see this note here in the database about "trimming 3 and 3" off something—what does "3 and 3" mean?

That will be a note for the editor. So just please trim 3 and 3, at top and tail of a shot.

So the note is talking about trimming three frames of animation.

Yeah. As we're talking frames. You would think, "Oh, that's not much room then if it's literally just compiling one shot after the other, and there's a couple of frames of overlap."

Because you've got "handles," those extra frames of action at the ends in case the editors need more than you planned for?

Yes. We gave eight frames at the front and ten at the end, so there's not a lot to play with. But the amount of fiddling we do . . .

So there is some editing going on, as far as adjusting—?

There is loads of editing. There's loads of stuff that we move around, change positions, try timing options, retime stuff.

Traditionally, in live-action shooting, the most you're going to get during the shoot is something like a rough assembly cut. But you're saying at this point Wes and [editor] Ralph Foster are doing fine work on the edit? Three frames seems like pretty fine-grain work.

Pretty much. . . . Because we have to do that to a certain degree, because a lot of the time, we have to know where we are before we can go on to the next shot. And Wes has already spent quite a lot of time working on the edit in the animatic, to hit certain beats at certain times. It's sort of like music.

So Wes has been partitioning off the postproduction part of his brain as well, even while you're shooting.

Oh, very much. I mean, once the shoot's complete, there will probably be an overview, a re-edit, to tighten up.

But it's pretty close already.

Yeah. It's not like, "Oh, you're going to add another shot in here, and we're going to change this around."

I wonder if you could also speak to some of the differences between *Fox* and *Isle of Dogs*, too, as you see them from your position.

Fox was already an established children's story, even though he adapted it. It's got Wes Anderson's fingerprints all over it, but you sort of knew that's what it was.

But *Isle of Dogs*, being a completely new thing—it's interesting. Because I'm still not quite sure that everybody really knows the number of levels that this is playing at. Not that *Fox* wasn't, but you know, it was a children's book. There were some added bits and pieces that Wes obviously had brought in about family relationships and themes that he's put in all his other films. Which this one also has.

But there's lots of stuff in this. Lots of levels—topical themes about leadership, about authority, about animal cruelty, about . . . almost touching on, sort of, genocide. That sort of treatment of individuals or groups, approaches to life and how you deal with that . . . I mean, you can go down into those levels, which are all there in the film. And it'd be interesting, when we've actually completed it, how much of that punches through, and how much Wes *wants* to punch through as well, or whether he wants to keep

it a little bit hidden. . . . Whether it'll just be there if you notice it or whether he wants to bring that out a little bit more upfront, to push that forward.

And lot of that is going to depend on scoring and a lot of things we can't know yet . . .

Yes, all those sorts of things. But you can sort of feel that there's a definite sense that he's wanting this in there, and he's steering it to show that sort of stuff. He's not shying away from it.

I think people don't associate that with him, although I think they very much could. It has sort of always been there. I think a lot of people found it to be more pronounced in *The Grand Budapest Hotel* than it had been in a lot of previous movies because there was quite a dark ending there. But I don't think this is what people may be expecting on this film.

No. I don't think so either. I think they're probably expecting another *Fantastic Mr. Fox* . . . "Oh, it's talking dogs." But it will be so much more than that.

LEFT: **A mass of frightened dogs on set, Oracle chief among them**

OPPOSITE: **"We had to try to find out what these dogs were like, what the rules were,"** Mark says. **"Do they do human things? There were a few bits that were storyboarded where they were doing human activities—when they were building a raft, they were doing carpentry, holding saws with their teeth, and picking things up. I think one of them had a paintbrush. There were only a few little concessions to that, even then. But now they're purely dogs in a dog's world."**

ACCOMPANYING THE DRAMA

AN INTERVIEW WITH
TAIKO COMPOSER/ADVISOR Kaoru Watanabe

AFTER KAORU WATANABE graduated from the Manhattan School of Music with a degree in jazz flute and saxophone, he did a musical and cultural one-eighty: he moved to Japan and joined the elite taiko ensemble Kodo. Kaoru was the first non-native Japanese person to join the group. "I'd been going through a lot of these big existential moments, growing up Japanese American, playing jazz and classical music, thinking about my connection to those musics—then moving to Japan, trying to understand traditional Japanese music, and where my place is."

OPPOSITE: Portrait of Kaoru Watanabe, by Bryce Craig

ABOVE: Character design of the three taiko drummers, by Félicie Haymoz

After nearly a decade with Kodo, he moved back to the United States, where he works in his own hybrid form: both Japanese and Western, traditional and contemporary. Kaoru spoke about working with Wes to create the traditional and not-so-traditional sound of the *Isle of Dogs* score.

Are you actively working on your pieces for the film now, or are you done with that?

We're in the thick of it, as it were. I just had some people over in my studio to record a little voice thing.

There's a vocal somewhere?

Yeah, there's a scene where there's maybe ten seconds of a play that's happening . . .

Oh, the Kabuki performance?

Yes, exactly. There are kids singing, and they needed to fill that with a song, so I threw together a little song. A friend's kids are actually coming over in a couple hours to record some stuff.

So what does your role on this film look like? How has it developed?

It's been changing a lot over the last year or so. A year ago Wes and I were in the studio, and I would play a rhythm, and he would ask me to add or take away parts of it, or try different ideas and sounds and patterns. I thought that would be it. But then, over the course of the last year, he's been emailing to say, "Can you come up with this kind of vibe or this kind of rhythm?" Or, "I need a little snippet of this sort of thing," and I would send things. It's been a really interesting process.

Did you know Wes before this project?

No, the music supervisor, Randy Poster, is the one who introduced me to Wes. After half a year of talking to Randy, one day Randy emails me and says, "I'd like to bring Wes to your studio, tomorrow." And I was like, "Uh, OK!"

So Wes shows up. And within about five minutes of him walking through the door, we were jamming. He'll be the first to say that he's not a musician and definitely not a drummer. But he is a very intuitive

with music. I handed him sticks, and he started playing and coming up with these little figures and riffs, and I started improvising with him. I didn't know that he was working on a movie about, you know, *this* movie. But then, within five minutes of jamming, he says, "So when can you come to the studio?" And I was like, "What? Why would I come . . . ?" [LAUGHS] I was like, "What are you talking about?" It was a really wonderful meeting. I've been a huge fan for years. Musically, we were able to just kind of fall right into each other's groove, if you will.

It seems like drums are a big motif in the film. I've only seen a bit of footage in its early stages, but there was a scene where we first meet the Hero Pack. It was scored with a temp track, which if I identified it right, was Fumio Hayasaka's opening drum music from *Seven Samurai*. It seems like drums might be functioning as kind of a heartbeat for the film, from what I can tell—in the scenes I saw, it was very subtle but almost constant, and it kept the pulse rate of the scene up. Are drums primarily what you're doing on this film?

I consider myself a flute specialist as much as, if not more than, a drummer. And half-jokingly, every time I see Wes, I suggest, "You know, we could really use more flutes." [LAUGHTER] To be honest, I don't know how much drumming is in the whole movie. It might just be two minutes in the middle of the movie for all I know. But it seems to me that, at this point, the opening sequence is going to be drums, and some of the key moments in the movie

ABOVE LEFT: **Wes has always taken pleasure in the earnest dramatic endeavors of adolescents—the R-rated stage adaptations of the Max Fischer Players, Margot Tenenbaum's violent juvenalia, Suzy Bishop's turn as the raven in *Noye's Fludde*.**

ABOVE RIGHT: **A snapshot of the Kabuki choir, supervised by their teacher**

OPPOSITE LEFT: **The pudgy adolescents of Megasaki High give it their darnedest. It was this footage of a Kodo performance taken from a Wowow television broadcast and uploaded to YouTube, that inspired Wes to film this sequence. It's the video that galvanized Andy Gent back in 2015.**

OPPOSITE MIDDLE: **The svelte men of Kodo, consummate masters of the taiko drum, send ripples of frisson through the audience.**

OPPOSITE FAR RIGHT: **Portrait of Kaoru Watanabe, by Yuki Kokubo**

are going to be very drum-heavy. I've just created a bunch of stuff over the last year, and I don't know what's going to come out of it. I'm very excited to see what happens.

So, the taiko boys that open the movie—is that you?

I'm not a twelve-year-old boy, but . . .

[LAUGHS] No, no, is it your *music*?

Yeah, yeah, that is my music [LAUGHS]. Friends of mine saw the trailer, and they jokingly asked me if I wore one of those motion detection suits . . .

Oh, motion capture, yeah.

And I did not [LAUGHS]. But I do remember when we were recording last year, Wes had his iPhone out, and he was videotaping me quite a bit, from various angles. So . . . I don't know how much of me is in there.

When he first approached me, he did talk about that scene. At that point, it was just a storyboard drawing, but he said there's going to be three kids, and we even talked about whether I knew any kid drummers that he could film playing, and we went back and forth about that. It's interesting that he did have that image very early on in the whole process.

One thing about the type of drumming used in the opening sequence: It's not necessarily traditional. I always consider that more of a contemporary thing, something that started post–World War II.

In traditional contexts, taiko drums were always used as accompaniment to something else. Whether it was for theater, like Kabuki or Noh, festival music, or accompaniment to dancing, singing, or sacred rituals, the drumming was always one element within something larger. Not until the 1950s did people start taiko groups, where the feature and the focus is primarily on the drumming. So if you've ever seen a group of taiko drummers on stage and their playing is not part of a ritual or theater, more than likely, that's something that's only been around since the 1950s.

And you've performed in that kind of group, right?

I have—Kodo is considered one of the top contemporary taiko performing arts ensembles. But having said that, going back to the idea of what is traditional, groups like Kodo study various festival music, Noh theater, Kabuki theater, and other older traditional musics, and then incorporate elements from them into their performance.

So you might look at a piece, and while the origins of the piece might be traditional, the presentation of it is contemporary. It's a fine line—a blurred line—of whether something is a traditional thing or a new thing. It gets a bit confusing. Kabuki theater is definitely a traditional art form. And I guess Wes just had the idea of throwing that into a school play, which is, I think, great. However, the drumming in that scene, with the guys standing behind their drums, that's definitely not how Kabuki musicians would play the drums.

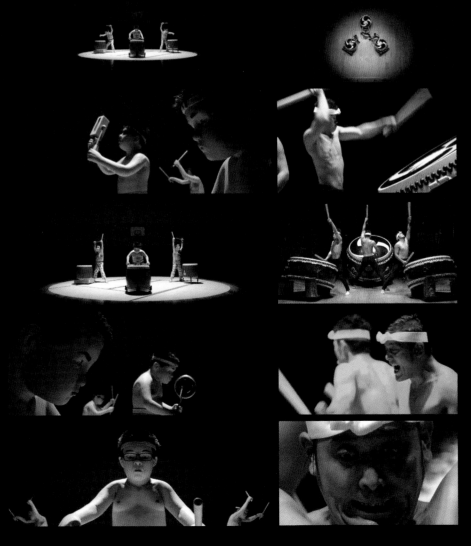

This movie is set in the twentieth century, getting released in the twenty-first, but as we've been discussing, it has a lot of nods to, sometimes remixes of, traditional Japanese arts, between taiko, Kabuki, sumo, lots of others. How are these traditional arts perceived in Japan today? How often do they come up in contemporary pop-cultural settings, as in a film like this? What do people make of it when they do?

Things like sumo wrestling or Kabuki theater are still very common. I mean, sumo wrestling maybe is more for the older generations of people, but everybody knows who the top sumo wrestlers are. You might not have teenage kids tweeting about it or anything, but it's a very present thing in Japanese culture.

It's funny, when you're watching a lot of the old Japanese films from the '50s that *Isle of Dogs* is referencing, you see a lot of little kids watching television and getting really whooped up about sumo.

[LAUGHS] Right, I'm not sure if that's still the case now. Kabuki theater is interesting because a lot of its stars are also in movies. And they're on TV or on billboards selling tea or Coca-Cola or whatever.

They're celebrities. And it's a beautiful thing, you know? They're coming from a five-hundred-year-old traditional art form, but they're also ubiquitous in pop culture as well.

I haven't seen the sumo scene in the movie, so I don't know how it's being presented. The Japanese are very conscious of details and proud of their culture, right?

And Wes is obviously famous for his attention to detail. When I saw the Kabuki scene for the first time, I noticed right away that the drummers were actually all wrong, that it wasn't the right type of drumming for Kabuki theater. But this is a school presentation of it so it actually makes perfect sense that if you couldn't find these specialized drummers, you'd have to use a more common form of drumming . . .

The kids at school who already know how to drum.

Exactly. So it didn't really cause any sort of conflict or confusion. When I saw it I was like, "Oh, that's fun. That's funny." [LAUGHS] You know? "That's an interesting take on it." But it didn't look wrong or misguided, in that sense.

You've recently worked on something for Martin Scorsese's *Silence*, **yes?**

Yes. That was another one of those things, where I spent the whole day in the studio trying different ideas. In the end, to be very honest, they used very little of what I did. Very, very spacious, just a very gentle *don . . . don . . .* You know? **[LAUGHS]** Just single hits for about two minutes. When I saw the movie, part of me was a little disappointed. I had recorded all these different rhythms and different ideas. For my ego's sake, I wanted to hear more of me. But in terms of the overall effect, of course, Martin knows what he's doing. It turned out to be very nice—perfect, actually.

But it's wonderful because, as I mentioned earlier, the function of the taiko drums, historically, has always been accompaniment to something. While they didn't have films hundreds of years ago, taiko were used to help convey a story in the theater or create the proper mood and energy in festivals—it's always been a tool of communication between people and their community, people and their gods, people and their ancestors. These kinds of functions have always been a part of taiko drumming. What we did for this movie actually falls right in line with the roots of what the drums are about, you know?

In my own performance, there's a lot more improvisation, a lot more musical complexity. The music is about conveying the spirit of the compositions or the emotions of the players. However, for a movie soundtrack, or even for traditional theater, the music should be a little bit more repetitive, less obtrusive. The music doesn't have to speak for itself; it's more about supporting the feeling of the drama or the mood of whatever's happening, right?

I think a lot of composers who come from concert music and move into film work tend to notice what you're talking about—the degree to which they're forming an ensemble with other art forms, with cinematography, and with editing and whatnot.

Yes. In film, with so many other moving parts in it and with so many different elements, it's easy for everything to become garbled if the music is too complex. It's definitely a different kind of perspective and, in a way, closer to the older traditional perspective, for me to be working on a movie

soundtrack. And I do love it. It's been really a great learning experience for me and a lot of fun.

Oh, actually, I remembered something I was thinking about earlier.

What's that?

I mentioned how very quickly Wes and I started to jam together, and then soon after we were in the studio together, and how he asked me to lay down a rhythm, and I would play one, and he might say, "OK, something maybe slower . . . something faster . . . maybe more busy. Less busy." And I would try to accommodate. He would get very specific: "OK, instead of hitting two on the high drum and then three on the low side, how about two on the high, then one on the low, then two more high . . ."

It was surprising how specific he got, musically. It was kind of shocking. I've worked with a lot of different non-musicians, but he really heard something in his mind very clearly. And in the end, it was always *good*. It always felt like, "Oh yeah, this is a good and balanced use of the different drums . . ."

I've had the great pleasure of working with some really, I guess you could consider, genius artists and musicians, and I would definitely rank Wes in there, you know? Someone who, without being a specialist or a musician or a composer, has a very clear idea of what he likes. But without being completely married to it. We would try things and like them, but as soon as we'd start to feel, "Oh, maybe this isn't the right path," we'd discard it and move on to something else. So it was very easy and fun to spend all that time with him, working all these ideas out. And of course, I think all that's reflected in his movies too: The balance, the pacing, and the timing is always impeccable. Often startling and surprising and very moving but somehow all in order.

What you're saying is very much like what you'd want to hear from an actor about a good director. That, at the same time, the performance feels like it is totally yours, but also that the director was totally attentive to everything you were doing. That he was constantly involved and making changes, but based on exactly the things you would want someone to be noticing and being attentive to in your performance—demonstrating that he's paying attention to the good things you want him to see about it too.

I hadn't thought of it that way, but that's exactly correct. Yes, he never offered an idea in a way that made me feel like I'd made a mistake, just "Oh, what about trying it this way?" It was very easy to make adjustments. I'm not an actor, so I hadn't thought of it in those terms, but that's exactly how it felt.

Wes Anderson with the *Isle of Dogs* puppets in Berlin

SURPRISED BY WHAT IT IS

A SECOND INTERVIEW WITH Wes Anderson

○○○○○○○○○○○○○○○○

'M IN PARIS to meet Wes, and it feels right. Wes Anderson makes sense in Paris. The city feels production-designed, done in a palette of cream and slate blue, weathered with a perfect patina, all the buildings rhyming. Gorgeous compositions form right before your eyes every time you round the corner. The balcony scene in "Hotel Chevalier" could have been shot out of any window.

We meet outside a nearly empty café on a nondescript side street in Paris's Montparnasse neighborhood. Wes's look is summer-sharp—an off-white pinstripe linen suit, a windowpane check shirt, yellow and purple on white, and his signature tan chukka boots. At one point, he slips on a pair of round, thick-framed, olive-green glasses to look at his phone.

When Wes Anderson looks at you, you feel seen. He notices things. At one moment a breeze threatens to topple a menu at a nearby table, and he gently and instinctively lays it flat. At another, a young woman mounts a bicycle with the strap of her bag hanging out of the front basket, and Wes

quietly voices his concern, far out of her earshot: "I hope that strap is not going to get caught in the tire. . . . I would put it in the basket, myself." He's calm, intent, and attentive, his energy tilted ten degrees forward in its seat. There's a lightness to his presence, which calls to mind Kristofferson's mantra from *Fantastic Mr. Fox*: as if he "weighs less than a slice of bread."

In conversation, Wes is a listener. He wants to see where you're going to take something; often, he lets an idea hang in the air, content not to resolve it. When he says "maybe," he really means maybe—it may or may not be, he'd have to think about it. When he says, "I don't know," it has the air of "Ask me in two years." He's reticent to say anything definitive, either about his

work or someone else's. It seems that he treats ideas the same way he treats a choice about an edit or a sound effect or a color—looking at options, wanting to see things laid out against each other, passing over some, turning one over in his hand..

It's a workday, and the crew at 3 Mills is shooting, but we're taking the studio's lunch break to sneak in a talk over coffee. Despite the fact that his phone is actively filling up with questions from set, he manages to stay surprisingly present. A waitress comes and takes our orders—a *café* for me, a *café crème* for him.

So this shoot is two years, as opposed to, say, six weeks. I know that when a director does a six-week shoot, you have to be intensely "on" for that period of time, and then there's breathing room on the other side. What is it like to be "on" for two years?

井の中の蛙大海を知らず

海の物山の物

大海は芥を択ばず

行き当たりばったり

日和よう

帰心矢のごとし

荒野

ボイド・フラッ゛ンセ゛ー

大海元史

Atari and the gang before the Yamato-e–style mural in the Tug-boat on the Dune

Well, you're really not because it's such a totally different process. It's not like a live-action movie. Everything happens simultaneously. We have numerous shots going at once, and the process of editing, mixing, visual effects—all the things that are normally postproduction are happening—

All at the same time.

Right. It's just much less *intense*. Everything's going to happen very slowly anyway. On a live-action movie, we might have eight or ten or twelve weeks of actual, full-fledged, real, whole-crew shooting, and then little bits that get spread out into the preproduction time, and we've kind of tried to make little special units to break up the shoot in some way, so it's not always a whole big gang. With a live-action movie, I don't like to work anywhere near where anybody lives. I want us all to be on location.

Which maybe creates a sort of summer-camp atmosphere.

Well, anyway, if we are all away from home, we sort of are forced to . . .

To do *it*.

Yes, to just live in the movie. With an animated movie like this, you wouldn't want it that way. It takes too long. It wants to be incorporated into everybody's normal life.

Sure, that makes sense. My impression visiting 3 Mills was that it's almost like an incredibly efficient, well-oiled . . . office, that you go to. Isle of Dogs Industries.

Yes, right.

Our waitress comes out to our sidewalk table bearing our coffee, depositing my espresso and Wes's café crème—which, rather than the traditional espresso with a side of cream, has been made into a cappuccino. If you are a coffee person, it is decidedly not the same thing.

Wes briefly considers clarifying his order, trying to make eye contact with the waitress.

Over the course of a second, he weighs the cost in social attrition of requesting a new drink, deciding not to press on it the moment he can tell the waitress is uninterested: "Oui, c'est bon, c'est bon." *When she saunters back into the café, Wes discloses wryly,* "This is not really what I meant by café crème."

He's not bothered in any serious way. But there was a moment in which he was presented with something small but not-quite-right, in which he had to decide whether to take the step to make it right or to let it go.

This was my only in-person glimpse of Wes Anderson practicing the art of directing.

(He did not accept my offer to switch coffees.)

I've just come from seeing all these sets at the studio, and right now the film feels very expansive to me. Do you see *Isle of Dogs* as an epic?

Hmm. Well, there's a big, dramatic, kind of political event. There's quite a long journey these animals take. You know, I don't know how long the events of this story take place, from when this boy crashes onto this island, until the end of it all. For all I know, it's three days. I don't know. They do go on a sizeable journey. And there are a lot of characters, I guess. There are crowds of dogs and people and soldiers and fleets of vehicles and so on.

But you know, really, what makes it epic is that it feels epic when somebody watches the thing, and I have no idea whether it will or not. Most of this movie is a boy and five dogs doing simple things together. Dogs having conversations. Most of it is like that. I don't really know how epic that could be.

When we were writing the script, we had the sense that they'd made a vast journey, but once we kind of figured out the shots of it, I realized, you know: they don't come across many other dogs. Sort of none. There's Jupiter and Oracle, two dogs they meet along the way—

And then there are also the former lab test dogs.

When they arrive. That's the end of that big journey across the island. But somehow, I pictured that there were going to be all these little episodes along

the way . . . and we don't really have that. It wasn't ever even in the script, I just *thought* it was. So I don't know, we'll see how it feels.

I wanted to talk a bit with you about some of the film references that you started with or that you've found yourself returning to for this.

There's a sort of ongoing list of movies we've been keeping and expanding with Jason and Roman, Jeremy [Dawson] and Paul Harrod, maybe Andy Gent, a few people like that. I don't think any of the cast had anything to do with these; not really that many people. But it's all a couple of years ago now.

During the last movie, *The Grand Budapest Hotel*, we had a whole bunch of movies in the place where we all lived, and people *would* watch them, the actors would watch them. But those things sort of find their way in in the beginning, and then really, it's just about, "What are we doing tomorrow morning? And how are we going to get from this to this in time, and what's going to happen after that?"

Right. So here I am, trying to have a conversation with you about all these influences, and you're just worried about the shots they're setting up this afternoon. And I understand the difficulty of that.

It's a different phase of the thing. It's not like anybody desperately wants to get movie references into the movie in the first place. Not at all. It's just about, "What is it supposed to be like?" And now we *know* what it's supposed to be like. We've done most of the movie, or a lot of the movie, and it's all sort of in front of us. But it still evolves and grows, and there's always . . . When you *need* something, when we reach a point in the movie and there's a blank space, then you sort of go through the Rolodex of "What did we have in mind in the first place?"

I was watching *Fantastic Mr. Fox* with your commentary, and you mentioned something about how you had Mark Rothko paintings in mind for the skies. And I realized, a reference can

come from anywhere. It can be anything. It doesn't have to be meant to be caught. It's to help the people designing the thing and making the thing know what you were envisioning, and it isn't necessarily some kind of Easter egg, or something that you're putting in there for someone to find.

No. The only time I ever put in something that I want people to find is if I think it might be funny if somebody saw it.

Well, the Hokusai wave with the dogs on it, that's in this movie. People will see that.

Yes. At first, Rothko was just a way of describing something . . . but then I thought, well, it could be kind of funny if somebody actually recognized it that way. But it's not, really. I mean, you probably wouldn't see it that way, if you saw the movie.

Are there intentional ones that you've put into *Isle of Dogs*, then, that you want people to catch?

I don't think so. Not that I can think of.

I talked to a lot of people at 3 Mills about Ozu—some of his films were on the list of movies you sent around to the department heads. Your style has been compared to Ozu's in the past, because his shots are kind of straight-on and the sets are sort of impeccably dressed, with everything in its place. Do you feel any affinity to Ozu's work?

Maybe it's mostly a comparison about something on the surface, something that people might latch onto to kind of categorize.

In the case of most movies, the identity of the thing comes mostly from the story that was cooked up, and the characters you wanted to bring to life, and the setting and the world of it, and, eventually: how are we going to do it? And usually for us, for our little group, that's going someplace and wandering around there, and then going home, and then going back, and thinking some more about it, and circling around it, and slowly finding it.

ABOVE: **One of the layered skies in *Fantastic Mr. Fox*. Wes made reference to the paintings of abstract expressionist Mark Rothko when describing the look he wanted.**

OPPOSITE: **The cesspool from *Drunken Angel* (TOP) reappears on Trash Island (BOTTOM).**

And so, the question "How do you want to frame the shots?" is just the tiniest, tangential sliver of what you're doing. You could say, "Well, Kurosawa wouldn't do it like this, but Ozu might." Except Ozu would never have the slightest interest in making this movie. He wasn't really the key inspiration, even though he's a director whose work I love very much. We thought about Kurosawa every day.

So the comparison is perhaps a bit superficial . . . ?

It's about shots. Which is a perfectly reasonable thing to compare.

Well, I mean, the phrase "mise-en-scène," or what's placed in the scene, in the shot—I did get quite a sense of that when I visited 3 Mills and I saw that each individual set inside the studio is essentially a proscenium stage. That there's a camera at one end of it, and you have built exactly what is going to go in the frame a lot of the time.

Especially with an animated movie, that's sort of what you do. But even with a live-action movie, especially if it's a period movie, you can usually only go so far outside the frame before you've left the decade or maybe century. If you work on soundstages and you build big sets, and you're a big movie, then sometimes you can say, "Let's turn around. Let's look over here and do this part another way we hadn't thought of." But usually for us, most of the time, there isn't a whole set, because, well, we didn't build it.

And that decision not to build more than appears in the shot is a producing decision. That's something that I think is under-known about you, that you're producing, and that you are very conscious about how you're spending your resources.

Part of the thing I like is figuring out our systems and methods. That's sort of entertaining to me. And often I feel like those things become part of what the movie is. But the people I know who've been doing movies for a while, they tend to be pretty nuts-and-bolts about how this is going to happen. Maybe in the case of some of the big Hollywood-movie filmmakers, those people might have a producer who runs the operation, and the director is more like a high-level employee, and they go away to a trailer, and they wait until the light is ready, and so on. But maybe not? I expect even somebody like Steven Spielberg, the biggest big-movie kind of filmmaker, helps formulate the plan for how it's going to happen, and he's very efficient. That's my impression from people who've worked with him.

That makes sense. But then there's also the artistic choice to build more—like Kurosawa would build sets that were bigger than necessary, actually, and he would say that it would impart some kind of ineffable something to the actors, that they would know that their character's bedroom was in the other room if they needed to go to their bedroom.

That sounds good to me. You want to make sure every drawer in the chest has something in it. Maybe something interesting, too. Visconti, where every layer of the clothing is of the period, and that sort of thing. I'm sure actors feel that and respond to that and love that.

You've said that *Isle of Dogs* is your homage to Japanese cinema, but that Kurosawa is at the center of it, and maybe we can talk about his directing style a little. I guess maybe I'll start by saying that the first Kurosawa film I saw was *Drunken Angel*.

That's a good one.

It is. I was struck by the conceit of having this film sort of set around this cesspool—that that's where it starts. And that film is full of so many moments that are managed so carefully, that are sort of choreographed. His use of music—those guitar songs that somebody plays across the water.

Yes. We have one of those in our movie.

I've only seen a little bit of *Isle of Dogs*, but I recognized that song immediately.

Well, I don't know whether we'll use it, really, or we might redo it. It's just the opening titles of *Drunken Angel*. But that one I love. I always loved that setting you're describing—this filthy slum on some kind of canal. But it's very artificial, you know? It's a set.

They also made a stage play of it—with the same actors, with Kurosawa.

Is it based on a play?

I don't think so. I think they wrote it as an original script, but then sort of took the show on the road.

Adapted it.

They did sort of a *Drunken Angel* tour. But you can see how that would have worked because it has those very—

It's quite confined.

I'm thinking of the brilliance of that first confrontation between [Takashi] Shimura and [Toshiro] Mifune, the way they really built those characters to clash.

Yes. Even the dramatic structure of it is sort of suited for the stage.

One thing that's funny about Kurosawa, and maybe you don't even hear about this in your circles, but in critical circles

Kurosawa's crew and colleagues described him as probably the "world's greatest editor." His techniques shaped the course of film editing in Japan and America; modern action filmmaking can trace a straight line back to *Seven Samurai*'s battle scenes. His cuts reveal a keen sense of weight, momentum, and visual congruence. One of his most famous sequences shows six of the seven samurai running to the rescue (ABOVE). The rapid match cuts emphasize their common speed, shape, and purpose. The Hero Pack's journey to the Middle Fingers (OPPOSITE) makes a nod to this editing pattern.

Kurosawa was also fond of using an "axial cut" for emphasis—the camera doesn't change its angle of view but jumps straight forward or straight backward for a new shot. Kurosawa frequently places the scene's most interesting listener, rather than the scene's most talkative speaker, in the deep foreground. Kurosawa uses both techniques in this scene from *Stray Dog* (BOTTOM); Wes uses both in this scene from *Isle of Dogs* (OPPOSITE BOTTOM).

OVERLEAF: Atari and the pack kneel before a dog's remains.

anyway, Kurosawa is, I think, considered, I don't know, not the refined choice in Japanese cinema. That it's considered more sophisticated to like Mizoguchi, maybe, or Ozu.

Yes, well, I think Kurosawa . . . there are a lot of genre movies. And in a way, the opposite of Kurosawa is sort of like Ozu or Mizoguchi.

They're sort of refined, and restrained, and elegant in some way.

Yes. And I think Kurosawa you could say is extremely refined, and extremely elegant, and *not* particularly restrained. The films are dynamic. And they're dynamic in kind of western ways too. I mean, he adapted Shakespeare. The connections between some of his samurai movies and westerns is established in both directions.

Have you heard about his response to going to see *A Fistful of Dollars*?

No, what was it?

Well, essentially, I guess that Sergio Leone did not let him know that it was a remake of *Yojimbo*, and so Kurosawa's response to Leone was something like, "I've seen your movie. It's a very good movie. Unfortunately, it's my movie."

[LAUGHS] That's good. Leo McCarey might have had a similar reaction to *Tokyo Story*. For this movie, we were thinking mostly about the city movies, you know? That tends to be more kind of what we felt like we were drawing on. But, I mean, we have—at least right now—we have music from *Seven Samurai*, and we had some from *Yojimbo*.

It doesn't do that much good to keep going back to the well again and again, though, does it? More like: take it all in and internalize it. Then see what you invent.

Somehow it will speak within the work that you make.

Yes. And it wasn't like I watched a bunch of Kurosawa movies and then decided, "Let's make this dog movie." I've been watching these movies for thirty-five years or something like that, and so finally I think, "Is there something related to these movies?" and "Maybe we can use this." And Roman in particular, he's interested in those movies. We're not doing what Sergio Leone did: a remake. It probably wouldn't have been a bad idea, but we didn't see a plot that was going to work for our dog story so, well, we just made up our own.

One thing that's interesting to me about Kurosawa, unlike some of the Japanese directors that have come up, is that he doesn't necessarily have one hyper-recognizable film style—that he does vary it from picture to picture.

Yes. He made all kinds of stories, but I do think we can envision some signature varieties of Kurosawa shots. Especially the ones in widescreen, black and white, often with seven or nine different characters in the frame, blocking using a

Pan-focus allowed Kurosawa to create deep stagings where different kinds of action happen in the foreground and background—two scenes running in parallel within the same shot, providing context and implicit commentaries for one another. In this shot from *High and Low* (ABOVE TOP RIGHT), he uses the width of the anamorphic widescreen frame for the same purpose—creating, in essence, two adjacent "shots" in screen right and screen left. One establishes the action, one lets us in on the reaction. Another

filmmaker may have chosen to cut two shots together to accomplish what Kurosawa does here in one composition. The Sheep Dogs confer in the frame-right foreground in a shot from *Isle of Dogs* that uses this same technique (TOP LEFT).

Taken to an extreme, this kind of blocking introduces an element of humor, as it does (for me, anyway) in these shots from *Yojimbo* (SECOND FROM TOP RIGHT) and *Rashomon* (THIRD FROM TOP RIGHT). It has something to do with the

visual contrast between the awkwardly intimate foreground figure who stands nose-to-nose with us, and the awkwardly distant figures who have been quietly miniaturized in the deep background. A lot of the visual comedy of *Isle of Dogs* seems to be based on this principle (SECOND AND THIRD FROM TOP LEFT).

Before the move to widescreen, Kurosawa managed to pack an extraordinary number of figures into an Academy-ratio shot by making the most of the height of the frame. He often uses high camera angles,

diagonal or curvilinear blocking of bodies, and a variety of seated, kneeling, and standing positions to keep anyone from upstaging and eclipsing anyone else. This set of hardbitten peasant profiles from *Seven Samurai* (BOTTOM RIGHT) is the kind of shot Wes was imitating with this diagonal Hero Pack lineup (BOTTOM LEFT).

OPPOSITE: Publicity still of Maxim Munzuk, who plays the title role in *Dersu Uzala*

lot of depth, and very dramatic in the staging and so on. Somebody very close to the camera, and somebody very deep.

Especially in *The Bad Sleep Well* and *High and Low*, those two together, the way he deals with exposition in those movies is fascinating and peculiar. They say things that you know they would not say to each other. They already know it all. They're telling us.

I think sometimes people think of something like *Seven Samurai* as an "action film" and think of Kurosawa as an action filmmaker. Which you're pretty quickly reminded isn't the whole truth, when you go back and watch it. It actually reminds me of the way that you just spoke of *Isle of Dogs*: Maybe it's an epic, but there's a lot of parts where it's just them talking. In *Seven Samurai*, there's a lot of issues of the group of samurai relating to the people in the town, and how they relate to each other, and there's a little romance happening in the sides there.

Yes. They're like westerns.

And I could be wrong about this, but my initial impression of what is going on in *Isle of Dogs* is that there is something you, perhaps, are doing with tempo and with pacing that does seem more Kurosawan to me, compared to your other films. But you may or may not be able to speak to that at this phase of the process.

Well, this one has some sequences that are much more quiet and slow than I anticipated them being. There are long scenes where it's just kind of silent. Especially when the boy and the one dog end up alone together. They stop talking. That sort of surprised me along the way, I think. When we were making the animatic, we found ourselves saying, "Well, once again, this is a scene where it's mostly just the wind blowing, and they're walking around and quietly doing something." And I could see that kind of being a bit Kurosawa. People in fields or lanes in the middle of a desolate village or in abandoned vacant spaces not saying anything, and waiting, and looking, and the wind blowing. It's not really something I expected from the script.

It just happened that way.

It's just the way it *is*.

There is something thematically about Kurosawa's films, a moral vision of the world, and a lot of the stuff that he makes is about what human beings owe to one another, and the idea of responsibility. Like, *Red Beard* is a great example of that.

Yes.

It's about somebody learning to . . . not just be a good person, but realizing that you're sort of obligated by something that you don't even know what, but you need to do it. And I see a bit of that in *Isle of Dogs*, in the character of Chief. And again, that may not be something you were consciously thinking of.

It could be a dog thing. If we're going to anthropomorphize them, but keep them dogs, then they're there to serve people. They're domesticated.

Well, they're masterless, in the same way that ronin are masterless.

They *want* a master.

The dogs want a master. That's just a thing about them being dogs.

Yes. That is not particularly a theme that I would be drawn to in any other context. I can't think of a movie where I would be especially connected to a human character who is looking for a master.

Yeah, that'd be a strange idea.

It also could be a legitimate idea for something. Somebody could want a master, a teacher. And I mean, I guess I've had that—but in this case, they're not looking for a teacher, they're looking for a master to be the servant of forever. And that's maybe more of an animal thing.

So that theme came from the fact that they are dogs.

I think so. And that they are dogs that have been abandoned, and so on. But also, I could say, or maybe you could say, it could read a bit like: they're friends. I mean, the dogs are friends with each other, but their masters are maybe their closest friends, or their real families, or something like that.

Yeah. I'm thinking back to the moment—it's a very tender moment—the flashback to the meeting of Atari and Spots, in the hospital.

Yes, when they're first introduced.

And they clearly care about each other.

Yes, they form a quick bond.

I was about to say, they're people who care about each other, but of course one is a dog. Have you seen the film *Dersu Uzala*?

Yes!

One of the things that Dersu says is "people"—his word in his language for animal. He calls all creatures "people."

I love that.

And that's one of the things I think Kurosawa found really admirable about the character. There's a section where they're throwing away their extra meat, burning it in the fire, and Dersu says, "What are you doing? People might want that." And the guys say, "What people? We're the only people around." And he's like, "For instance, a badger!"

That's a good bit. He made that one in Russia, right? Where was it?

I don't know exactly where in Russia.

It was a Russian production, even, wasn't it?

It was. That was kind of during a rough patch, as far as . . .

Kurosawa getting a movie made.

Right. Well, *Dodes-ka'den* was the one he made with his new production company that he tried to launch, with Kobaysahi, Kinoshita, and Ichikawa—

And that didn't go over well.

No. So he was kind of exiled in a certain way. *Dodes-ka'den* is another film that came to mind for me when I saw what I've seen of *Isle of Dogs*—

And we've sort of re-created sets from that movie a bit. I mean, not for any reason other than that it's a very good reference for Japanese kind of garbage dumps. Every now and then, we go back to stills from *Dodes-ka'den*, you know. We use anything we can.

Yes. But when you watch that movie, it has a sweetness about it—the music from it has this kind of warm quality, and it's very colorful. It's Kurosawa's first color film. It's a strange thing, that you can almost have a really fond memory of watching it; but then turn it on again and you realize, "Oh, there's some quite dark material in here."

Yes, maybe we are in similar territory there. I really don't know. I don't know what the balance of dark and light is going to be in this movie. I mean, on the surface it's a bunch of dogs exiled to a garbage dump island—

To die!

Right, to die. And eventually, to be killed, in the story. But I don't know how much it will feel like an adventure, given that context. It obviously just depends on how the sort of chemicals mix together in relation to somebody watching it. Really, you just can't tell. I think.

It's interesting to hear you say, "I don't know" or "I can't tell" just because, on some level, you are *the* person who would know. You know, the movie's in your head. You do have control over it. So when you say you don't know, you're speaking of . . . when you talk about the chemical reaction, you're talking about the audience, but perhaps is there still some work in postproduction that you're wondering how it's going to come together?

No, not even that. I mean, yes! But I do think you can have planned out anything you want, and the movie's still unknown. There are too many variables. I mean, I feel like people outside of making a movie, people who haven't made a movie, tend to think of *control* over a movie in a different way than people who have done it.

Absolutely. Well, the word "control" even has this negative connotation. You don't want to be perceived as a "controlling" director, but it's like, how do you direct a film? You have to have control.

I don't even see a negative connotation to it. I wouldn't think about it one way or the other. I just think that, if you do it, you know that most of your job is not about controlling. It's about getting it to work, getting it to *happen,* and, really, just taking a blank canvas and filling it. It's not like the movie exists, and you're trying to force it to be this and that. You've got to *do* the thing! And, so, if somebody says, "Oh, this person is very controlling," well, that might just mean that that's somebody who's *interested* in *aspects* of the thing you're noticing. If you see what I mean. It's sort of . . . I don't remember how exactly we got into it. Where did it come from, control, in our conversation? Where were we before that?

Where were we . . . That's funny, I really sort of don't remember. Oh! I was talking about how *you* know what the film is going to be like, in a certain sense, but then you were also talking about how you kind of don't know what the experience of watching the film is going to be like.

You definitely don't know how the movie is going to make someone feel when they watch it. But you don't even know, even if you've written the scene, and you've planned the set, and you've sort of blocked it, and you've—you've *made* the thing. When you put it all together, often you say, "Well, that is a weirdly sad scene." Or *not* very sad. Or a scene you thought was simple and realistic somehow is kind of surreal.

You find yourself surprised by how things strike you emotionally or tonally?

You're just surprised by *what it is*. You're just surprised by how it came out. By what comes out of the oven, you know? You make decisions. And then the thing that is a result of that is *this,* and that's . . . maybe it turned out like you wrote it in the recipe and maybe it didn't but it's still kind of edible. It's a different dish. Even if nothing changed radically from the plan. I bet a lot of directors would say the same thing.

It's fascinating to hear that from *you,* because having spent time on the set and having heard firsthand from your department heads the degree to which you are involved in decisions about lots of small things—

[LAUGHS] How much I'm trying to control everything!

And I don't mean it in a negative way!

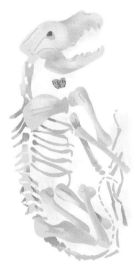

OPPOSITE TOP: **Medium-scale Hero Pack puppets**

OPPOSITE BOTTOM: **Anxious dogs in medium scale**

[STILL LAUGHING] You don't have to qualify it!

Just that you care about the details—

Yes, I know, even half the time, I'm like—[FOLDS ARMS, FURROWS BROW, LETTING OUT BREATH] "I could let this one go, but . . . but I just don't want to." [LAUGHS]

But to hear that "Wes Anderson," of all people, who cares about all these very small details of design and camera placement and whatever, *still* doesn't have control over what the thing ends up being—I think people would be surprised to hear that.

Oh, boy. Well, with a live-action movie, it's . . . you don't know what the relationship between an actor and a scene is. It's *them,* you know? They take whatever you give them, but they have to play and make something.

And also just however they are that day.

Yes. I mean, *they* don't know what they're doing. They may not *want* to. And it isn't even just that day—take three versus take six could be something totally different. And you don't really want to force an actor to be what they aren't. You have to sort of let them show you. And also, you know, on a movie set, something changes and *everything* changes. The clouds come in, and you're in a different place.

[INDICATING OUR SURROUNDINGS, FULL OF LOUD TRAFFIC NOISES AND SHIFTING LIGHT AND SHADOW FROM PASSING CLOUDS] **These would be terrible conditions to be shooting us right now.**

Well, you'd find a way. You'd say, "I know we planned it like this, but now let's see what it's like if they have to yell the breakup scene." I mean, some people are better at that than others. Ridley Scott, anything could happen, and he'd figure out how to make it . . .

He's kind of a genius at that.

I think so. I gather he's really like a director and a director of photography. With the animated ones, too, animators are like actors, and you watch what happened that day, and you say, "Yes, this person is doing well, and this is happening," and then the next day something happens, and you think, "That's a little . . . Well, I could say something . . . " But sometimes you don't want to guide them because as soon as you step in—

They get self-conscious?

Or they just make a change and it makes it worse, and now what are you going to do? Because now

you've helped them. They were going to do something that might not be what you wanted, exactly, but they were following a train of thought, and now you've tried to steer them, but they haven't found the rhythm for it.

They're trying to follow your direction, but they had something they were doing before—

And it might not work. But sometimes you give somebody a little nudge, and they say, [SNAPS] I get it. It's just the same as with actors. There are a lot of similarities between actors and animators. The biggest difference—other than that it's sort of a metaphor, in a way—I think is just time. How it happens in time is so different. And that's a strange thing with this kind of movie.

You're dealing with a lot of emotional subtlety in these films. They're not broad comedy.

Right. I mean, in a lot of them, it's like, if they don't give a performance like a person, then it's just not going to be interesting. The scene is not going to be worth doing. The thing to me, in particular, is just because those heads are just tiny! They're the biggest heads we've got, but they're quite little. And you saw that with the humans we're doing a different kind of animation. With *Mr. Fox,* we had rubber faces with paddles under them, the same way the animals are. And this, we're doing a completely different thing, which I think is better because I just wasn't happy . . . With *Mr. Fox,* we didn't have that many scenes of talking humans, but they didn't hold up well in time, the faces just disintegrated. They were quite limiting. And the problem with this is, when you get there and you say, "Now that we're seeing this moment, it needs to be more like this or more like that," then it's like, "Well, we need to sculpt, and we need to cast—so that's three weeks," which is tricky.

As far as managing subtle emotional moments in this film, the dogs cry. The humans cry.

Yes, there's a lot of crying. An unexpected amount of crying.

Is that one of the things that surprised you when you ended up seeing it, or did you plan that ahead of time?

Well, I think, usually, it's something we had in the script. But . . . I had no clue we had this much crying. I mean, "Are we really going to have them cry again here?" And sometimes we've added *more.* But you've just got to follow your instinct about it, you know? I would tend to think, it's not usually that moving just to see somebody cry. I mean, it's not a good way to make something moving, necessarily.

I feel like I haven't seen characters cry in most animated films the way they do in this one.

Maybe not. I mean, in stop motion they don't cry as much because—

It's difficult to produce.

Well, in ours, like, you're putting some kind of grease on these puppets that rolls down, you know, I mean, when you make people cry frame by frame, it's a sort of odd thing. But I like it! I like the way we've done it, and the moments seem right to me. So, we may end up in the cutting room saying, "We need to figure out how to digitally take out some tears." But I bet we won't.

This film—we've talked about how there's some darkness and blood, but there's also incredible tenderness, I think. But I don't mean to ask you what the movie's "about." You have this great quote in an interview with Matt Zoller Seitz, in which he asked a thematic question and you said something like, "That's a little too much the whole thing." Donald Richie says that once when he asked Kurosawa that sort of question, about what this or that movie meant, Kurosawa said something like, "If I could have told you in words, I wouldn't have had to make the movie."

I did some interviews with Kent Jones, for his *Hitchcock/Truffaut* documentary, and he asked me some questions. When I saw it, I realized the things I was talking about were nothing like what the other directors who were interviewed in the movie were talking about. They focused very significantly on *Vertigo*, and the emphasis was on Hitchcock's interest in certain kinds of psychological situations. It was about emotion and psychology. Which mine wasn't, and I think I missed the whole idea of it.

What did you want to talk about?

Rear Window. Not so much the voyeurism in it, and not even so much the strange dynamic in the relationship between Jimmy Stewart and Grace Kelly (which is one of my favorite movie romances ever, by the way). But what I seem to have chosen to focus on about the movie was the atmosphere of the place itself and this group of people living there together. It's not just that there's a murder, it's that it's like a little community.

The apartments.

Yes. These different buildings all centered on this one little space. It evokes something.

It's very obviously on a set.

It's a great set, and it has a sort of storybook quality to it, and it has a lot to do with the way he's bringing us into that story, which is from this room.

Yes. It expands outward slowly, so that you get a bigger picture of what's actually happening—

And you, obviously, never get a bigger picture of what's happening from any other position.

Exactly.

It's all through him.

There's a limitation placed on it. It's a challenge, kind of, for the filmmaker.

It's a challenge—and it's a reason to bother.

[LAUGHS] Do you think a filmmaker needs a reason to bother?

I think that probably, for Hitchcock, he said, "I see a thing that interests me, a thing I could do with this story." I'm sure he said, "I know how to do it." And probably he would not have said, "Let's do this one," if he hadn't had this idea of the point of view.

It interests me, insofar as I think that the tendency of an interviewer is often that psychological stuff. You know, "I want to get you talking about what you meant to do, how this is supposed to make us feel, or what it means." I mean, even with *Isle of Dogs*, there could be a political thing read into it: Is it about exile, or refugees, this or that, and . . . I imagine you don't want to talk about it. [LAUGHS]

Interpretation. In my experience, what most people find in a movie I've made, well, what they see might be partly what I was thinking about and working through, and also maybe it's partly what I was reading or sort of studying. But I rarely, if ever, think, "And my additional comments about this will really serve the experience of watching the movie." I mean, usually my comments will offer absolutely nothing.

You're living your life, and you're absorbing what's going on in your world, but maybe you're not making the thing to be an intentional statement on anything?

Yes, and me adding to the movie with some paragraph? That doesn't add to it. It takes away, a bit. So that's why I usually kind of . . . I mean, probably when Kurosawa . . . What was the Kurosawa line that you had about that—?

Oh, that "If I could have summed it up in a sentence, I wouldn't have had to make a movie about it."

He's gone to the extent to communicate it *this* way, which was elaborate and complex and time consuming, and it probably does undermine it a little to then reduce it to a statement in words. That's perfectly fine for somebody who *sees* it to do, and maybe that's part of what their contribution is as an audience.

And that's kind of how I see my role, or the role of a critic, to try to be kind of an ideal viewer of something, and to be in part a liaison between filmmakers and audiences, offering a

OPPOSITE: **The dangers of Dog-Flu, as drawn by Gwenn Germain**

bit about how this was achieved, and offering a way you can perhaps appreciate what's going on here.

Yes.

Somebody needs to do that, and it doesn't have to be the director's job to advise on exactly how you should watch the movie.

No.

I liked that "reason to bother" line you just had. Do you have a reason to bother about this movie?

Well, I mean, that may not be apples to apples. In the one case, there's a short story, and someone is making a script, and Hitchcock is saying, "Do I do this one or should somebody else do this one?" On the other hand, for our movie, there's nothing until we start saying, "Well, I do have this idea. A pack of dogs. And this garbage dump island in Japan. And a little airplane." So in a way, it's more like, the fact that it even happens at all is the reason to bother.

You just mentioned about this island of trash. I am betting that there will be all kinds of prose written about how Wes Anderson has made this movie about trash because it's not neat, it's not tidy, and people associate that with your work. Have you enjoyed getting into the aesthetics of trash for this movie?

I always loved the idea of a garbage dump. It was just a chance to work with a garbage dump. I will

say, it's probably the most neatly organized garbage dump—

[LAUGHS] It has sections.

Yes. Well, because we've got probably forty minutes of this movie on this garbage dump, maybe more. And if it's all just continual garbage together, then it's just going to turn into nothing. We've got to have identities to the different kinds of garbage.

Then we can track their journey through the different sections of it.

That's right. So we've tried to give some kind of "rooms" on the island. But it ends up being quite neat, actually. [LAUGHS]

But it is a chance, aesthetically, to explore something totally different for you. It's a city film, it's in Japan, there's garbage—I mean, it's one-eighty from a lot of the things you've done most recently.

Yes. But I feel like that with every single movie, though! Usually, when the movie comes out, I always get the exact same response: "This one is even *more*—he's gone further towards himself than ever." But I think, "This is nothing like what I did . . ."

Is that maddening?

Professor Watanabe, Assistant-Scientist Yoko-ono, and the Junior Scientists prepare to toast their success with drinks in the lab bar.

It's not maddening because it's not hugely distracting to me. But sometimes I do feel like, "I know what you're going to say." And, you know, that's all right because that's just somebody saying . . . Well, if they hate it, then that's what that is; and if they like it, they could just as easily have the same thought. It's just somebody saying, "I can recognize the hand behind the camera here." And that's fine. It doesn't matter, really. I mean, I'm not expecting people to say about this movie, "Now, this is a real change of pace." Probably people are going to say, "Hmm, this is just how I thought he would do a Japanese garbage dump." So that's just how it is.

Well, you're you, you know?

[LAUGHS] I know. And it's very easy for someone at this stage of the game to just not go to—if they don't like what I'm doing, it's easy not to see it, I think. It doesn't take much effort to skip it.

There are all kinds of other things to do.

Yes, for sure. Not that I want to discourage—I'm happy if someone's hated everything I've done, if they want to still give it another shot. I'd prefer that.

Do you think this film is different, though? Do you feel that way about it?

I think that every single one of them is different. I mean, I did a movie set in the '30s in central Europe; I did a sort of Norman Rockwell, '60s Americana kind of setting . . . There's one set in India that's about brothers. I did an animated one that's, you know, about foxes . . .

They sound very different when you lay them out like that.

Mostly I'm just describing settings, I guess, but certainly the last one, I don't know how much overlap there is, even in the kinds of characters or anything. But anyway.

Gustave, from *Grand Budapest*, is a totally different creation, I think. And maybe I'm reading into this, but the films are getting bigger, in a certain sense. That there is kind of a ramping up. *The Life Aquatic with Steve Zissou* was the first globe-trotting one—

Well, that one, it's a bigger story. It takes place in different time periods, it has a huge hotel and a

war and a ski chase, but the production itself was a much more kind of focused thing than *Life Aquatic*.

I think you managed to create a feeling of bigness with *Grand Budapest*. Especially the hotel set itself.

We found a good way to do the hotel. And also, part of it was, when we did *Life Aquatic*, I was not opposed to just letting it be big. I thought, "Well, this is how you do this." And my experience of working that way wasn't—I had a great time making the movie, but it's a strange sort of story. Probably, if we had made it ninety-three minutes long and did it with twenty-five million dollars instead of fifty-five million, then it probably would have been good for the movie. I don't think those things would have harmed it. And the ways to do that would have made it more fun to make the movie because instead of spending a hundred something days filming, we would have shot it in sixty-five days, something like that.

Well, it was your first very big film. And one thing that I think is perhaps true of the kinds of stories that you've made, or the kinds of films that you've made—*Bottle Rocket* and *Rushmore* hew closer to your own life experience.

Yes.

It makes sense that as you've become a person who has become more well-traveled and has done and seen more things . . .

Well, those movies also, like *Bottle Rocket*, we were writing something that we thought we'd be able to make on our own. We didn't expect to be able to build sets, or anything like that. And *Rushmore* kind of falls into the same category. Even though we might have had more resources to do the movie, we wrote the story before we thought we could paint on a bigger canvas. But *Life Aquatic* is a movie that, well, we have the basic idea for the movie long before we made *Bottle Rocket*. In fact, I wrote a little short story about it in college! So it kind of predates it.

So my theory's a little off.

I'm sure your theory is probably basically right, but it's slightly undermined by that fact. [LAUGHS]

Wes has to get back to his day of directing, and after a genial wave goodbye, he takes off toward his apartment at a good clip. His ill-begotten café crème rests on the table, untouched.

BIBLIOGRAPHY

Resources on Akira Kurosawa

Anyone who wants to read more about Akira Kurosawa should start with the memoirs of the *Kurosawa-gumi*. Kurosawa's own *Something Like An Autobiography* (New York: Vintage, 1983) demonstrates his genius as a writer and student of human nature. It also includes some of Kurosawa's words of advice to young filmmakers. He compares a good screenplay to a battle flag, for example—a quote I refer to on page 75. The autobiography leaves off at the release of *Rashomon*. Shinobu Hashimoto, *Rashomon*'s co-writer, picks up the story in *Compound Cinematics: Akira Kurosawa and I* (New York: Vertical, 2015), an insider's account of Team Kurosawa's unique writing process. Anecdotes from Kurosawa's sets are supplied in *Waiting on the Weather: Making Movies with Akira Kurosawa* (Berkeley: Stone Bridge Press, 2006). It's written and wryly illustrated by Teruyo Nogami, Kurosawa's longtime script supervisor and later production manager, and, today, one of the most tireless caretakers of his legacy. All three are beautifully written and quite touching.

Video interviews with Kurosawa and his team can be found in his son Hisao Kurosawa's 2000 documentary *A Message from Akira Kurosawa: For Beautiful Movies*, as well as in the 2002 Toho Masterworks series *Akira Kurosawa: It Is Wonderful to Create*. Episodes of the latter can usually be found as special features on the Criterion Collection's editions of Kurosawa films.

Any study of Kurosawa depends in part on the work of the late Donald Richie. Even if you disagree with his critical observations on the films, he remains indispensable as an eyewitness to Kurosawa's career, and his personal impressions of Kurosawa the man are just as valuable as his frequent quotations from his own conversations with the director. One of the most colorful is found in "A Personal Record" (*Film Quarterly* 14, no. 1, Autumn, 1960); here, he quotes Kurosawa's opinion that too few of his fellow directors care passionately enough about "people." Richie's *The Films of Akira Kurosawa* (University of California Press, first published in 1965 and now in its third edition, 1999) was one of the first book-length studies of any individual filmmaker's complete works; the debt *The Wes Anderson Collection* owes to this book is therefore twofold. Richie includes quotes from his interview "Kurosawa on Kurosawa," originally published in *Sight and Sound* (33, nos. 3 and 4, Summer/Autumn 1964); I quoted and paraphrased from it on pages 54 and 250. Thanks to Criterion for granting permission to print an excerpt from Richie's 2009 piece for *The Current*, "Remembering Kurosawa," on page 16.

Joan Mellen's *Voices from the Japanese Cinema* (New York: Liveright, 1975) contains a wide-ranging interview with Kurosawa; Kurosawa shares a memory of his days as a young sometime Marxist, which this book mentions on page 57.

Stuart Galbraith IV's biography of Kurosawa, *The Emperor and the Wolf* (New York: Faber and Faber, 2002), also tells the life story of Kurosawa's leading man Toshiro Mifune. Exhaustively thorough, it remains the best place to find all the known facts about Kurosawa's life arranged chronologically, and it fills in gaps in the narrative with new details from Japanese sources that English-language studies too rarely consulted in the past. One of these sources, his daughter Kazuko's memoir *Papa Akira Kurosawa* (Tokyo: Bungei Shunju, 2004), offers a rare glimpse of the Kurosawas' home life—it's from Galbraith, citing Kazuko Kurosawa, that I learned that Kurosawa loved spending time with his dogs (Poni, Mini, Sonny, Putti, and Leo).

Some Other Works Consulted

There have been far too few book-length studies on Miyazaki in English; I benefited from Dani Cavallaro's pioneering effort *The Anime Art of Hayao Miyazaki* (Jefferson, NC: McFarland, 2006). *Starting Point* and *Turning Point* (San Francisco: VIZ Media, 2014), two collections of Miyazaki's writings and interviews, are also recommended. I share Jason Schwartzman's opinion that Mami Sunada's Ghibli documentary *The Kingdom of Dreams and Madness* (2013) is not just good, it's great.

Zengakuren: Japan's Revolutionary Students (Berkeley: Ishi Press, 1970, reprinted 2012) is supposedly not the most academically rigorous book on the history of Japan's student movements, but I found it by far the most intriguing of the ones I read. It was also the most lucidly written and patiently explained. It was written by Japanese students at Waseda University, edited and introduced by their teacher, Stuart J. Dowsey. Another compelling primary source is Hiroshi Hamaya's 1960 photo series of the Anpo protest, *A Record of Rage and Grief*, which has been presented, with accompanying essays, as a kind of online museum exhibit by MIT's Visualizing Cultures at https://ocw.mit.edu/ans7870/21f/21f.027/tokyo_1960/. William Andrew's *Dissenting Japan: A History of Japanese Radicalism and Counterculture, from 1945 to Fukushima* (London: Hurst, 2016) and Shunsuke Tsurumi's thoughtful *A Cultural History of Postwar Japan 1946–1980* (London: Routledge and Keagan Paul, 1987) also contributed to my understanding of the student and citizens' protest movements. Tadao Sato's story of modern Japan through its movies, *Currents in Japanese Cinema* (New York: Kodansha, 1987), directed me to Japanese protest films I had not seen before.

For a general introduction to ukiyo-e, I've liked Tadashi Kobayashi's *Ukiyo-e: An Introduction to Japanese Woodblock Prints* (New York: Kodansha, 1997). In the section on ukiyo-e in this book, I probably also included something I learned from two old editions of Hokusai's *The Thirty-Six Views of Mount Fuji* and Hiroshige's *The Fifty-Three Stages of the Tokaido* (Honolulu: East-West Center Press, 1966) that were introduced by the art scholar Ichitaro Kondo. For readers interested in learning more about ukiyo-e and Yamato-e, a good place to start is the Metropolitan Museum of Art's online Heilbrunn Timeline of Art History, which contains several great introductory essays on Japanese art. I visited exhibits at The Met, the British Museum, and Japan Society while writing this book and learned much from each.

The photographs of haikyo in this book were taken by Jordy Meow. To explore more Japanese ruins, you can buy his book *Abandoned Japan* (Versailles, France: Jonglez Publishing, 2015) or visit his websites, haikyo.org and offbeatjapan.org.

Takeshi Murakami's *Little Boy* (New York: Japan Society; New Haven: Yale University Press, 2005), a book of lavishly illustrated essays and interviews not unlike this one, is a favorite guide to *tokusatsu*, vintage Japanese comics, and the experience of being a young geek in the futuristic zeitgeist of Japan's sixties and seventies. Fans of *Isle of Dogs* will find much to explore there.

Acknowledgments

Thanks first to the other crew members we interviewed, whose perspectives on *Isle of Dogs* were essential to writing this book: animation producer Simon Quinn, art director Curt Enderle, animation supervisor Tobias Fouracre, music supervisor Randy Poster, co-producer Octavia Peissel, and producer Jeremy Dawson. Thanks also to 1st AD James Emmott for showing us around the units, and to the many crew members who took time out of their workday to answer our questions. Thanks to consulting producer Molly Cooper for facilitating our communication with Wes and Fox. Special thanks to associate producer Ben Adler who guided us on set and supplied us with a huge collection of images from the production.

Thanks to Jackson Clark for the many weeks spent helping us collect and optimize other images in this book. Thanks to Seth Myers for his research on Wes's screenwriting in earlier films, and to Paddy O'Halloran for his thoughts on the writings of Richard Adams. Thanks to JP Murton for giving us time off work for writing and travel, and for his good counsel about our mission and our values throughout this process. Thanks to Chad Perman and the editorial team at Bright Wall/ Dark Room for their continual support, patience, flexibility, and friendship while this project was underway. Thanks to our friends Lana Kitcher and Elliott Brichford for sharing their knowledge of Japan and their command of Japanese. Thanks to Roger Stevenson and to Rachel Stevenson for their command of English, for their help in refining our writing and our thinking, for bringing much wit, insight, and clarity to the language in this book.

Thanks to Taylor and Tony, Max and Martin—it's been an honor to collaborate with you. Thanks to Matt, for creating this series and trusting us with it. Thanks to transcriber David Jenkins, copyeditor Annalea Manalili, designer Liam Flanagan, and assistant editor Ashley Albert for all their work. Above all, thanks to editor Eric Klopfer for shepherding us through the hardest writing job we've ever done and never losing faith that we could all pull it off.

CREDITS AND COPYRIGHT

Lauren Wilford and Ryan Stevenson

are editors at Bright Wall/Dark Room, a magazine that publishes longform, carefully considered takes on film. They have been married and collaborating since 2015 and are currently based in Providence, Rhode Island.

Matt Zoller Seitz is the editor in chief of

RogerEbert.com, the TV critic for *New York* magazine, the author of *The Wes Anderson Collection, The Wes Anderson Collection: The Grand Budapest Hotel, The Oliver Stone Experience,* and *Mad Men Carousel,* and the coauthor of *TV (The Book).* He is based in New York City.

Taylor Ramos is a 2-D animator and video

essayist. She studied both classical hand-drawn and 3-D animation and has worked as an animator and designer for television and mobile games. She is the cocreator, with Tony Zhou, of the video essay series "Every Frame a Painting." Their joint work has been featured in the Criterion Collection and on the streaming service FilmStruck. She currently works as a 2-D animator for television and resides in Vancouver, British Columbia.

Tony Zhou is a filmmaker and video essayist.

He has worked for more than a decade as a video editor, with experience in television, documentary, corporate video, and independent film. He is the cocreator, with Taylor Ramos, of the video essay series "Every Frame a Painting." Their joint work has been featured in the Criterion Collection and on the streaming service FilmStruck. He is an occasional lecturer and has given talks on filmmaking at Walt Disney Animation Studios and Apple University. He currently works as an animatic editor for television and resides in Vancouver, British Columbia.

Max Dalton is a graphic artist living in Buenos

Aires, Argentina, by way of Barcelona, New York, and Paris. He has published a few books and illustrated some others, including *The Wes Anderson Collection* (Abrams, 2013). Max started painting in 1977, and since 2008, he has been creating posters about music, movies, and pop culture, quickly becoming one of the top names in the industry.

OVERLEAF: Poster for the Japanese release of *Isle of Dogs* by Katsuhiro Otomo, creator of the manga *Akira* and director of its anime version.

Image Credits:

Isle of Dogs unit photography by Ray Lewis and Valerie Sadoun; 90, 102, 220: Andy Gent. © 2018 Twentieth Century Fox Film Corporation. All Rights Reserved; 20, 48, 54 60, 235: Photos by Charlie Gray. © 2018 Twentieth Century Fox Film Corporation. All Rights Reserved; 72: *Cock*, Attributed to Katsushika Hokusai. The Metropolitan Museum of Art, New York. H. O. Havemeyer Collection, Bequest of Mrs. H. O. Havemeyer, 1929; 72: *Chidori Birds*, School of Katsushika Hokusai. The Metropolitan Museum of Art, New York. Gift of Annette Young, in memory of her brother, Innis Young, 1956; 80: Photo by Ryan Stevenson; 82: *Rotatory Gallop: The Dog*, Eadweard Muybridge, 1887; 134: *The Whirlpools of Awa*, Hiroshige, 1857. The Metropolitan Museum of Art, New York. Henry L. Phillips Collection, Bequest of Henry L. Phillips, 1939; 136: *Full Moon at Kanazawa, Province of Musashi.* Utagawa Hiroshige, 1857. The Metropolitan Museum of Art, New York. Henry L. Phillips Collection, Bequest of Henry L. Phillips, 1939; 153: "A La Recherche de Mickey" and "The Screw Coaster," photos by Jordy Meow; 158: *Scenes in and Around the Capital*, Edo Period, 17th Century. The Metropolitan Museum of Art, New York. Mary Griggs Burke Collection, Gift of the Mary and Jackson Burke Foundation, 2015; 159: *Ichikawa Sadanji II*, Toyohara Kunichika, from Album of Thirty-Two Triptychs of Polychrome Woodblock Prints by Various Artists. The Metropolitan Museum of Art, New York. Gift of Eliot C. Nolen, 1999; 161: Woodblock print from crepe book *Momotaro, or, Little Peachling.* Illustrations by Kobayaski Eitaku, text by David Thompson, published by Hasegawa Takejiro (Tokyo: Kobunsha, 1886); 163: *View of the Kabuki Theaters at Sakai-cho on Opening Day of the New Season*, Utagawa Hiroshige, ca. 1838. The Metropolitan Museum of Art, New York. Purchase, Joseph Pulitzer Bequest, 1918; 164: *Under the Wave off Kanagawa*, Hokusai, c. 1830–1832. The Metropolitan Museum of Art, New York; 165: Seven-ri Beach, Province of Soshu, by Hiroshige, date unknown. The Metropolitan Museum of Art, New York; 165: *Oi Station*, by Hiroshige, c. 1835. The Metropolitan Museum of Art, New York; 165: *Narumi, Meisan Arimatsu Shibori Mise*, by Hiroshige, 1855. The Metropolitan Museum of Art, New York; 226: Photo by Bryce Craig; 229: Photo by Yuki Kokubo; 233: Photo by Daniel Torres; 256: © 2018 Twentieth Century Fox.

Editor: **Eric Klopfer**
Assistant Editor: **Ashley Albert**
Designer: **Martin Venezky**
Production Manager: **Kathleen Gaffney**

Library of Congress Control Number: 2017945115

ISBN: 978-1-4197-3009-2
eISBN: 978-1-68335-296-9

Text copyright © 2018 Lauren Wilford

ISLE OF DOGS film artwork © 2018 Twentieth Century Fox Film Corporation. All rights reserved.

Printed and bound in the United States
10 9 8 7 6 5 4 3 2 1

Abrams books are available at special discounts when purchased in quantity for premiums and promotions as well as fundraising or educational use. Special editions can also be created to specification. For details, contact specialsales@abramsbooks.com or the address below.

Abrams® is a registered trademark of Harry N. Abrams, Inc.

ABRAMS The Art of Books
195 Broadway, New York, NY 10007
abramsbooks.com